District Gazetteers of India Series 194

RAJPUTANA DISTRICT GAZETTEERS

AJMER-MERWARA

Owing to the antiquity and rarity of this book, certain pages are regrettably absent, and readability is compromised due to the blurring of the original text. If you possess any insights regarding the availability of these missing sections, kindly inform us. Your assistance is crucial in ensuring the completion of this significant work for the benefit of future generations.

District Gazetteers of India Series 194

RAJPUTANA DISTRICT GAZETTEERS

AJMER-MERWARA

(TEXT AND STATISTICS TABLES)

COMPILED BY

C. C. WATSON

3 VOLUMES

(VOL. I[st] - A & B)

GYAN

Published by

Gyan Publishing House
5, Ansari Road
Daryaganj, New Delhi-110002
Phone: 011-47034999, 9811692060
E-mail: books@gyanbooks.com

Distribution Network
gyanbooks.com
India, USA, Canada, UK, Australia, France

ISBN: 978-93-6208-478-1 (Set) 3 Volumes
978-93-6208-899-4 (PB)

First Published, 1904

2nd Impression 2024

Printed at: Gyan Press, Delhi.

RAJPUTANA DISTRICT GAZETTEERS (Vol. I[st] - A & B)
Compiled By: C. C. WATSON

LIST OF VOLUMES

S. NO.	ISBN NO.	VOLUME	TITLE	AUTHOR	PRICE	PAGES
			ASSAM DISTRICT GAZETTEERS			
1	9788121285926	1st	Cachar	B. C. Allen	600	300
2	9788121285919	2nd	Sylhet	B. C. Allen	750	378
3	9788121285902	3rd	Goalpara	B. C. Allen	400	203
4	9788121285896	4th	Kamrup	B. C. Allen	675	344
5	9788121285889	5th	Darrang	B. C. Allen	725	364
6	9788121285872	6th	Nowgong	B. C. Allen	560	280
7	9788121285865	7th	Sibsagar	B. C. Allen	675	343
8	9788121285858	8th	Lakhimpur	B. C. Allen	690	347
9	9788121285841	9th	Naga Hills and Manipur	B. C. Allen	580	294
10	9788121285834	10th	The Khasi And Jaintia Hills, The Garo Hills And The Lushai Hills	B. C. Allen	675	363
11	9788121285827	11th	The Sadiya and Balipara Frontier Tract	B. C. Allen	375	190
			BENGAL DISTRICT GAZETTEERS			
12	9788121218672	1st	Angul	L. S. S. O'Malley	340	168
13	9788121259637	2nd	Bakarganj	J. C. JACK	970	194
14	9788121218696	3rd	Balasore	L. S. S. O'Malley	450	228
15	9788121259590	4th	Bankura	L. S. S. O'Malley	1000	199
16	9788121218375	5th	Bhagalpur	J. Byrne	390	194
17	9788121218290	6th	Birbhum	L. S. S. O'Malley	300	150
18	9788121259651	7th	Eastern Bengal and Assam - Bogra	J. N. Gupta	940	188
19	9788121218351	8th	Burdwan	J. C. K. Peterson	450	227
20	9788121259538	9th	Calcutta District Gazetteer - Statistics, 1901 - 02		340	68
21	9788121218313	10th	Champaran	L. S. S. O'Malley	410	205
22	9788121259613	11th	Eastern Bengal District Gazetters - Chittagong	L. S. S. O'Malley	1080	216
23	9788121259552	12th	Chota Nagpur Tributary		130	26
24	9788121259415	13th	The Cooch Behar Gazette: Statistics		1460	292
25	9788121218412	14th	Cuttack	L. S. S. O'Malley	490	248
26	9788121261357	15th	Eastern Bengal District Gazetteers Dacca	B. C. Allen	400	207
27	9788121218436	16th	Darbhanga	L. S. S. O'Malley	360	180
28	9789362089335	17th	Darjeeling	L. S. S. O'Malley	500	248
29	9788121259453	18th	Eastern Bengal District Gazetteers - Dinajpur	F. W. Strong	890	178
30	9788121259392	19th	Faridpur	L. S. S. O'Malley	700	140
31	9788121218474	20th	Gaya	L. S. S. O'Malley	540	270
32	9788121214032	21st	Bihar and Orissa District Gazetteer: Hazaribagh	E. Lister	715	234
33	9788121218337	22nd	Hooghly	L. S. S. O'Malley	680	340
34	9788121218191	23rd	Bengal District Gazetteer Howrah	L. S. S. O'Malley	390	199
35	9788121259293	24th	Eastern Bengal and Assam - Jalpaiguri	John F. Gruning	890	178
36	9788121259279	25th	Jessore	L. S. S. O'Malley	960	192
37	9788121259231	26th	Khulna	L. S. S. O'Malley	1100	220
38	9788121259217	27th	Malda	G. E. Lambourn	670	134
39	9788121267854	28th	Manbhum	H. Coupland	600	313
40	9788121218498	29th	Midnapore	L. S. S. O'Malley	500	252
41	9788121218597	30th	Monghyr	L. S. S. O'Malley	560	280
42	9788121259156	31st	Murshidabad	L. S. S. O'Malley	1250	250
43	9788121259576	32nd	Bengal District Gazetteers - Muzaffarpur	L. S. S. O'Malley	940	188
44	9788121259132	33rd	Mymensingh	F. A. Sachse	960	192
45	9788121259118	34th	Nadia	J. H. E. Garrett	1070	214
46	9788121259095	35th	Eastern Bengal and Assam - Noakhali	J. E. Webster	580	115
47	9788121218450	36th	Feudatory States of Orissa	L. E. B. Cobdenramsay	790	395
48	9788121259071	37th	Pabna	L. S. S. O'Malley	710	142
49	9788121218511	38th	Palamau	L. S. S. O'Malley	380	190
50	9788121218634	39th	Patna	L. S. S. O'Malley	500	250
51	9788121218535	40th	Puri	L. S. S. O'Malley	650	328
52	9788121218757	41st	Purnea	L. S. S. O'Malley	440	220
53	9788121258937	42nd	Rajshahi	L. S. S. O'Malley	1080	216
54	9788121256681	43rd	Bihar and Orissa District Gazetteers: Ranchi	M. G. Hallett	1350	278
55	9788121258913	44th	Eastern Bengal and assam - Rangpur	J. A. Vas	890	178
56	9788121218559	45th	Sambalpur	L. S. S. O'Malley	480	242
57	9788121214056	46th	Santal Parganas	L. S. S. O'Malley	940	308
58	9788121218610	47th	Saran	L. S. S. O'Malley	380	190
59	9788121218658	48th	Shahabad	L. S. S. O'Malley	380	190
60	9788121256704	49th	The Gazetteer of Sikhim	H. H. Risley	960	481
61	9788121218573	50th	Singhbhum, Saraikela And Kharsawan	L. S. S. O'Malley	560	280
62	9788121259439	51st	Eastern Bengal District Gazetteers - Tippera	J. E. Webster	730	146
63	9788121259033	52nd	24 Parganas	L. S. S. O'Malley	1420	284

S. NO.	ISBN NO.	VOLUME	TITLE	AUTHOR	PRICE	PAGES
			CENTRAL PROVINCES DISTRICT GAZETTEERS			
64	9789362081728	1st, Vol. A	Akola (Descriptive)	A. E. Nelson, C. Brown	870	436
65	9789362085481	2nd, Vol. A	Amraoti (Descriptive)	S. V. Fitzgerald, A. E. Nelson	1050	524
66	9789362089267	3rd,Vol. A	Balaghat (Descriptive)	R. V. RUSSELL	430	216
67	9789362083494	4th, Vol. A	Betul (Descriptive)	R. V. RUSSELL	610	306
68	9789362085146	5th, Vol. A	Bhandara (Descriptive)	R. V. RUSSELL	580	292
69	9789362088390	6th, Vol. A	Bilaspur (Descriptive)	R. V. RUSSELL	870	434
70	9789362086044	7th, Vol. A	Buldana (Descriptive)	A. E. Nelson	1090	543
71	9789362089014	8th, Vol. B	Chanda (Descriptive)	R. V. RUSSELL	470	234
72	9789362086938	9th	Chhattisgarch Feudatory State	E. A. De Brett	880	440
73	9789362082961	10th	Chhindwara (Descriptive)	R. V. RUSSELL	550	274
74	9789362089342	11th, Vol. A & B	Damoh (Descriptive and Statistical Tables 1891-1901)	R. V. RUSSELL	830	414
75	9789362081230	12th, Vol. A	Durg (Descriptive)	A. E. Nelson	460	232
76	9789362086037	13th, Vol. A	Hoshangabad (Descriptive)	R. V. RUSSELL	860	430
77	9789362086792	14th, Vol. A	Jubbulpore (Descriptive)	A. E. Nelson	950	474
78	9789362089663	15th, Vol. A & B	Mandla (Descriptive and Statistical Tables 1891-1901)	R. V. RUSSELL	370	186
79	9789362086419	16th, Vol. A	Nagpur (Descriptive)	R. V. RUSSELL	790	394
80	9789362080646	17th, Vol. A	Narsinghpur (Descriptive)	R. V. RUSSELL	510	257
81	9789362084835	18th, Vol. A	Nimar (Descriptive)	R. V. RUSSELL	600	299
82	9789362087737	19th, Vol. A	Raipur (Descriptive)	A. E. Nelson	790	396
83	9789362080264	20th, Vol. A	Saugor (Descriptive)	R. V. RUSSELL	570	285
84	9789362081117	21st, Vol. A	Seoni (Descriptive)	R. V. RUSSELL	460	232
85	9789362084965	22nd, Vol. A	Wardha (Descriptive)	R. V. RUSSELL	600	302
86	9789362083401	23rd, Vol. A	Yeotmal (Descriptive)	R. V. RUSSELL	550	277
87	9789362080325	24th, Vol. I, Pt. I	Gwalior (Text and Tables)	R. V. RUSSELL	980	489
88	9789362087133	24th, Vol. I, Pt. II	Gwalior (Maps)	R. V. RUSSELL	400	198
89	9789362086341	24th, Vol. I, Pt. III	Gwalior (Village List)	R. V. RUSSELL	810	406
90	9789362085467	24th, Vol. I, Pt. IV	Gwalior (Photos)	R. V. RUSSELL	1400	698
91	9789362087393	25th, Vol. II	Indore (Text and Tables)	C. E. Luard	1050	524
92	9789362084422	26th, Vol. III	Bhopal (Text and Tables)	C. E. Luard	540	272
93	9789362086815	27th, Vol. IV	Rewah (Text and Tables)	C. E. Luard	500	250
94	9789362087584	28th, Vol. V, Pt. A	Western States - Malwa (Text)	C. E. Luard	1520	762
95	9789362087300	29th, Vol. VI, Pt. A	Eastern States - Bundelkhand (Text)	C. E. Luard	930	463
96	9789362082169	30th, Vol. VI, Pt. B	Eastern States - Bundelkhand (Tables)	C. E. Luard	830	417
			GAZETTEER OF THE BOMBAY PRESIDENCY:			
97	9788121283441	1st, Part I	History of Gujarat	Ed.: James M. Campbell	3220	644
98	9788121285582	1st, Part II	History of the Konkan Dakhan and Southern Maratha Country	Ed.: James M. Campbell	4200	840
99	9788121285568	2nd	Gujarat, Surat and Broach	Ed.: James M. Campbell	2990	598
100	9788121285544	3rd	Kaira and Panch Mahals	Ed.: James M. Campbell	1690	339
101	9788121285520	4th	Ahmedabad	Ed.: James M. Campbell	1860	372
102	9788121285506	5th	Cutch, Palanpur, and Mahi Kantha	Ed.: James M. Campbell	2390	478
103	9788121285483	6th	Rewa Kantha, Narukot, Cambay, and Surat States	Ed.: James M. Campbell	1450	290
104	9788121285469	7th	Baroda	Ed.: James M. Campbell	3260	652
105	9788121285445	8th	Kathiawar	Ed.: James M. Campbell	3790	758
106	9788121285421	9th, Part I	Gujarat Population - Hindus	Ed.: James M. Campbell	3170	636
107	9788121285407	9th, Part II	Gujarat Population - Musalmans and Parsis	Ed.: James M. Campbell	1520	304
108	9788121285384	10th	Ratnagiri and Savantvadi	Ed.: James M. Campbell	2500	501
109	9788121285360	11th	Kolaba and Janjira	Ed.: James M. Campbell	2550	513
110	9788121285346	12th	Khandesh	Ed.: James M. Campbell	3190	638
111	9788121285322	13th Part I	Thana	Ed.: James M. Campbell	2050	413
112	9788121285308	13th Part II	Thana	Ed.: James M. Campbell	1770	357
113	9788121285285	14th	Thana - Places of Interest	Ed.: James M. Campbell	3290	659
114	9788121285261	15th Part I	Kanara	Ed.: James M. Campbell	2340	348
115	9788121285247	15th Part II	Kanara	Ed.: James M. Campbell	1740	348
116	9788121285223	16th	Nasik	Ed.: James M. Campbell	3490	698
117	9788121285209	17th	Ahmadnagar	Ed.: James M. Campbell	3860	772
118	9788121285186	18th Part I	Poona	Ed.: James M. Campbell	2930	586
119	9788121285162	18th Part II	Poona	Ed.: James M. Campbell	2680	537
120	9788121285148	18th Part III	Poona	Ed.: James M. Campbell	2500	503
121	9788121285124	19th	Satara	Ed.: James M. Campbell	3450	692
122	9788121285100	20th	Sholapur	Ed.: James M. Campbell	2730	547
123	9788121285087	21st	Gazetteer of the Bomaby Presidency: Belgaum	Ed.: James M. Campbell	2570	514
124	9788121285063	22nd	Dharwar	Ed.: James M. Campbell	4200	841
125	9788121285049	23rd	Gazetteer of the Bombay Presidency:Bijapur	Ed.: James M. Campbell	3550	712
126	9788121285025	24th	Kolhapur	Ed.: James M. Campbell	2250	450

S. NO.	ISBN NO.	VOLUME	TITLE	AUTHOR	PRICE	PAGES
127	9788121285001	25th	Botany	Ed.: James M. Campbell	2040	408
128	9788121284981	26th, Part I	Materials Towards a Statistical Account of the Town and Island of Bombay - History	Ed.: James M. Campbell	2500	504
129	9788121284967	26th, Part II	Materials Towards a Statistical Account of the Town and Island of Bombay - Trade and Fortifications	Ed.: James M. Campbell	2690	538
130	9788121284943	26th, Part III	Materials Towards a Statistical Account of the Town And Island of Bombay - Administration	Ed.: James M. Campbell	2450	702
131	9788121284929	27th	General Index	Ed.:R. E. Enthoven	2190	428
			MADRAS DISTRICT GAZETTEERS			
132	9788121258814	1st	Anantapur	W. Francis	1140	227
133	9788121258555	2nd	Malabar	C. A Innes & F. B Evans	3010	602
134	9788121258791	3rd	Bellary	W. Francis	1890	377
135	9788121258777	4th	Statistical Appendix For Chingleput		280	56
136	9788121258753	5th	Coimbatore	K. N. Krishnaswami Ayyar	3420	628
137	9788121232814	6th	Madras District Gazetteers District Gazetteer Cuddapah	C. F. Brackenbury	1120	285
138	9788121258715	7th	Statistical Appendix For Ganjam		370	73
139	9788121256766	8th, Vol. 1st	Godavari District Gazetteer	F. R. Hemingway	650	320
140	9788121256803	8th, Vol. 2nd	Godavari District Gazetteer	F. R. Hemingway	160	83
141	9788121258678	9th	Statistical Appendix For Kistna		640	127
142	9788121258654	10th	Statistical Appendix For Kurnool		270	54
143	9788121258616	11th	Madura	W. Francis	1900	379
144	9788121258579	12th	Statistical Appendix For Madura		740	148
145	9788121258630	13th	The Nilgiris	W. Francis	2190	437
146	9788121234276	14th	Madras District Gazetteers Gazetteer Of The Nellore District Brought Upto 1938		1150	386
147	9788121258517	15th	North Arcot		590	118
148	9788121258494	16th, Vol. 1, Part I	Salem	F. J. Richards	1710	343
149	9788121258593	16th, Vol. 1, Part II	Salem	F. J. Richards	1800	360
150	9788121258456	17th	South Arcot	W. Francis	2400	480
151	9788121258470	18th	Statistical Appendix For South Canara		400	80
152	9788121258432	19th, Vol. 1st & 2nd	Tanjore: Main Volume and Statistical Appendix		2070	401
153	9788121258395	20th	Tinnevelly	H. R. Pate	2740	547
154	9788121258418	21st	Statistical Appendix For Tinnevelly		320	64
155	9788121258371	22nd, 1st & 2nd	Trichinopoly: Main Volume and Statistical Appendix	F. R. Hemingway	2440	487
156	9788121241953	23rd	Vizagapatam District Gazetteer	W. Francis	760	385
			PUNJAB DISTRICT GAZETTEERS			
157	9788121255943	1st	Ambala District 1883-84		620	124
158	9788121255967	2nd	Amritsar		1180	236
159	9788121255981	3rd	Delhi		1300	260
160	9788121256001	4th	Ferozepore		950	188
161	9788121256025	5th	Faridkot		350	70
162	9788121256049	6th	Gujranwala 1893-94		1270	254
163	9788121256063	7th	Gujrat	C. E. Luard	1140	228
164	9788121256087	8th	Gurdaspur 1891-92		1260	252
165	9788121256100	9th	Gurgaon 1883-4		1020	203
166	9788121256124	10th	Hazara	H. D. Watson	2290	458
167	9788121256148	11th	Hissar district and Lohar State		1840	367
168	9788121256162	12th	Hoshiarpur		1420	283
169	9788121256186	13th	Jhang		1070	213
170	9788121256209	14th	Jhelam		1010	202
171	9788121256223	15th	Jalandhar District 1883-84		540	108
172	9788121256247	16th, Vol. XIV-A	Jullundur District, with maps and Kapurthala		1990	398
173	9788121256261	17th, Pt. I	Kangra (Proper)		1450	290
174	9788121256285	17th, Pt. II	Kangra (Kulu, Lahual, Spiti)		1800	357
175	9788121256308	18th	Karnal		1930	386
176	9788121256322	19th	Kohat		1540	307
177	9788121256346	20th	The Lahore District 1883-84		1220	244
178	9788121256384	21st	Ludhiana and Maler Kotla		1680	335
179	9788121256407	22nd	Lyallpur		735	147
180	9788121256421	23rd	Mianwali		1170	234
181	9788121256445	24th	Montgomery	P. J. Fagan	1590	318
182	9788121258364	25th	Multan (1901-02)	E. D. Maclagan	2400	480
183	9788121258708	26th	The Rohtak District 1883-84		980	196
184	9788121258746	27th, Vol. III A	Dujana State 1904		500	16
185	9788121256483	28th	Shahpur District		1780	356
186	9788121256506	29th	Simla District		800	159

S. NO.	ISBN NO.	VOLUME	TITLE	AUTHOR	PRICE	PAGES
187	9788121256520	30th	The Chamba State		2040	408
188	9788121256544	31st	The Chenab Colony 1904		1550	310
189	9788121256568	32nd	Kalsia State		270	53
190	9788121256582	33rd	Suket and Mandi		770	154
191	9788121256605	34th	Phulkian States, Patiala Jind And Nabha 1904		2070	414
192	9788121256643	35th	Simla Hill States		2220	443
193	9788121256667	36th	Sirmur		920	183

RAJPUTANA DISTRICT GAZETTEERS

S. NO.	ISBN NO.	VOLUME	TITLE	AUTHOR	PRICE	PAGES
194	9789362088994	1st, Vol. I-A & B	Ajmer-merwara (Text and Statistics Tables)	C. C. Watson	1230	246
195	9789362080882	2nd. Vol. II-A & B	Mewar Residency (Text and Statistics Tables)	K.D. Erskine	1700	339
196	9789362088444	3rd, Vol. III-A & B	The Western Rajputana States Residency And The Bikaner Agency	K.D. Erskine	3590	718

UNITED PROVINCES OF AGRA AND OUDH DISTRICT GAZETTEERS

S. NO.	ISBN NO.	VOLUME	TITLE	AUTHOR	PRICE	PAGES
197	9789362087560	Vol. I	Agra	H. R. Nevill	2260	452
198	9789362082466	Vol. II	Aligarh	H. R. Nevill	1300	260
199	9789362089779	Vol. III	Allahabad	H. R. Nevill	2050	409
200	9789362081346	Vol. IV	Almora	H. G. Walton	1670	333
201	9789362085658	Vol. V	Azamgarh	D. L. Drake Brockman	1750	349
202	9789362080547	Vol. VI	Bahraich	H. R. Nevill	1410	281
203	9789362085214	Vol. VII	Ballia	H. R. Nevill	1750	350
204	9789362084668	Vol. VIII	Banda	D. L. Drake Brockman	1750	349
205	9789362086518	Vol. IX	Bara Banki	H. R. Nevill	1720	344
206	9789362084101	Vol. X	Bareilly	H. R. Nevill	1640	327
207	9789362086631	Vol. XI	Basti	H. R. Nevill	1610	321
208	9789362083814	Vol. XII	Benares	H. R. Nevill	2290	458
209	9789362086105	Vol. XIII	Bijnor	H. R. Nevill	1820	363
210	9789362081674	Vol. XIV	Budaun	H. R. Nevill	1890	378
211	9789362086891	Vol. XV	Bulandshahr	H. R. Nevill	2100	419
212	9789362081520	Vol. XVI	Cawnpore	H. R. Nevill	2210	442
213	9789362088031	Vol. XVII	Dehra Dun	H. G. Walton	1710	342
214	9789362088710	Vol. XVIII	Etah	E. R. Neave	1600	320
215	9789362082992	Vol. XIX	Etawah	D. L. Drake Brockman	1390	277
216	9789362082220	Vol. XX	Farrukhabad	E. R. Neave	1620	324
217	9789362083869	Vol. XXI	Fatehpur	H. R. Nevill	1890	377
218	9789362085962	Vol. XXII	Fyzabad	H. R. Nevill	1700	339
219	9789362087997	Vol. XXIII	Garhwal	H. G. Walton	1270	254
220	9789362089892	Vol. XXIV	Ghazipur	H. R. Nevill	1600	320
221	9789362085436	Vol. XXV	Gonda	H. R. Nevill	1650	330
222	9789362080271	Vol. XXVI	Gorakhpur	H. R. Nevill	1890	378
223	9789362086129	Vol. XXVII	Hamirpur	D. L. Drake Brockman	1390	277
224	9789362087638	Vol. XXVIII	Hardoi	H. R. Nevill	1680	336
225	9789362081636	Vol. XXIX	Jalaun	D. L. Drake Brockman	1180	236
226	9789362084309	Vol. XXX	Jaunpur	H. R. Nevill	1750	350
227	9789362084187	Vol. XXXI	Jhansi	D. L. Drake Brockman	1960	391
228	9789362089168	Vol. XXXII	Kheri	H. R. Nevill	1650	330
229	9789362086778	Vol. XXXIII	Lucknow	H. R. Nevill	1760	352
230	9789362088635	Vol. XXXIV	Mainpuri	H. R. Nevill	1740	348
231	9789362080424	Vol. XXXV	Meerut	H. R. Nevill	2170	434
232	9789362081087	Vol. XXXVI	Mirzapur	D. L. Drake Brockman	2430	486
233	9789362085443	Vol. XXXVII	Moradabad	H. R. Nevill	1900	380
234	9789362082763	Vol. XXXVIII	Muttra	D. L. Drake Brockman	2140	428
235	9789362089915	Vol. XXXIX	Muzaffarnagar	H. R. Nevill	2260	451
236	9789362086143	Vol. XL	Naini Tal	H. R. Nevill	1890	377
237	9789362086761	Vol. XLI	Partabgarh	H. R. Nevill	1560	312
238	9789362081124	Vol. XLII	Pilibhit	H. R. Nevill	1570	314
239	9789362084453	Vol. XLIII	Rai Bareli	H. R. Nevill	1610	322
240	9789362088284	Vol. XLIV	Rampur	H. R. Nevill	1170	234
241	9789362083654	Vol. XLV	Saharanpur	H. R. Nevill	2190	438
242	9789362083142	Vol. XLVI	Shahjahanpur	H. R. Nevill	1510	302
243	9789362083623	Vol. XLVII	Sitapur	H. R. Nevill	1590	317
244	9789362089939	Vol. XLVIII	Sultanpur	H. R. Nevill	1330	266
245	9789362080851	Vol. XLIX	Unnao	H. R. Nevill	1530	305

RAJPUTANA DISTRICT GAZETTEERS.

VOLUME I.—A.

AJMER-MERWARA.

TEXT

COMPILED BY C. C. WATSON, I.C.S.

AJMER:
SCOTTISH MISSION INDUSTRIES CO., LTD.

1904.

PREFACE.

The Gazetteer of Ajmer-Merwāra compiled by Mr. J. D. (now Sir James Digges) LaTouche in 1875, is the basis of the present work The arrangement has been altered in accordance with Government's general scheme for the new District Gazetteers, and it has been brought up to date, but except where recent investigations have thrown new light on any subject, the matter, and in many cases even the wording of the original have been retained. I am indebted to Mr. R. C. Bramley for the use of material collected for his article on Ajmer-Merwāra in the Imperial Gazetteer at present under issue, to Colonel Melvill for helpful criticism and advice, and to many members of the District Staff for useful notes on various subjects. My clerk Munshi Kanahaya Lal has given much assistance throughout.

C. C. W.

Abu, 21st August 1904.

CONTENTS.

PART I.—DESCRIPTIVE.

CHAPTER I.—*Physical Aspects.*

CHAPTER II.—*History.*

CHAPTER III.—*Population.*

PART II.—ECONOMIC.

CHAPTER IV.—*Agriculture.*

CHAPTER V.—*Rents, Wages and Prices.*

CHAPTER VI.—*Forests.*

CHAPTER VII.—*Arts and Manufactures.*

CHAPTER VIII.—*Commerce and Trade.*

CHAPTER IX.—*Communications.*

Chapter X.—*Famines.*

Part III.—ADMINISTRATIVE.

Chapter XI.—*Government.*

Chapter XII.—*Legislation and Justice.*

Chapter XIII.—*Finance.*

Chapter XIV.—*Land Revenue and Tenures.*

CHAPTER XXI.—*Medical.*

CHAPTER XXII.—*Surveys.*

TEXT.

CHAPTER I.

PHYSICAL ASPECTS.

Ajmer-Merwāra is an isolated Province of British India in Rājputāna, lying between 25° 24′ and 26° 42′ North Latitude and 73° 45′* East Longitude. The Province is composed of two districts (1) Ajmer and (2) Merwāra, and is entirely surrounded by Native States.

Boundaries. The Ajmer district is bounded on the north and west by Mārwār, on the south by Mewār, on the south-west by Merwāra and on the east by Jaipur and Kishangarh. Merwāra is bounded on the north and west by Mārwār and Ajmer, on the south and east by Mewār and on the north-east and to some extent on the north by Ajmer.

Dimensions. The length of the Ajmer district is some 80 miles from north to south, while it is 50 miles in breadth. Merwāra is a narrow strip about 70 miles long, and with a varying breadth of from 15 miles to 1 mile. They have a total area of 2,711 square miles, of which Ajmer has 2,070 and Merwāra 641. The population according to the census of 1901 is 4,76,912 or 175·93 persons to the square mile.

Origin of name. The Sanskrit word *Meru*, a hill is a component part of the names of both districts. In Ajmer it is combined with the name of Rājā Aja, the traditional founder of the fort and city: in Merwāra it expresses the physical features of the country only.

Divisions. The boundaries are territorial: there are no natural divisions. The two tracts originally formed distinct districts, and each possesses a history of its own. The number of villages on the Government rent roll according to the last census is 740, of which 425 are in Ajmer, and 315 in Merwāra. The Land Revenue in 1902-03 amounted to Rs. 2,63,845, Ajmer contributing Rs. 2,09,111 and Merwāra Rs. 54,734. The gross revenue for the Division, including the District Funds, was Rs. 14,49,200.

Of the 2,711 square miles of area *khālsa* and *jāgīr* villages occupy 1,399 square miles, the *istimrāri* estates in Ajmer 1,272 square miles, and towns 40 square miles.

Hill system. The distinguishing feature of the country is the Aravalli range, the strong barrier which divides the plains of Mārwār from the high tableland of Mewār. The range, which commences at the "Ridge" at Delhi, comes into prominence near the town of Ajmer, where it appears in a parallel succession of hills. The highest point, on which is perched the fort of Tāragarh, rises immediately above the city of Ajmer to a height of 2,855 feet above the level of the sea,

---

* 75° 24′.

and between 1,300 and 1,400 feet above the valley at its base. The "Nāgpahār," or Serpent hill, 3 miles west of Ajmer city, attains a scarcely inferior elevation. About 10 miles from Ajmer the hills disappear for a short distance, but in the neighbourhood of Beāwar form a compact double range which approach each other at Jawāja, 14 miles further south, and finally meet at Kukra in the north of the Todgarh *tahsīl*, from which village a succession of hills and valleys extends to the furthest extremity of the Merwāra district. Thence the range gradually becomes bolder and more precipitous, till it finally terminates in the south-east corner of the Sirohi State, near Mount Abu.

Configuration and Watershed.

The plateau on which the town of Ajmer stands marks the highest point in the plains of Hindustan; and from the hills, which hem it in, the country slopes away on every side. The range of hills between Ajmer and Nasīrābād marks the dividing watershed of the continent of India. The rain which falls on the southern or Nasīrābād side, finds its way by the Chambal into the Bay of Bengal; that which falls on the other side is discharged by the Luni into the gulf of Cutch. Further south the watershed is still more clearly marked, and is the high wall of rock which separates Mārwār from Merwāra. The portion of Ajmer east of the range, which connects Srinagar with Rājgarh, including the pargana of Rāmsar and the estates of the *istimrārdars* generally, is an open country with a slope to the east and broken only by gentle undulations. West of the Nāgpahār the pargana of Pushkar stands quite apart from the rest of the district, and is a sea of sand.

Passes.

In Merwāra there are no important mountains; the highest hills occur near Todgarh, where the peak of Goramji attains an elevation of 3,075 feet above the level of the sea. The average level of the valleys is about 1,800 feet. In the *tahsīl* of Beāwar there are four well-known passes. The Barr Pass on the west is a portion of the Imperial road from Agra to Ahmadabād and is metalled throughout. On the eastern side are the Pakheria and Sheopura Ghāts, the first leading to Masuda and the second to Mewār. There is also the Sura Ghāta pass which leads to Mewār. In the Todgarh *tahsīl* there are the Kachbali, Pipli Undabāri, Sarupa Ghāta and Dewair passes leading from Merwāra into Mārwār. There are no passes deserving of the name in Ajmer except where the road to Pushkar, six miles west of Ajmer city, traverses a dip in the Nāgpahār range.

River system.

Owing to their position on the watershed of the continent, the districts do not possess rivers of any importance. The principal stream is the Banās, which takes its rise in the Aravalli range, about 40 miles north-west of Udaipur, and enters the Ajmer District at the extreme south-east corner, not far from the cantonment of Deoli. During the rains this river is frequently in flood, and travellers from Kōtah and Deoli are ferried across at the village of Negria, in Jaipur territory, 5 miles from Deoli. Besides the Banās there are four streams, the Khāri Nadi, the Dai Nadi, the Sagarmati and the Sāraswati. All are mere rivulets in the hot weather, but become torrents in the rains: neither they nor the Banās are used for the transport of produce. The Khāri Nadi rises in the hills near the village of Birjāl in the Merwāra district, and after forming the boundary between Mewār and Ajmer for a short distance, falls into the Banās at the northern extremity of the Sāwar pargana. The Dai Nadi, flowing from west to east across the Ajmer district, is arrested in the early part of its course by the Neārān embankment. Thence it flows by Sarwār, belonging to Kishangarh, and, leaving the district close to Baghēra, eventually also empties itself into the Banās. The Sagarmati rises near the Bisla tank in Ajmer, and after flowing through and fertilizing the Ajmer valley, takes a sweep northwards by Bhaonta and Pisāngan to Govindgarh. Here it meets with the Saraswati, which carries the drainage of the Pushkar valley, and the united stream from this point until it falls into the Rann of Cutch is designated the Luni, or salty river, and it is on this stream that Mārwār chiefly depends for what fertility it has. The affluents of these streams are many, and there are some independent rivulets running northwards into the Sāmbhar lake. None of them have obtained a name, as they are mere drainage channels running only in the rainy season.

Scenery.

In striking scenery Ajmer district is deficient, although Ajmer itself is an exception. The ancient city, with the frowning heights of Tāragarh as a background, makes an effective picture, even when the hot weather has stripped the hills of all their covering. But the general aspect of the country at that season is desolate and forbidding. A change comes with the burst of the monsoon, when the arid plain and rocky hills are transformed by a covering of verdure, which contrasts pleasantly with the blue of the sky. The sunset effects are at times very striking. The most beautiful scene of all is the Anasāgar embankment and lake on a night when the moon is at its full and the marble *chatris* of Shāh Jahān are mirrored in the waters.

Merwāra scenery with its hills has a certain rugged grandeur at all times. But when the autumn and spring harvests are standing in the valleys, some parts are remarkably pretty, and the effect is heightened by the glimpses of water in the numerous tanks and the fresh foliage on the hill side trees. The view from the top of the Dewair pass looking down is singularly beautiful, and also the view from the top of the pass which separates Barākhan from Todgarh. Comparing small things with great, an enthusiast has called the Todgarh district the "Alps of Rājputāna."

It is regrettable that there are few *topes* of trees to be met with either in Ajmer or Merwāra. Except on the embankment of Jawāja tank it is difficult to get shade for tents and animals. Even in the forests the trees are generally mean and scrubby in appearance, and round Ajmer the humble euphorbia supplies their place on the hill-sides. Only near wells or in the watered gardens of the towns do they attain any height or luxuriance of foliage.

Low cover is scanty, both on the slopes of the hills and in the valleys. After good rains the grass grows to a height of two or three feet, but it is soon cut and utilized as fodder.

In ordinary years during the cold weather any traveller through Ajmer-Merwāra will find the districts covered with lakes of all sizes.

With four exceptions all the water reservoirs are artificial, and most of them have been constructed since the establishment of British rule. Of these last the great majority owe their existence to the unaided and untiring energy of one man, who ruled Merwāra from 1836 to 1842, and the united districts from 1842 to 1857, when he died at Beāwar. The name of Colonel Dixon will be remembered in Ajmer and Merwāra for many generations. For years he worked steadily at this single object without help or sympathy, and without much encouragement; for until the works were completed they attracted but little attention, and the district was too remote to allow of the Government of the North-Western Provinces taking at first an intelligent interest in the work. With such help as his *tahsildars* and a few trained *chaprasis* could give, Colonel Dixon constructed these works, and it was only in 1853, when his tanks had been completed, that the appointment of an uncovenanted European Assistant was sanctioned. Nothing worthy of note was done after Colonel Dixon's death till the establishment of the Ajmer Irrigation Division of Public Works in the beginning of 1869. Most of the tanks thereafter constructed are the products of famine labour during the calamities which have since come upon the country.

Besides the artificial reservoirs there are four natural lakes which, in less dry countries, would hardly deserve mention. Of these are the sacred lake of Pushkar and the lake known as Old Pushkar, near the former. Both are depressions among sand-hills without any outlet, but exercise a considerable influence by percolation through the sand-hills on the low sandy bottoms in their vicinity. In Merwāra there are two natural basins, that of Sārgaon and that of Karāntia, both near Beāwar. A passage for the escape of the water of the former has been cut through the encircling sand-hills, and the bed is now regularly cultivated for the spring crop. That of Karāntia lies among hills, and is of no use for irrigation. There are no *jhils* in the districts *i.e.*, extensive swamps such as are met with in the United Provinces of Agra and Oudh, which in the cold weather teem with duck and snipe.

Geology. The geology of the province is that of the Aravalli range, which extends throughout it. The rocks consist of gneiss, biotite, horn blendic schists and limestone, mostly in the form of marble and quartzite, which is probably the Alwar quartzite. The whole are much disturbed, most frequently nearly vertical, and repeated several times in the section. It is the Alwar quartzite, the rock highest in the section within the range, broken, repeated and placed upon end that forms all the long narrow ridges, which rise to a considerable height above the general level of the range, and of which an example is the Tāragarh hill near Ajmer. The best sections of the range in the province are exposed in the Dewair and Pipli passes in Merwāra, ascending from the western plains. The rocks of the former consist of schists and bands of white marble, the actinolite schists occurring at the top. There is also a section of mica schists frequently felspathic and often including bands of limestone. The Pipli pass is similar but contains more frequent quartzite ridges. Granitic intrusions are common and increase in the direction of Todgarh. Towards Beāwar gneiss and granite predominate, hardly any other rocks being exposed. Quartzite in contact with a large pile of gneiss is the characteristic formation of the Chāng and Sendra hills. Towards Ajmer granite alternates with limestone, dark mica schists, and gneiss being not much more than a quartzite containing some felspar. At Ajmer the section across the range differs from the others in the number and size of the ridges of quartzite which cross it. Tāragarh hill, formed of Alwar quartzite rises to a height of upwards of 1,300 feet above the level of the surrounding country, and the same quartzite is repeated in the ridge east of the Anasāgar. East of Ajmer the Alwar quartzites are repeated five times in the section, the intervening low grounds being occupied by schists and limestone, in which intrusive granite is of frequent occurrence. North of Ajmer, the range becomes very broken, and near the Sāmbhar lake it consists almost entirely of the Alwar quartzites, repeated five or six times, forming high narrow parallel nearly vertical ridges a mile or so apart, the intervening ground being covered with blown sand. Under some of the ridges a small thickness of the schists is exposed, and at Makrāna on the western side of the range, the famous white marble quarries are situated. The hills are schistose for the most part, and in appearance often serrate, and are probably volcanic. The cultivated soil is a natural mixture of one-third stiff yellow loam and two-thirds sand, consisting of disintegrated mica schist and felspar. Pure silicious sand is rare.

Botany.

Owing to its geographical position and limited rainfall the flora of Ajmer-Merwāra is not a rich one. Indigenous species are limited, and few of them are attractive in appearance. Several centuries of civilization have practically denuded the Ajmer hillsides of all timber. Even in Merwāra—"the impenetrable jungle" of 1819—only within the reserved areas are trees still found in any quantity. The district has no species peculiar to itself, every plant in it being found also either in the adjacent provinces, or in the dry regions of the Deccan and southern India.

As in other parts of India with a similar vegetation, the majority of the trees and shrubs flower during the hot season, while the herbaceous plants blossom chiefly in the rains. Many of the latter are annuals which wither and die at the approach of the cold weather. Among the larger trees which yield both fuel and building timber are the semul (*bombax malabaricum*), the khejra (*prosopis spicifera*), the kurr (*sterculia urens*), the two *acacias* (*leucoplhœa* and *catechu*), *anogiesus latifolia* and *pendula*, *dichrostachys cinerea*, *lordia rothisi* and the aonla (*phyllanthus emblica*). On the roadsides the babul (*acacia arabica*) nīm (*melia indica*) kurrus (*pangamia glabra*) and jal (*salvadora persica*) are commonly planted, as they thrive well and give good shade. The pīpal (*ficus religiosa*), the banyan (*ficus bengalensis*), the gular (*ficus glomerata*), the tamarind (*tamarindus indica*), and the mango (*mangifera indica*), are found usually in gardens or near villages throughout the district. The shrubby vegetation, which is everywhere more prominent than the arboreal, consists largely of capers, jujubes, tamarisks and grewias. Of the *capparideae*, the *gynandropsis pentaphylla* is common in waste lands, as is also the small jujube (*zizyphus nummularia*). Tamarisks of several species abound in the watercourses, while the *grewias pilosa* and *populifolia* are found everywhere. The *euphorbia nivalia* occurs near Ajmer and in the Merwāra hills.

The herbaceous vegetation consists of *leguminosae* of the genera *alysicarpus, desmodium, crotalaria, cassia, etc.*, of various widely distributed species of *compositae* and *rubiaceæ*. During the rains a few *convolvulaceæ* appear, and grasses and sedges are abundant. The only ferns ever seen are *adiantum lunulatum and candatrum*, *nephrodium molle* and *actiniopterus radiata*. The latter is found only on walls, where it is associated with *funaria hygrometrica*, the only moss at all common in the region. In wells the maidenhair (*adiantum capillus veneris*) is occasionally met with.

Wild Animals.

There is little cover for large game. An occasional tiger is to be met with in the Merwāra forests, while leopards and hyænas are found in the hills from Nāgpahār to Dewair. Wolves are rare. Wild pigs are found in most of the *istimrāri* estates. They are preserved by the Thakurs, as pig-shooting is a favourite amusement of Rajputs. A Tent Club has recently been revived at Nasirābād, but the pig love the shelter of the hills, and the country is broken and hard to ride. Black buck (*antelope bezoartica*), ravine deer (*gazella bennettii*) and nīlgāi (*portax pictus*) are met with in Ajmer. A few sāmbhar (*rusa aristotelis*) are to be found in the hills of both districts. Rewards are given for the destruction of wild animals—Rs. 7 for a tiger, Rs. 5 for a leopard, Rs. 3 for bears, hyænas or wolves; and 2 annas for snakes. The reward for snakes is increased to 6 annas during the two months immediately preceding the breeding season, *i. e.*, May and June. Of small game the great Indian bustard is occasionally found in Ajmer, and florican is a visitor during the rains. Geese duck and snipe are found about the tanks in the cold weather, but good snipe ground is very limited. The small sand grouse is found in abundance; the large sand grouse is rare. Quail are moderately plentiful in the cold weather, and hares and grey partridge are common at all seasons.

Climate and Seasons.

The climate is healthy. In summer it is dry and hot, in the winter cold and bracing, especially in December, January and February, when hoar frost not infrequently covers the ground.

Temperature.

During the 20 years ending in 1900, the maximum temperature recorded in the shade was 116·9° F. in June 1897, the minimum being 35° F. in December 1892. In 1902 the maximum recorded was 108° 5′ F. in May, and the minimum 36° 8′ F. in December.

Rainfall.

The rainfall is precarious and partial. The province is on the border of what may fairly be called the arid zone, and is the debateable land between the north-eastern and south-western monsoons, and beyond the full influence of either. The south-west monsoon sweeps up the Narbada valley from Bombay, and, crossing the table-land at Nimach, gives copious supplies to Mālwa, Jhālawār and Kōtah, and the countries which lie in the course of the Chambal river. The clouds which strike Kathiawar and Cutch are deprived of a great deal of their moisture by the influence of the hills in those countries, and the greater part of the remainder is deposited on Abu and the higher slopes of the Aravalli range, leaving but little for Merwāra, where the hills are lower, and still less for Ajmer. It is only when this monsoon is in considerable force that Merwāra gets a plentiful supply from it, and only the heaviest storms get as far as Jodhpur, where the average rainfall does not exceed 13 or 14 inches, while beyond lie the Jaisalmer State, with an average fall of 6·7 inches, and the rainless land of Sind. The north-eastern monsoon sweeps up the valley of the Ganges from the Bay of Bengal and waters the northern part of Rājputāna, but hardly penetrates further west than the longitude of Ajmer. On the conflicting strength of these two monsoons the rainfall of the province depends.

The prevailing wind during the rainy season is a south-westerly one, but there is little rain from this direction. The south-west monsoon is exhausted before it reaches even Merwāra, and if this monsoon is in the ascendant, the weather may be cloudy and there may be little and partial showers, but no heavy rain. It is from the north-east that Ajmer, Beāwar and Todgarh obtain their heaviest rainfalls, though the south-western monsoon has naturally more effect at Todgarh than at Ajmer. The central portions of the province often receive heavy falls from the north-west, the north-east monsoon being apparently diverted from its course by the winds from the desert. Not only, however, is the rainfall most precarious and partial, varying much in total amount from year to year and from place to place, and falling with fury on one side of a hill, while the other side is perfectly dry, but it is most irregularly distributed over the rainy season, and most uncertain in the intensity of the fall. The last is a most important question with reference to the filling of the reservoirs. If the rain comes in light showers, even though it be on the whole an average fall, the soil will absorb it, the *nallas* will not run and the tanks will remain empty. If the fall is sudden and heavy, and at the same time general within the catchment area of a tank, the chances are that the embankment will be damaged. The best rainy season is one which includes a fall of 3 or 4 inches in the 24 hours in June, and a similar fall in September, with intermediate showers. Then the tanks fill and are replenished for the *rabi* harvest, and the *kharif* crop is not drowned with excess of moisture. These peculiarities may be illustrated from the history of the twenty years before 1899-1900. In 1881-82 the rainfall in Ajmer was 17·9 inches. The early rainfall was deficient and the *kharif* crops failed, but heavy showers in September filled the tanks and the irrigated *rabi* crops were good. In 1882-83 the monsoon began well, but the *kharif* crops were injured by excessive rainfall in September. This filled the tanks and gave a good irrigated *rabi* crop, but the *barani* or dry crop failed through want of light showers after September. The rainfall was 24 inches: much the same happened in 1884-85, when the rainfall was 23·9 inches in Ajmer and 28·5 in

Merwāra. The heavy September rains filled the tanks but ruined the maize and cotton crops sown as *kharif.* In 1885-86 the rains recorded were 19·3 inches. There was a good fall in July and August but hardly a drop in September. The tanks did not fill nor did the early crops ripen properly, so both *kharif* and *rabi* were comparative failures. In 1887-88, 22 inches fell in Ajmer and 20·3 in Merwāra, but it came principally in June and July and in the form of constant drizzle, with a result to the crops similar to that in 1885-86. In 1888-89 only 18·7 inches were recorded in Ajmer and 20·9 in Merwāra, but though slightly deficient in quantity it was well distributed. Heavy rain fell in July and September, with intermediate light showers: the tanks filled and the crops were good.

In 1889-90 there was promise of excellent harvests, but although there was a total rainfall of 21·4 inches in Ajmer and 16·8 in Merwāra, it ceased early in September and the out-turn was below the average in both crops. In 1890-91 the rain was very deficient, 12·05 inches in Ajmer and 13·56 in Merwāra. It set in early but soon ceased The following year was one of famine. The rainfall was 8·50 inches in Ajmer and 10·24 in Merwāra. These two successive years of shortage produced a water as well as a crop famine. In 1892-93 the total rainfall was large, averaging 37·3 inches in both districts, but owing to its late commencement the *kharif* out-turn was only fair. In 1893-94 the rains were timely and well distributed and crops were good. In 1894-95 the rains, 25·33 inches in Ajmer and 28·51 in Merwāra, were above the normal but were badly distributed. Want of heavy showers in September left the tanks half empty, and the consequent irrigation suffered. In 1896-97 heavy showers fell in September and filled the tanks, but there was no rain later, and the dry crops were a failure. In 1897-98 the rain was over the average and well distributed. In 1898-99 only 14·05 inches fell in Ajmer and 10·66 in Merwāra. The rain began early but stopped entirely by the end of July. The *kharif* suffered severely and, as the tanks did not fill, the *rabi* cultivated area was insignificant. It was followed by the famine year of 1899-00, when 8·36 inches fell in Ajmer and 4·92 in Merwāra. The greater part came in June; the *kharif* crops failed to reach maturity and, as the rains ceased entirely after a few showers in September, tho *rabi* crops were lost also.

The average annual fall during the 20 years was 19 inches in the Ajmer district and 20 inches in Merwāra. The maximum rainfall during this period was 37 inches in each district in 1892-93 and the minimum 8 inches in Ajmer and 5 inches in Merwāra in 1899-1900, as already stated. The rainfall in 1900-01 was 28 inchesin the Ajmer district and 30 in Merwāra.

Storms, Cyclones, Earthquakes.

There have been no cyclones or floods within Ajmer-Merwāra during the last three decades. On the 12th June 1897 slight shocks of earthquake were felt at 4-45 P.M. in Ajmer. They came from west to east, and were felt horizontally about 5 or 6 times within the duration of 15 minutes. But for the fact of their rarity they would be hardly worth mentioning.

CHAPTER II.

History.

(a.) Ajmer.

Hindu Period.

The early history of Ajmer is, as might be expected, legendary in its character, and commences with the rule of the Chauhāns, the last born of the Agnikulas, and the most valiant of the Rājput races. According to tradition, the Fort and City of Ajmer were founded by Rāja Aja, a descendant of Anhal, the first Chauhān, in the year 145 A.D. Aja at first attempted to build a fort on the Nāgpahār, or Serpent Hill, and the site chosen by him is still pointed out. His evil genius, however, destroyed in the night the walls erected in the day, and Aja determined to build on the hill now known as Tāragarh. Here he constructed a fort, which he called "Garh Bitle," and in the valley known as Indrakōt he built a town, which he called after himself, and which has become famous as Ajmer. This Prince is generally known by the name of Ajaipal, which, Colonel Tod explains, was derived from the fact that he was a goat-herd "whose piety in supplying one of the saints of Pushkar with goats' milk procured him a territory." The name probably suggested the myth, and it is more reasonable to suppose that the appellation was given to him when, at the close of his life, he became a hermit, and ended his days at the gorge in the hills about ten miles from Ajmer, which is still venerated as the temple of Ajaipal.

It has been shown, however, by more recent research that Aja or Ajāya flourished about 1000 A.D., and that the foundation of Ajmer must be ascribed to this period. The Chauhāns came to Rājputāna from Ahichhatrapur on the Ganges about 750 A.D., and their first capital was Sāmbhar. Their possessions included the tract now known as Ajmer, but there was at that time no known city there. Ajāya's son Anā (or Arno) constructed the fine Anāsāgar embankment, on which the Emperor Shāh Jahān subseqently erected a magnificent range of marble pavilions. An inscription discovered at Chitōr by Pandit Gauri Shankar of Udaipur shows that Anā was alive in 1150 A.D. Vigraharāja III, otherwise known as Visaldeo, a son of Anā, was the most famous of the Chauhān dynasty of Ajmer. He conquered Delhi from the Tuars, and constructed the Bisal-Sāgar Tank in his ancestral territory. The latest inscription under his reign is dated 1163. Prithvi Rāj, nephew of Visaldeo, was king of Delhi and Ajmer at the time of the invasion of Shahāb-ud-dīn Muhammad Ghorī. In 1191 he defeated the latter in a great battle and forced him to fly. But in 1193 Muhammad Ghorī returned with a fresh army recruited in Afghānistān and Central Asia. The Rājput chiefs were weakened by feuds, and Prithvi Rāj was defeated, taken prisoner, and murdered in cold blood. Muhammad Ghorī shortly afterwards took Ajmer, massacred all the inhabitants who opposed him, and reserved the rest for slavery. After this expedition he made over the country to a relation of Prithvi Rāj under an engagement for a heavy tribute. In the following year Muhammad Ghorī prosecuted his conquests by the destruction of the Rāhtor kingdom of Kanauj, an event of considerable importance in the history of Ajmer, in that it led to the emigration of the greater part of the Rāhtor clan from Kanauj to Mārwār.

The Delhi Sultans.

The new Rāja of Ajmer was soon reduced to perplexities by a pretender, and Kutab-ud-dīn Eibak, then Viceroy and afterwards the first of the slave dynasty at Delhi, marched to his relief. Hari Rāj the pretender was defeated, and Kutab-ud-dīn, having appointed a governor of his own faith to control the Rāja, proceeded with his expedition to Gujarāt. A year or two afterwards, however, the Rāja, uniting with the Rāhtors and Mers, attempted independence. Kutab-ud-dīn, marched from Delhi in the height of the hot season and shut up the Rāja in the fort. Here finding no means of escape, he ascended the funeral pyre as is related in the *Tajul Maasir*. Kutab-ud-dīn then marched against the confederated Rāhtors and Mers, but was defeated and wounded, and obliged to retreat to Ajmer, where he was besieged by the confederate army. A strong reinforcement from Ghazni, however, caused the enemy to raise the siege, and Kutab-ud-dīn annexed the country to the kingdom of Delhi, and made over the charge of the fort of Tāragarh to an officer of his own, Sayyid Husain, whose subsequent tragic fate has caused him to be enrolled in the list of martyrs, and whose shrine is still the most conspicuous object on the hill he was unable to defend. On the death of Kutab-ud-dīn in A.D. 1210, the Rāhtors joined the Chauhāns and made a night attack upon the fort. The garrison was taken unprepared, and massacred to a man. Their tombs, as well as those of Sayyid Husain and his celebrated horse, may still be seen on Tāragarh in the enclosure, which bears the name of *Ganj Shahīdān* or treasury of martyrs.

Shams-ud-dīn Altamsh, the successor of Kutab-ud-dīn, restored the authority of the Kings of Delhi, and it was maintained till the disastrous invasion of Taimur. Rāna Kumbho of Mewār profited by the relaxation of all authority, which ensued upon the sack of Delhi and the extinction of the house of Tughlak, to take possession of Ajmer, but on his assassination the territory fell into the hands of the Kings of Mālwā, with whom the Rāna had been perpetually at variance, and for 15 years had waged war.

The Kings of Mālwā obtained possession in A.D. 1469, and held Ajmer till the death of Mahmud II in A.D. 1531, when the kingdom of Mālwā was annexed to that of Gujarāt.

On the death of Mahmud II, Mal Deo Rāhtor, who had recently succeeded to the throne of Mārwār, took possession of Ajmer among other conquests. He improved the fortress of Tāragarh, and commenced the construction of a lift to raise water to the fort from the "Nur Chashma" spring at the foot of the hill. The work still stands, as solid as on the day it was built, but the scheme was never completed. The Rāhtors held Ajmer for 24 years, but the country was one of the earlier acquisitions of Akbar, and from 1561 A.D. to 1730, a period of 170 years, Ajmer was an integral part of the Mughal Empire.

Mughal Emperors.

Akbar included Ajmer in a *sūbah* or province, which gave its name to the whole of Rājputāna. The great importance of the fort and district of Ajmer as a *point d' appui* in the midst of Rājputāna was early recognized by the Muhammadan rulers. It commanded the routes from northern India to Gujarāt on the one side, and to Mālwā on the other. Ajmer itself was a centre of trade, with a well-nigh impregnable fort to protect it. The situation was strong, central, and picturesque, and was well watered as compared with the arid tracts around. The Mughal sovereigns, like their predecessors, were not slow to grasp the advantages of the place, and Ajmer became an appanage of the royal residence.

Akbar had made a vow that, if a son were born to him and lived, he would go on foot from Agra to Ajmer, and offer thanks at the tomb of the saint Muin-ud-dīn Chishti, a holy man who came from Gor to India in 1143 A.D., and whose tomb, known as the Dargāh Khwāja Sāhib, has been a place of Muhammadan pilgrimage for several centuries. Salīm, afterwards Jahāngīr, was born in A.D. 1570. Ten years later Akbar built a fortified palace, the Dar-ul-Khair, just outside the city. Jahāngīr and Shāh Jahān both spent a considerable portion of their time at Ajmer, and it was here that the former received Sir Thomas Roe, the Ambassador from King James I, who reached Ajmer on the 23rd December 1615. He had his first audience with Jahāngīr on the 10th January 1616, and was received by the Mughal Emperor with "courtly condescension." Near Chitōr, on his way to Ajmer from Surat, Roe met the eccentric Thomas Coryat, whose mania for travelling brought him on foot from Jerusalem to Ajmer. The "World's foot post," as he describes himself, wrote a pamphlet, "From the Court of the great Moghul, Resident at the Town of Asmere in Eastern India," which is a quaint and early specimen of travellers' tales. Roe himself remained at Ajmer until November 1616, and afterwards accompanied Jahāngīr in his March to Ujjain. Although it appears doubtful whether he managed to obtain any substantial advantage for the East India Company as a result of his mission, his Journal has left us a vivid picture of the life both in Ajmer and in camp. It was at Deora, near Ajmer, that in A.D. 1659 Aurangzeb crushed the army of the unfortunate Dārā and forced his brother into the flight which was destined to terminate only by his imprisonment and death. The celebrated traveller Bernier met and accompanied Dārā for three days during the flight, and has given a graphic description of the miseries and privations of the march. During the war with Mewār and Mārwār, which was brought about by the bigotry of Aurangzeb, Ajmer was the head-quarters of that Emperor, who nearly lost his throne here in 1679 by the combination of Prince Akbar with the enemy.

Rāhtors of Mārwār.

On the death of the Sayyids in 1720 A.D., Ajīt Singh, son of Jaswant Singh of Mārwār, found his opportunity in the weakness consequent on the decline of the Mughal Empire to seize on Ajmer, and kill the Imperial governor. He coined money in his own name and set up every emblem of sovereignty. Muhammad Shāh collected a large army and invested Tāragarh. The fort held out for four months, when Ajīt Singh agreed to surrender his conquest. Ten years later Abhay Singh, the accomplice in the assassination of his own father, Ajīt Singh, was appointed by Muhammad Shāh Viceroy of Ajmer and Ahmadābād, and Ajmer became practically a portion of Mārwār. The parricide Bakht Singh obtained Nagaur and Jalor from his brother, Abhay Singh. Abhay Singh was succeeded by Ram Singh, who attempted to wrest Jalor from his uncle. This led to the battle of Merta, where Ram Singh was defeated and forced to fly. He determined to call in the aid of the Marāthās, and at Ujjain found the camp of Jai Appa Sindhia, who readily took the opportunity of interference. Meanwhile Bakht Singh had been poisoned, and his son, Bijai Singh, opposed the Marāthās. He was defeated and fled to Nagaur, which withstood a year's siege, though meanwhile all the country submitted to Ram Singh. At the end of a year Jai Appa was murdered by two soldiers of Bijai Singh, who sacrificed themselves in their master's interest. With Jai Appa removed, the siege languished, and eventually a compromise was agreed upon. Bijai Singh surrendered to the Marāthās in full sovereignty the fort and district of Ajmer as *mundkati* or blood-money for the death of their leader. The Marāthās on their side abandoned the cause of Ram Singh. A fixed triennial tribute was to be paid to the Marāthās by Bijai Singh. Ram Singh obtained the Mārwār and Jaipur share of the Sāmbhar Lake, and resided there until his death. These events occurred in A.D. 1756.

Marāthās.

For 31 years the Marāthās held undisturbed possession of Ajmer, till in 1787, on the invasion of Jaipur by Madhoji Sindhia, the Jaipur Rāja called in the Rāhtors for aid against the common foe. The call was promptly answered, and at the battle of Tonga the Marāthās suffered a signal defeat. The Rāhtors re-took Ajmer, drove out Mirza Beg, the Marāthā governor, and annulled their tributary engagements. The success was, however, transient, for in three years time the Marāthās, led by De Boigne, defeated the Rāhtors utterly at Patan. General De Boigne then marched on Ajmer. On the 21st August 1791, he arrived under the walls: the next day the town was taken and the fort invested. The citadel, however, had been provisioned for a year and was defended by a numerous garrison. After 17 days' operations De Boigne, converting the siege into a blockade, marched with the greater part of his troops against the Rājputs, who had assembled on the plains of Merta. On the 10th September the Rājput army was surprised before daybreak and nearly annihilated, and by three o'clock on the same day the town of Merta was taken by assault. The Rāhtors now submitted and agreed to pay tribute. Ajmer reverted to the Marāthās and was held by them till its cession to the British Government.

Cession to the British Government.

Singhi Dhanraj was Governor of Ajmer during the three years it was held by the Rāhtors. The best known of the Marāthā *sūbahdārs* was Govind Rao, who appears to have been a strong and good governor. By the treaty of 25th June 1818, Daulat Rao Sindhia, after the Pindari war, ceded the district of Ajmer, valued in the treaty at Rs. 505,484, to the British Government; and on the 28th July 1818, Mr. Wilder, the first Superintendent of Ajmer, received charge of the district from Bāpu Sindhia, the last Marāthā *sūbahdār*.

The history of Ajmer from 1818 is the history of its administration. The long roll of battles and sieges is closed. The district, worn out by the incessant warfare of half a century, at length enjoys rest, and the massive battlements of Tāragarh begin to crumble in a secure peace. Mr. Wilder and his successors worked hard to improve the condition of the people, and the long incumbency of Colonel Dixon, who took charge of the district in 1842 in addition to Merwāra, was productive of much good. Irrigation works were vigorously pushed forward. Commerce and agriculture were encouraged, and in 1851 the district came under a regular settlement. The measures taken to win the confidence of the people were successful, and the mutiny of 1857 passed over the province like a cloud. On the 28th May two regiments of Bengal Infantry and a battery of Bengal Artillery mutinied at Nasirābād. The European residents, however, were sufficiently protected by a regiment of Bombay Infantry, while a detachment of the Merwāra Battalion made a forced march to Ajmer and protected the Treasury and Magazine. There was no interruption of civil government. The mutinous regiments marched direct to Delhi, and the agricultural classes did not share in the revolt.

Mutiny of 1857.

Since then famines alone have troubled the district. The more noteworthy are described in their proper place. The opening of the Rājputāna-Mālwā Railway in 1879 ushered in a period of material prosperity. The population of Ajmer city has nearly doubled, and the place will probably continue to grow in size and importance. The district, although severely affected by recent famines will, given a series of good years, quickly recuperate. These natural calamities alone disturb its peaceful progress.

(b.) Merwāra.

Early History.

The history of Merwāra before the occupation of Ajmer by the British authorities in 1818, is practically a blank. Hardly anything was known of the country, except that it was a difficult, hilly tract, inhabited by an independent and plundering race, who cared not for agriculture, and who supplied their wants at the expense of the surrounding territories. Sawai Jai Singh of Jaipur had penetrated no further than Jhāk in an endeavour to subdue the country, and Amir Khan had failed in an attempt to chastise the plunderers of Jhāk and Chāng. Mr. Wilder, the first Superintendent of Ajmer, entered into agreements with the villages of Jhāk, Shāmgarh, Lūlwa, Kāna Khera and Kheta Khera, the nucleus of what is now *Khālsā* Merwāra, binding them to abstain from plunder. The pledge, however, was little respected, or could not really be enforced by the headmen, and in March 1819, a force was detached from Nasirābād for the attack of these places. No opposition was encountered, the villages were taken one after the other, and all levelled to the ground. The inhabitants escaped into the adjacent hills. Strong police posts were stationed at Jhāk, Shāmgarh, and Lūlwa.

In November 1820 a general insurrection broke out. The police posts were cut off and the men composing them were killed. The thorough subjugation of the country was then determined on. A force, stronger than the former retook Jhāk, Lūlwa, and Shāmgarh, and after some correspondence with the governments of Udaipur and Jodhpur, and after co-operation promised on their part, the force advanced into Mewār and Mārwār-Merwāra to punish the refugees of Jhāk Lūlwa, and Shāmgarh, and the men who had given them an asylum.

Bōrwa was the first village of which possession was taken, and the attack was then directed against Hathun, where a repulse was sustained with a loss of three killed and twenty-three wounded. In the night, however, the garrison evacuated the fort. The troops then marched on Barār and took it after slight resistance. The capture of Mandlān and Barsawāra followed, and a strong detachment was then sent against Kōt-Kirāna and Bagri in Mārwār-Merwāra. These were taken and made over to Jodhpur, and the reverses of the Mers reached their culminating point in the capture of Rāmgarh, whither most of their chief men had retreated. These were nearly all killed or wounded or taken prisoners, and the remaining strongholds submitted in rapid succession. A detachment of cavalry and infantry was left at Jhāk, and the main body withdrew at the close of January 1821, the campaign having lasted three months. Captain Tod, in the name of the Rāna, undertook the administration of the portion belonging to Mewār. He appointed a governor, built the fort of Todgarh in the centre of the tract, raised a corps of 600 matchlock men for this special service, and began to collect revenue. A different policy was pursued by the court of Jodhpur. The villages which had been decided to belong to Mārwār were made over to the adjoining Thākurs: there was no controlling authority and no unity of administration. Ajmer brought all its share under direct management, but at first the Thākurs of Masūda and Kharwa were held responsible for the establishment of order, under the superintendence of Mr. Wilder. It soon appeared that this triple government was no government; the criminals of one portion found security in another; the country became infested with murderous gangs, and the state of Merwāra was even worse than before the conquest. In these circumstances it was determined that the three portions should be brought under the management of one officer, vested with full authority in civil and criminal matters, and that a battalion of 8 companies of 70 men each should be enrolled from among the Mers.

Treaties with Udaipur and Jodhpur.

The negotiations with Udaipur resulted in the treaty of May 1823, by which the management of Mewār-Merwāra, consisting of 76 villages, was made over to the British Government for a period of 10 years, the Rāna agreeing to pay Rs. 15,000 a year to cover civil and military expenses. In March, 1824, a similar engagement was, after some difficulty, concluded by Mr. Wilder with the Jodhpur Durbar. It was arranged that the sum of Rs. 15,000 should be paid annually on account of civil and military expenses, the Maharāna and Mahārāja receiving in each case the revenue of their respective portions. In March 1833, the arrangement with Mewār was continued for a further period of eight years, the Rāna agreeing to pay Rs 20,000 *Chitori* or Rs. 16,000 *Kaldār* on account of expenses. On the 23rd October 1835, the arrangement with Mārwār was extended for a further period of nine years. The transfer of Jodhpur territory was only partial, and many villages were left in the hands of the border ing Thākurs, though nominally under the police superintendence of the British authorities. Twenty villages were made over by the first treaty, and by the second treaty some were added, but these latter were returned to Marwār in 1842. About this year the agreements of 1833 and 1835 expired, and it became necessary to make further arrangements for their continuance. The Udaipur Durbar expressed its willingness to allow its villages to remain under British management so long as it might suit the convenience of the British Government, and the Jodhpur Durbār expressed its readiness to do the same. But no agreements were executed, and although an effort was made to procure the perpetual cession of their shares from the respective Durbārs, it was unsuccessful. On this unsatisfactory footing the British administration of Merwāra remained for many years. With Udaipur the question was finally settled in 1883 by the following arrangement:—

The British Government was to accept the revenues of Mewār-Merwāra in full discharge of the Udaipur State's contributions towards the cost of administration of the tract, the expenses of the Mewār Bhil Corps and of the Merwāra Battalion, and no demand was to be made upon the Durbār for arrears of payment. The Mahārāna was specifically assured that his rights of sovereignty over Mewār-Merwāra would be in no wise prejudiced by this arrangement; and that, should the yearly receipts for the district at any time exceed Rs. 66,000, which sum represents the contribution payable by the Durbār for the administration of Mewār-Merwāra and the expenses of the two local corps, the surplus money should be paid in full to the Durbār. The Resident at Mewār was to annually report to the Durbār the aggregate revenue received from the district. This arrangement is still in force.

In the case of Mārwār-Merwāra it was many years also before a satisfactory solution could be effected. Eventually in 1885 it was agreed that Jodhpur should retain its sovereign rights in its Mārwār-Merwāra villages and receive Rs. 3000 a year from them, and that in the event of a profit being derived from them by Government, the Durbār should receive 40 per cent. of it. On these conditions the Government of India have full and permanent administrative control over the villages.

Administration of Colonels Hall and Dixon.

Colonel Hall was the first officer appointed to the charge of the newly acquired district, and he ruled Merwāra from 1823 to 1836. He was fettered by no instructions, and was left to provide for the administration of the country. His system was simple and paternal, but well suited to the needs of the people. Civil and criminal justice were administered by *panchāyat* or arbitration of the assembled elders of the village. If two-thirds of the *panchāyat* agreed, the question was settled.

The jail was made self-supporting; each prisoner was supplied with a *seer* of barley-meal daily and with nothing else, but if the prisoner wished he might furnish his own flour. On his release he was obliged to pay for his food and for his share of the jail establishment as well as for any clothing that might have been given him, and this system of recovering the jail expenses from the prisoners and their relations lasted till Colonel Dixon's death, when, on the representation of Captain Brooke, it was abolished in 1858. The revenue was collected by an estimate of the crops, one-third of the produce being the Government's share, except in some special cases. The estimate was made by a writer on the part of Government, assisted by the *patels*, the *patwāris*, and the respectable landowners. In calculating the money payment to be made, the prices current in the country for 10 or 12 miles round were taken and an average struck. Cultivators who broke up new land or made wells received leases authorizing them to hold at $\frac{1}{6}$th and $\frac{1}{8}$th of the produce. The headmen of the villages paid $\frac{1}{4}$th.

This system of administration possesses historical value as being that under which the country throve until 1851, the year of Colonel Dixon's regular settlement. According to competent observers it was consistently successful, and to it much of the rapid progress made by the country was due. Another important factor in the civilization of the people was the Merwāra Battalion which was raised in 1822. By service in its ranks the wild mountaineers became brave and disciplined soldiers, and when they returned home they carried the leaven of law-abiding order into the villages.

Colonel Hall was followed by Colonel Dixon, who ruled Merwāra until 1842, and thereafter the combined districts of Ajmer and Merwāra until his death in 1857. He is still, and deservedly, remembered by the Merwāra people as their greatest benefactor. His administration was remarkable for the large number of tanks which were built in Merwāra for irrigation purposes, and they were all entirely due to his personal energy and enthusiasm. Their good effect can hardly be over-estimated. Agriculture became possible and profitable, and the area under cultivation increased rapidly. In order to make the people obtain the benefits of their industry and to attract traders to Merwāra, Colonel Dixon founded the walled town of Nayānagar, or Beāwar, in 1835. Mahajans flocked to it; the enterprise was at once successful; and the place is now the commercial and administrative capital of the district. The founder is probably the latest Englishman who has built a "fenced city." Before he died he had the satisfaction of seeing around him a people whose wants had been supplied, whose grievances had been redressed, and who were described as being "most prosperous and highly favoured."

Nothing can speak more plainly to the great social change which has been wrought in the inhabitants of Merwāra than the deserted and ruined state of their ancient villages. These were formerly invariably perched upon hills in inaccessible places for the sake of safety from the attack of their fellow-men and of wild beasts. The adoption of habits of industry and agriculture has rendered the retention of such dwellings alike unnecessary and inconvenient. The old villages are nearly deserted and are fast falling into decay. New hamlets have sprung up everywhere in the villages, and the tendency to settle near the cultivated land is still on the increase.

(c) Archæology.

Ajmer is rich in objects of archæological interest. The most important is the mosque known as the *Arrhāi-din-kā-Jhonprā* or "Two and a-half days' shed." This, originally a Brahmanical temple or college, was converted into a mosque by order of Muhammad Ghori, the legend being that as he passed the temple, he ordered that it should be ready for him to pray in on his return in two and a-half days. The pillars and the roof of the temple were permitted to remain, but the rest of the Hindu portion of the building was demolished and much of the carving on the remaining pillars defaced. A screen or facade of very remarkable beauty was erected, and forms the front of the present mosque, which was surrounded further by lofty cloisters with a tower at each corner of the quadrangle. The cloisters have largely fallen in, and the surviving portions of the towers are very imperfect. The facade of the mosque, however, and the mosque itself are in good preservation, having been extensively repaired in Lord Mayo's Viceroyalty, while considerable further restorations were carried out in 1900-1902. The mosque is a few years only later in date than the Kutab mosque, near Delhi, and is one of the best specimens of the mosques of its kind. **Arrhāi-din-kā-Jhonprā**

The embankment of the Anā Sāgar Lake supports the beautiful marble pavilions erected as garden or pleasure-houses by Shāh Jahān. Of the five original pavilions, four remain in good preservation: the remains of the fifth have been preserved but are very slender. The embankment, moreover, contains the site of the former *hammām*, the floor of which still remains. Of the five marble pavilions two were at one time built into residencies for British officials, while two others were converted into an office and a library. The houses and enclosures were finally swept away in 1900-1902, when the two south pavilions were re-erected, the marble parapet completely repaired, and the embankment restored as far as was practicable to its early conditions. **Bārādaries.**

The shrine of the "Dargāh Khwāja Sāhib," where is the tomb of the Muhammadan saint Muīn-ud-dīn Chishti, is another remarkable building, and is an object of pilgrimage to Muhammadans from all parts of the world. The shrine contains a mosque of Akbar, another by Shāh Jahān, and numerous more modern sacred buildings. The gateway, though disfigured by modern colouring, is picturesque and old. The shrine contains the large drums and brass candlesticks taken by Akbar at the sack of Chitōr, and given by him to the shrine. The saint's tomb is richly adorned with gold and silver, but only **Dargāh.**

Muhammadans are permitted to enter its precincts. The Dargāh was commenced in the reign of Shams-ud-dīn Altamash (circa 1211—1236 A.D.) and finished in that of Sultān Humāyūn The shrine is venerated and visited by Hindus as well as Muhammadans.

Magazine Fort.

The Ajmer Fort was built by the Emperor Akbar. It is a massive square building, with lofty octagonal bastions at each corner. The Fort was used as the residence of the Mughal Emperors during their visits to Ajmer, and was the head-quarters of the administration, both in their time and in that of the Marāthās. The main entrance faces the city and is lofty and imposing. It was here that the Mughal Emperors appeared in state, and here that, as recorded by Sir Thomas Roe, state criminals were publicly executed. The ground surrounding the Fort has been largely built over, and its striking appearance is thus considerably impaired. The interior was used as a magazine during British occupation until 1857, and the centre building, now used as *tahsīl* offices, has been so much altered that its original shape and proportions are difficult to trace and restore. With the Fort the outer city walls of the same period are connected. These surround the city, and are pierced by five gates named the Delhi, Madār, Usri, Agra and Tirpolia gates. These gates were at one time highly decorated, but the Delhi gate alone retains any traces of its earlier ornament.

Tāragarh Fort.

In the older city, lying in the valley beneath the Tāragarh hill and now abandoned, the Nūr-chashma, a garden-house used by the Mughals, still remains, as do the water lifts built by the Rāhtors and previously mentioned. The Tāragarh Fort or citadel which defended the earlier city is in fair preservation.

Pushkar.

Pushkar, seven miles north of Ajmer, is a celebrated place of pilgrimage, and the great sanctity of its lake, equalled, according to Colonel Tod, only by that of Manusarowar in Tibet, is due to the belief that here Brahmā performed the *yajna*, and that the Sarasvati here reappears in five streams. The legends connected with these two beliefs may be found in the "Pushkar Mahatma" of the "Padma Purāna." Brahmā was perplexed as to where he should perform the sacrifice according to the Vedas, as he held no temple on earth like other deities. As he reflected, the lotus fell from his hand, and he determined that where it fell, there would he perform his sacrifice. The lotus rebounding struck the earth in three places; water issued from all three, and Brahmā descending called the name of the place "Pushkar," after the lotus. Brahmā then collected all the gods, and on the 11th day of the bright half of Kārtik all was ready. Each god and *rishi* had his own special duty assigned to him, and Brahmā stood ready with a jar of *amrit* on his head. The sacrifice, however, could not begin until Sāvitri appeared, and she refused to come without Lakshmi, Pārvati, and Indrāni, whom Pavan had been sent to summon. On hearing of her refusal Brahmā became enraged and said to Indra, "Search me out a girl that I may marry her and commence the sacrifice, for the jar of *amrit* weighs heavy on my head." Indra accordingly went, but found none except a Gūjar's daughter, whom he purified by passing through the body of a cow, and then bringing her to Brahmā told what he had done. Vishnu observed: "Brāhmans and cows are in reality identical; you have taken her from the womb of a cow, and this may be considered a second birth." Shīva added that as she had passed through a cow she might be called Gāyatri. The Brāhmans agreed that the sacrifice might now proceed, and Brahmā having married Gāyatri and having enjoined silence upon her, placed on her head the jar of *amrit*, and the *yajna* commenced.

The sacrifice, however, was soon interrupted by a naked man, who appeared crying, "Atmat, atmat," and who, at the instigation of Shīva, threw a skull into the sacrificial ground. When it was attempted to remove the skull, two appeared in its place, and the whole ground gradually became covered with skulls, till Shīva, at Brahmā's request, finally agreed to remove them on condition that he should have a temple at Pushkar, there to be worshipped under the name Atmateswar. Meanwhile a number of Brāhmans, all ugly men, arrived from the Dakhin. As they bathed in the lake they became handsome, and the *ghāt* at which they bathed, called Sarup ghāt, is the resort of pilgrims on the 11th day of *Kārtik*. On the morning of the 12th day the Brāhmans came to Brahmā and asked where they were to bathe. In reply he directed them to bathe in the Prechi Sarasvati, the stream which passes by the village of Hokrān, and it is explained how the Sarasvati, after disappearing under ground to escape the heat of the fire which she is carrying to the sea, re-appears in five channels in the sacred soil of Pushkar; how two of these meet at Nānd, 5 miles from Pushkar; and how from the junction the river, thereafter called the Luni, proceeds to the sea. The sacrifice was disturbed this day by Bhattu Brāhman, who let lose a snake among the Brāhmans. The reptile coiled itself round Bhrigu Rishi, whose son imprecated a curse against Bhattu that he might become a snake. Bhattu, going to his grandfather Brahmā, was consoled by the promise that he should be the founder of the 9th order of snakes, and was directed to go to the Nāgpahār, where he should receive worship on the 5th day of the dark half of *Sāwan*, at the place called the Nāgkund.

The sacrifice proceeded till the 15th, each day having its appointed duties; for this day the Brāhmans were directed to make a circuit of the lakes and to bathe in "Gayākup," the tank now known by the name of "Sudā Bāi." Shortly after their return Sāvitri appeared, greatly incensed at the disregard which had been shown to her. Brahmā sought to pacify her, but to no purpose, and she went away in a rage to the hill north of the lake, where is her temple.

After the *yajna* was performed by Brahmā, Pushkar became so holy that the greatest sinners by merely bathing in it went to heaven. Heaven became inconveniently crowded, and the gods complained that no man any longer regarded them or his duty, so easy was it to get to heaven. Brahmā agreed accordingly that the *tirth* should only be on earth from the 11th day of *Kārtik* to the full moon, and for the remainder of the year he promised to remove the *tirth* to the air. Such is the legend given in the Pushkar Mahatma.

The legends concerning Pushkar after the *yajna* of Brahmā are rather confusing. The virtue of the lake is said to have been forgotten till it was re-discovered by Rājā Nahar Rao Parikar of Mandōr, who followed a white boar to the margin of the lake, and then, dismounting to quench his thirst, found on touching the water that he was cured of a skin disease. He is accordingly said to have had the lake excavated and to have built *ghāts*. Pushkar after this appears to have come into the possession of Chechi Gūjars, for there is a legend that some 700 years ago, a large body of Sanyāsīs came to bathe in Pushkar; they disapproved of the Gūjars being in possession of the *ghāts*, killed them all on the night of the Dewāli, and turning out the Kānphata Jogis, who had become priests of the temples, themselves left a representative at each temple.

There are five principal temples at Pushkar, those dedicated to Brahmā, Sāvitri, Badri Nārāyana, Varaha, and Shīva Atmateswara. They are all of comparatively modern construction, for the old temples suffered much at the hands of the Mughals, and Aurangzeb here, as elsewhere in India, enjoys the reputation of having destroyed many temples. A masjid which is still kept up was built by him on the site of a temple to Keshav Rāi. The temple of Brahmā was built by Gokul-Parak, an Oswāl Mahājan of Gwalior, and is said to be the only temple dedicated to Brahmā in India. The attendants at the temple are Puri Gosāins. The temple of Sāvitri is built on the north of the lake, and was constructed by the "purohit" of Ajit Singh of Mārwār. The temple to Badri Nārāyana was rebuilt by the Thākur of Kharwa some 100 years ago. That of Varāha, or the boar, was demolished by Jahāngir, and the present temple was built by Bakht Singh of Jodhpur. Goma Rao, *sūbahdār* of the Marāthās rebuilt the temple of Shīva Atmateswara.

The town is picturesquely situated on the lake, with hills on three sides; on the fourth side the sands, drifted from the plains of Mārwār, have formed a complete bar to the waters of the lake, which has no outlet, though filtration through the sand hills is considerable. Bathing *ghāts* have been constructed nearly all round the lake, and most of the princely and wealthy families of Rājputāna have houses round the margin.

A fair at Pushkar takes place in October or November, and like other religious fairs is used as an opportunity for trade. It is attended by about 100,000 pilgrims, who bathe in the sacred lake.

Other places.

Outside Ajmer and Pushkar there are few objects of archæological interest. In the south-west of the Ajmer district there are several remains of Hindu temples, the age of which is not known. It is possible that they date from the time of the Hindu kings of Tōda Raisen, the ruins of which lie some 30 miles across the border in Jaipur territory. Baghēra and Sakrāni contain the better known of these remains. The fort at Bhinai is a good specimen of the forts built by the smaller Rājput Chiefs.

CHAPTER III.

POPULATION.

The census of 1901 was the sixth of a series, which began in 1865. It was practically speaking a famine census. Nothing can show more clearly the vicissitudes of season to which this tract of Rājputāna is exposed, and their influence on the people, than the extraordinary fluctuations of the population during the last forty years, as noted in the margin. The year 1872 followed the severe famine of 1868-69, and the effects are seen in the reduction of population by over a lakh. The census of 1891 was taken after 20 years of unusual prosperity, in which the opening of the railway and establishment of Ajmer as a large railway centre took place. The reduction in the population of 1901 is the outcome of the natural calamities of the decade, which included two famines, that of 1891-92 and that of 1899-00.

1865—4,26,268.
1872—3,16,590.
1877—3,96,331.
1881—4,60,722.
1891—5,42,358.
1901—4,76,912.

Density.

The square mile density for the province, including urban areas, is 175·93, as compared with 200·08 in 1891 and 169·96 in 1881.

As regards density of the rural population, Ajmer and Merwāra have now changed places; Merwāra has the larger figure (136·9 to the square mile); the Ajmer figure is 130. Both are considerably less than those of 1891 (154·9 Merwāra, 159·8 Ajmer). The result is probably due to the better physique of the Mer population of Merwāra, where a larger birth rate has consistently obtained since 1872. During the actual famines the Mers came and remained upon relief works more readily than the inhabitants of Ajmer, and the latter suffered more severely from the epidemics that followed.

Towns and Villages.

The total population in the last census was 4,76,912—2,51,026 males and 2,25,886 females—distributed over four towns and 740 villages and living in 1,07,401 occupied houses. The number of persons per house was 4·44. Of the total population Ajmer claims 3,67,453, of whom the residents in urban areas number 1,03,386 and in rural areas 2,64,067. In Merwāra the urban and rural populations are 21,928 and 87,531 respectively.

The villages of Ajmer are larger and more compact than those of Merwāra, where 52·2 per cent of the population live in hamlets of less than 500 inhabitants. In Ajmer the average village population is 621, and 46·8 of the rural inhabitants live in villages containing from 500 to 2,000 persons. In Merwāra the average village population is only 278. The difference in the physical features of the two districts is primarily responsible for this. The open plains of Ajmer encourage the growth of large central villages. In Merwāra the small patches of culturable land are scattered among the valleys, and are separated from each other by rocky and difficult hill country. Each man likes to live where he can keep a watch upon his crops, so every valley has its little hamlet, while the fortified and inaccessible central village, the product of an age of war and plunder, is falling into ruins.

Movements of Population.

On the whole the population of Ajmer-Merwāra has decreased by 65,446 since the census of 1891, but with the exception of Kekri, the decrease has taken place entirely in rural areas.

Of the towns, Ajmer, with a population of 73,839, shows an increase of 4,996, which may be attributed to the rise in the number of workmen in the Railway carriage and locomotive shops and the influx of people from Native States during the famine. Beāwar and Nasīrābād, with returns of 21,728 and 22,494 respectively, are almost stationary. Kekri alone with 7,053 shows a decrease of 47. There are no other places treated as towns within the division. It is doubtful whether the decrease in the rural population during the last decade can be attributed to any general movement on the part of the inhabitants. The increase in Ajmer city may be due to some extent to an influx of unskilled labourers, who could no longer get employment upon the land. But such movement would only be temporary, and no general tendency to desert rural areas could be deduced from it. The decrease in the rural population is rather to be accounted for by positive causes affecting those who remained in their villages, *viz.*, a low birth rate and a high death rate. Abnormally high prices ruled during the last half of the decade, during the last three years of which the whole or part of the district was affected by famine, and they checked the natural growth of the population; while the famines were followed by epidemic diseases, among which that of malarial fever at the close of 1900 was by far the most conspicuous. In that year the recorded fever deaths alone numbered 44,236, and the recorded death rate reached the unprecedented figure of 119·97 per 1,000.

Migration.

Considerable immigration is believed to have taken place from Native States during the famines, but reliable statistics are not available. In Merwāra the practice of emigration is common among the Mers, but the prompt provision made for them in recent famines has reduced the tendency. During the year 1899, 7,938 persons left Merwāra with 37,978 head of cattle. Most of the emigrants returned, but the number of cattle brought back was only 13,868. There is always a large stream of emigration through Merwāra from the neighbouring Native States whenever there is a scarcity of grain or fodder in Mewār or Mārwār; the stream always follows the same well-defined routes, and the local officials are well accustomed to dealing with it.

Vital Statistics.

The record of the population by age periods exhibits clearly the effects of the recent severe famines. The infant population of less than a year in age in 1891 was 19,976. In 1901 it was 6,117. That between one and two years of age fell from 9,555 to 3,116. Children between the ages of 5 and 10 years numbered 52,549 in 1901, whereas in 1891 their number was 76,192. It was the infant population that the famine most heavily affected.

The mean age of males in 1901 was 25·53, and had risen since 1881. The mean age of females was 26·27, and had also risen. The figures again indicate the heavy mortality among children in the famine.

In the municipalities of Ajmer, Beāwar and Kekri the municipal authorities, and in Nasīrābād the cantonment authorities, make the necessary arrangements for collecting and reporting vital statistics, under rules sanctioned by the Local Government. In rural areas the police are the reporting agency. Village watchmen make reports of births and deaths to the police stations, while revenue officials (*patwāris*) and managers (*kāmdārs*) of *istimrāri* estates also submit weekly reports to the same quarter. These reports check each other. The weekly figures are sent to the Civil Surgeon, Ajmer, who submits the monthly statement, through the Commissioner, Ajmer-Merwāra, to the Chief Medical Officer for Rājputāna. No doubt the system by which vital statistics are obtained in rural areas is far from perfect, but an efficient reporting agency is very hard to find. It has, however, received much attention recently and is believed to be improved. The ratio of births per 1,000, which was 27·76 in 1881, fell in 1891 to 21·32, while in 1901 the effects of famine reduced it to 16·10 per 1,000. The death rate possesses the same features and stands at 33·13 per 1,000 in 1901, against 20·23 in 1891 and 23·33 in 1881. In 1902 the birth and death rates per 1,000 were 36·08 and 32·86 respectively.

The majority of deaths are due to fever and bowel complaints. The death rate from fever in 1901 was 27·45 per 1,000. The fever that supervened upon the famine was widespread and of a very fatal character, causing a mortality which exceeded that of the period when the famine prevailed. Small-pox is a not uncommon epidemic, but the continued decrease of blindness in recent census returns is satisfactory, and points to the steady progress made year by year in vaccination. Cholera often occurs at the commencement of the rainy season. The last serious outbreak was in 1900. Dysentery and diarrhœa are very prevalent during the rains, as also is rheumatism. Cases of ophthalmia are frequently met with. Diseases of the skin are very common; they assume various types and characters, from a common herpetic eruption to the most inveterate form of lepra. Pleurisy and pnemonia carry off many people in the cold weather. Boils and abscesses are very prevalent during the rains, and scurvy is common at this season. Guinea-worm is always more or less prevalent, and in some years hundreds of people are attacked by the malady. Unless the worm is extracted at an early stage, considerable irritation and inflammation supervene, and it may be weeks or months before the patient recovers. So far Ajmer-Merwāra has been fortunate in continuing practically free from plague, in spite of the fact that it has been raging in the Punjab, in Bombay and in the Central Provinces. A few imported cases have been detected, but prompt isolation has prevented any spread of the disease. Measures have been decided upon and will be put in force in the event of any outbreak, whether in rural or urban areas. At present the inspection of all passengers arriving by train in Ajmer is the only prophylactic measure in operation. **Diseases.**

There are 2,51,026 males and 2,25,886 females in the division according to the 1901 census. The proportion of females to males is **Sex and Civil condition.**

higher among the Hindus than among Muhammadans, and taking all religions the proportion is higher in Ajmer than in Merwāra. Among selected castes the proportion of females to males has been found to be lowest in the castes of high social status.

The unmarried population is 1,76,338 and the married 2,32,920, while widowers and widows number 20,614 and 47,040 respectively. There has been a decline in the number of married persons and increase in the number of widowed since 1891, due to the calamities of the decade. The seasons of marriage among the Hindus are determined by astrological considerations. As a rule marriages are avoided during the rainy season, as it is believed that the gods are asleep in those months. But among Rājputs the festivals of *Janam-Ashtami, Basant Panchmi, Rādha Ashtami and Akhey Tīj* are deemed propitious for marriage. Gūjars and Jāts also marry on certain specified festivals. Among the Jāts marriage is not allowed within the same *gōt*, and generally takes place later in life than in Upper India. A cocoanut and a rupee, emblems of fertility and wealth, are sent to the house of the bride. There the brotherhood is collected, and the contract is concluded by throwing the cocoanut and the rupee into the lap of the bride. The day is then fixed by the bride's parents, and the *barāt* which consists generally of 25 to 30 men, reaches the village in the evening. At the appointed time the bridegroom proceeds to the bride's house in red clothes and with a sword in his hand. A frame of wood called a *toran* is fixed over the door, and this the bridegroom strikes with his sword and enters the house. All castes put up *torans*, which is a cross-barred frame resembling a wicket, and the custom is probably a relic of the marriage by conquest. When the bridegroom has entered the house, the Brāhman causes him and the bride to go round a fire lit in the centre of the courtyard. This is the ceremony called *phera* and is the only one used. On the second day there is a feast, and the bridal party then disperses. The bridegroom's father spends about Rs. 200, the bride's father nearly as much, and the subsequent *gauna*, when the bride's father gives turbans to his son-in-law and relatives, costs him about Rs. 150 more.

Among the Jāts—as among the Gūjars, Mālis and all the tribes of Merwāra—widow marriage is the rule and is called *nāta*. A man cannot marry his younger brother's widow, but may marry the widow of his elder brother. The younger brother has the first claim on the widow's hand, but if he does not marry her, any one in the *gōt* may do so. It is probably a relic of the now obsolete custom of *niyoga*, which obtained in Vedic times. No disability of any kind attaches to the children of *nāta* marriage: young widows are married off by their husband's relations, who take money from the second husband. In the early accounts of the Mers the custom is stigmatized as revolting, under the name of sale of women. As a matter of fact, grown up widows choose for themselves, though when they do the *panchāyat* generally orders a certain sum to be paid to the deceased husband's relations. These orders are often contested and are not enforced in the courts. It must, moreover, be noted that a widow cannot contract a valid *nāta* marriage except with a man of her own caste. If a widow chooses to remain so, she is not forced to marry, and in all castes a widow who has no sons retains her deceased husband's property till her death or re-marriage. She cannot mortgage except to pay her husband's funeral expenses, his debts, or to marry her daughter. The condition of widows under this custom is infinitely preferable than if they were forced to remain unmarried all their lives. Colonel Hall has recorded that, while he was complaining that women were sold as sheep, the women themselves so far from considering it a grievance, were flattered by the payment of a high price as a testimony to their beauty and usefulness. The Muhammadan law permits re-marriage of widows, but curiously enough the Muhammadan Khādims (Sayyids) of the Dargāh Khwāja Sāhib at Ajmer follow the custom of the superior Hindu classes. Rājputs and Brāhmans do not practice *nāta.* With Rājputs the custom of *sati* used to be optional, but it is now obsolete. Infant marriage is very restricted and polygamy is rare. Among Rājputs the marriageable age of a bride, as fixed by the rules of their *Sabha,* is 14 years, and that of the bridegroom 18 years. The rules are enforced by the *Sabha,* and any contravention of them is punished by fine. Divorce is only allowed among Muhammadans, according to their laws. The proportionate number of unmarried Muhammadans exceeds that of the Hindus.

Formerly large sums of money were wasted at marriages and similar festivals. But in 1891 rules were drawn up with a view to reducing such expenses among the Mer *zamindārs* in Merwāra. A reasonable scale of expenditure was laid down for all ceremonies, and it is believed that an improvement in the direction of economy is being effected.

Inheritance.

Among the Mer clans inheritance through the mother prevails. In the event of there being sons from two or more wives, the property is divided *per capita* of the wives and not *per capita* of the sons. In Ajmer primogeniture is recognized among the Rājputs.

Education.

Education generally has receded since 1891, the number of literate males per 1,000 having fallen from 108·3 to 103·7. Female education is still insignificant, but a slight increase is recorded. According to the last census there are 30,166 literate males and 1,922 literate females. The numbers of males and females literate in English are 4,152 and 646 respectively. In English education only has a considerable extension taken place during the last decade, and it has been entirely among the native population. The decline in education other than English is due to the recent famine, in which many village schools were closed while the children were on relief works. The heavy mortality in 1900 among children of a school-going age has also affected the figures. The Jains, who include the extensive trading communities of Ajmer and Beāwar, predominate among the literates, and after them come the Brāhmans. In Ajmer education is considerably more extended than in Merwāra.

Language.

Local dialects and Hindi form the language of the great bulk of the population. Whether the former are off-shoots of Hindi or whether they and Hindi are derived from a common parent may be ascertained from experts. The dialects are rough and difficult to understand, and are used by a largely illiterate and backward population.

Castes, Tribes, and Races.

Brāhmans.

Of the various castes, Brāhmans come first on the list of social precedence. They number 25,045, or 6·5 per cent. of the Hindu population of the province. The Panch Dravid Brāhmans have the highest rank socially but are few in number. Panch Gaudas come next. They number 11,583 persons and include, among others, the Gaudas, Kanaujias and Sāraswats. The Gaudas again include six castes, locally known as the Chhanayātis. These are Gaudas, Dāymās, Gūjar Gaudas, Pārikhs, Sikhwāls and Khandelwāls. Dāymās do not follow the marriage rules of the *shāstras* but rather those of the Mahājans and other castes. Some Brāhmans of Merwāra eat meat and have no dealings with other Brāhmans. They are not generally cultivators, but hold revenue free land in nearly every village. As none of their caste sub-divisions are peculiar to Ajmer-Merwāra, a full description of them is beyond the scope of this article, and belongs rather to the Imperial Gazetteer of India.

Vaishyās.

The Vaishyās, or Mahājans are the most numerous class of the community and number 37,027, or 7·8 per cent. of the total population of all religions. Their principal sub-divisions are the Oswāls, who trace their birth-place to Osa-nagri in Mārwār, and the Agarwals, who derive their name from Agarsen, who lived at Agroda in Hariāna. Other Vaishya castes are the Masheshwaris and Bijbargis. The Seths of Ajmer are the leading members of this portion of the community, whose occupation is trading. They are generally well off, but during the last famine Mahājans came on relief works in both Ajmer and Merwāra. This shows how severely they were affected, and gives some clue to the decrease in their numbers since the 1891 census.

Kāyasthās.

Kāyasthās have been classified as a caste allied to Kshatryas, Rājputs and Khattris. Some of them wear the Brahmanical thread. They number 2,620, and their chief sub-divisions are Māthur, Bhatnāgar, Shrivāstava, and Saksena. They are much employed in offices and educational establishments. There are three distinct families in Ajmer, known by the names of their *parganās*—Ajmer, Rāmsar and Kekri—and these acknowledge no relationship. They have been hereditary *kānūngoes* since the time of the Emperors, and hold about 1,000 acres of revenue free land, along with certain perquisites from *jāgīr* and *istimrāri* villages.

Rājputs.

Among the land-owning castes, the highest socially are the Rājputs. But they hold hardly any land except on *bhūm* and *istimrāri* tenures. The great majority of proprietors belongs to other castes. No Rājput will touch a plough unless forced by hard necessity to do so; and the crown tenants, as well as the tenants of the *jāgīr* estates, are mainly the descendants of the ancient cultivators of the soil who have held their land in all the dynastic changes through which Ajmer has passed. Where every man who dug a well became owner of the land irrigated therefrom, and where a cultivator without a well is considered a waif, with no tie to bind him to the village where he may reside, the land-owning castes must be nearly co-extensive with the cultivating castes, and such is found to be the case. Of the 195 Ajmer *khālsa* villages, 52 are held by Jāts, 41 belong to Mers, 35 to Gūjars, 4 to Rājputs, 4 to Merāts, 6 to Chitās, 2 to Deswāli Musalmāns ; 8 castes hold one village each—Māli, Sayyid, Pathān, Mughal, Bānjāras, Ahir, Fakir and Christian. In the remaining 43 villages there is no exclusive caste ownership ; the principal castes in these villages are 14 in number—Mālis, Telis, Mers, Merāts, Deswālis, Gūjars, Brāhmans, Rājputs, Mahājans. Kāyasthas, Khārols, Ahirs, Rebāris and Regars. The remaining land-owning castes have few representatives, and are scattered over many villages.

The four villages belonging to Rājputs are Arjanpura Jāgīr, Arjanpura Khālsa, Gōla and Khori. The two former belong to Gor Rājputs, the two latter to Rāhtors. This exception, however, only proves the conclusion of the foregoing paragraph. Arjanpura Jāgīr was given on condition of protecting the road, and assimilates to a *bhūm* tenure. Arjanpura Khālsa stands quite alone as the only *zamindāri* tenure in the district, with the exception of Muhammadgarh, where the tenure has been created by ourselves. Gola was held on *istimrāri* tenure till shortly before the establishment of British rule. Khori was originally a Mer village, but the Rāhtors held a large amount of *bhūm* in it, and gradually turned out the Mers. In short, where Rājputs hold *jāgīr* or *khālsa* land, it will generally be found that it is the relic of a tālukdār tenure, or of a *jāgīr* grant, or of an encroachment by *bhūmiās*. All the *istimrārdārs* of Ajmer are Rājputs, and they constitute the native aristocracy of the district.

Rājputs are returned in the census papers at 15,430. It is a curious fact, illustrative of the great vicissitudes of early times, that though Ajmer was held for over four hundred years by the Chauhāns, there are now comparatively few in the province. They must be looked for in Hāraoti, in Alwar, and in the desert of Nagar Pārkar, whither they have been pushed by the Rāhtors, who have occupied their place as the ruling tribe, and who in numbers, wealth and power greatly preponderate over the other Rājput clans in the district. These are three in number—Gor, Sesodiā, and Kachhwāha, and it will be convenient to consider them in the order of their arrival in the province, for a definite date can be fixed for the arrival of each.

In the time of Prithvi Rāj Chauhān (circa 1190 A.D.) Rājā Bach Rāj, and Rājā Bāwan, Gor Rājputs from Bengal, came to Ajmer on the customary pilgrimage to Dwārka. Prithvi Rāj engaged the brothers in an expedition against Daya Singh of Nāgaur which was successful, and subsequently each of them married a daughter of Prithvi Rāj. Rājā Bāwan settled at Kuchāwan in Mārwār ; Rājā Bach Rāj remained in Ajmer. In course of time Junia, Sarwār, Deolia and the adjacent country fell into the hands of the Gor Rājputs, and to the head of the clan Humāyūn gave a *mansab* of Rs. 7,000. In the time of Akbar Rājā Bithal Dās founded the town of Rājgarh, and called it after the name of his grandson, Rāj Singh. The son of the latter took Srinagar from the Ponwar Rājputs, who have now disappeared from the district. This, however, was the climax of the prosperity of the Gor Rājputs, for soon afterwards they were ejected from Rājgarh and all their territory by Kishen Singh Rāhtor. After 25 years of dispossession Gopāl Singh recovered Rājgarh, and the Gors were in possession when the country fell into the hands of the Marāthās. The latter in 1817 resumed Rājgarh and the 12 villages attached to it, as the Rājā was unable to pay a contribution of Rs. 10,000 *fauj kharch*. On the establishment of British rule these villages were returned on the condition of payment of *nazarāna*; but as the *nazarāna* was not, or could not be paid the whole was resumed with the exception of one small village, Kothāj, and remained *khālsa* until 1874. In March of that year the town of Rājgarh was presented by Government in *jāgīr* to Rājā Davi Singh, the representative of this ancient but fallen house. The Gor Rājputs hold land in 14 villages. The descendants of Bithal Dās are *jāgīrdārs* of Rājgarh and Kothāj and *bhūmiās* of Dānta and Jatiā. Bithal Dās had 5 brothers, whose descendants are the *istimrārdārs* of Manoharpur and the *bhūmiās* of Sanod, Nāndla, Neārān, Lavera, Dodiāna, and Jharwāsa. The descendants of Rājā Bāwan are *jāgīrdārs* of Arjunpura Jāgir, are owners and *bhūmiās* of Arjunpura Khālsa, and hold *bhūm* in Tabiji.

It is unnecessary in this place to give a detailed history of the Rāhtors, the great conquering race which, in the year 1194, abandoned the ruined capital of Kanauj and founded a kingdom in the desert of Mārwār Such an account belongs more properly to the Gazetteer of Jodhpur. There are 4,609 Rāhtors in Ajmer-Merwāra. All the tālukdārs of Ajmer, with the exception of the Thākur of Manoharpur, the Thākur of Sāwar and his relations, and the Chitās of Merwāra descent, who hold 4 villages on *istimrār* tenure, are Rāhtors, and have their descent from Sivaji, the founder of the monarchy. Of the 109 *bhūm* holdings in the district, 83 are held by Rāhtors, nearly all the younger sons and brothers of the *istimrārdārs*. The Rāhtors of Ajmer have the same characteristics as their brethren in Mārwār. Their physique is not remarkable; they are still warlike and indolent, and great consumers of opium. Each man carries at least a *dagger*, and, except under extreme pressure, none will touch a plough.

Sesodiā Rājputs hold the *pargana* of Sāwar at the south-eastern extremity of the Ajmer district on *istimrār* tenure, and the estate is a portion of a grant made by Jahāngir to Gokal Dās, who is said to have received 84 wounds in the service of the Emperor. There is a family of Sesodias who are *bhūmiās* in Nepoli. These are the only Sesodiās in the district.

The Kachhwāha Rājputs, like the Sesodiās, are to be found in the villages adjoining their respective States of Jaipur and Udaipur, and hold *bhūm* in 5 villages. They are found principally in the villages of Harmāra and Tilaurnia in the extreme north of the Ajmer district. Their number was returned as 666 at the last census.

Rājputs differ from other high-caste Hindus, in that they are exogamous so far as their different clans are concerned. A Rāhtor will not marry a Rāhtor, but will take his wife from the Sesodiās or Kachhwāhas.

The Jāts were numbered at the census at 27,952. They are first-rate agriculturists, and possess a fine physique. They, with the Gūjars, are the original cultivators of the soil. Nearly the whole of the Rāmsar *pargana* belongs to them. They are settled in Kekri and in the best villages of the Ajmer and Rājgarh *parganas*. Tabiji, Sarādhna, Makrera, Jethāna, Budhwāra and Pecholiān belong to Jāts. In the Beāwar *tahsīl* they hold 7 villages, chiefly in and about the old town of Beāwar, adjoining the Ajmer district, for they never penetrated far into Merwāra, and are not to be found in the Todgarh *tahsīl*. They are divided into three main families, Puniyo, Sishmo, and Harchitral, but their *gōts* are more than a hundred. They hold no revenue free land nor any *bhūm*; they have in Ajmer double as much land as the Gūjars and pay three times as much revenue, partly no doubt owing to their having monopolized the chief villages, but principally to their greater energy in making wells and improving the land. **Jats.**

The Gūjars hold 35 villages in all parts of Ajmer district and 4 in the Beāwar *tahsīl*, where they are settled in the outlying villages of Jetgarh, Bhairon Khera, Pillāni and Sheonāthpura. They are returned in the census at 36,278. They are careless cultivators and devote their energies to grazing cattle. Those who live in or near Ajmer sell milk and butter in the town. Their customs are identical with those of the Jāts, but the Gūjars of Merwāra follow the inheritance laws of the Mers. Gūjars and Jāts will eat together. Their chief men are called *Mir*. **Gūjars.**

The Merwāra clans consisting, as classified at the last census, of Rāwats 32,209, Mers 21,649 and Merāts 8,554, are supposed to be descended from a common ancestor. Their sub-divisions present peculiar features and deserve special notice. **Merwāra Clans.**

They do not claim to be, nor do they appear to have been the original inhabitants of Merwāra. Of these last, however, little is known. The country must have been an impenetrable jungle, and the majority of the sparse inhabitants were probably outlaws, or fugitives from neighbouring States. The caste of Chandela Gūjars is said to have dwelt on the hills about Chāng; the hills near Kālinjar, Sāroth and Bhāilān are assigned by tradition to the Brāhmans. On the east side, on the Bōrwa hills, the caste of Bhātti Rājputs is said to have been located, while the southern portion of the Todgarh *tahsīl* was occupied by Mīnas. There is a tradition that a Bhātti Rājput, Ajit Singh, bore the title of king of Merwāra.

Mer, which can be used promiscuously for all inhabitants of Merwāra, means a "hill man." It is not by origin a caste or tribe name, but signified the dweller on this portion of the Aravalli range. The two main tribes of Merwāra are known by the appellation of Chita and Barar, each class traditionally divided into 24 *gōts*, but new *gots* are constantly being formed which take the name of their immediate ancestor, and there are now many more.

Colonel Tod ("Rajasthan," Volume I, page 680) asserts that the tribes of Chita and Barar are Minas, and the traditions of the people themselves point to a Mina ancestry. Both tribes claim a common descent from Prithvi Rāj, the last Chauhān king of Ajmer, and the story is that Jodh Lakun, the son of Prithvi Rāj, married a girl of the Mīna caste, who had been seized in a marauding raid near Bundi, supposing her to be a Rājputni. When he discovered his mistake he turned her and her two sons, Anhul and Anup, away. The exiles wandered to Chāng in Beāwar, where they were hospitably entertained by the Gūjars of that place. Anhul and Anup rested one day under a *bar* or fig tree, and prayed that if it were destined that their race should continue, the trunk of the tree might be rent in twain. The instant occurrence of the miracle raised them from their despondency, and the splitting of the fig tree is a cardinal event in the history of the race, according to the following distich:—

> "Charar se chita bhayo, aur Barar bhayo Barghat,
> Shākh ek se do bhayo, jagat bakhāni jāt."

From the sound "charar" (the noise which is supposed to have reached Anhal from the splitting tree) the Chitās are called, and the clan Barar from the splitting of the fig tree. Both are descended from one stock. The world has made this tribe famous. In following the distribution of the clans, it is necessary again to bear in mind that there are 41 Mer villages in Ajmer, 214 in the Beāwar *tahsīl*, and 85 in the Todgarh *tahsīl*.

Anhul settled at Chāng in the north-west of Merwāra, and his descendants in course of time exterminated the Gūjars, who had given an asylum to Anhul and his mother. The clan waxed strong and multiplied, and gradually occupied all the strong places of Merwāra, where they founded the villages of Jhāk, Shāmgarh, Lūlwa, Hāthūn, Kukrā, Kotkerāna, Nāi and others. They appear to have held the remaining Mers in subjection, for they enumerate 16 castes of Mers, who, they say, used to pay them one-fourth of the produce of the soil, and of all plundering expeditions. The clan now holds 117 entire villages in Beāwar, besides portions of 53, and 10 entire villages in the Todgarh *tahsīl*, including the *pargana* of Kotkerāna. In Ajmer there are 21 entire *khālsa* and *jāgīr* villages belonging to Chitās, and they are to be found in all the Ajmer villages except four.

Of the sub-divisions of the clan, by far the most important and numerous is that of the Merāts, a term which is generally used as synonymous with Muhammadan Mer, but which is a patronymic derived from Mera, the common ancestor of the Kathāts and Gorāts. Harrāj, grandson of Mera, a Chita in the reign of Bābar, took service under the Emperor at Delhi. During a night of terrific rain he remained firm at his post as sentry, with his shield over his head. The Emperor, to whom the matter was reported, is related to have said: "In the Mārwār tongue they call a brave soldier Katha; let this man be henceforth called Katha." Harrāj soon after became a convert to Islam and is the progenitor of all the Kathāt Merāts, a very large family, who hold 78 villages in Beāwar, including all the principal places to the north and east of the *tahsīl*. Gora was brother of Harrāj, and his descendants are Hindus, and hold 21 villages in the centre and south-west of Beāwar, of which Kālinjar and Kābra are the chief. The Gorāts spread southwards, and have occupied 13 villages in the north of Todgarh; one village in Ajmer, Makhopura, belongs to them. The Kathāts, the most pushing of all the Chitās, spread northwards, and hold 9 of the 21 Chita villages in Ajmer. There they formed new *gōts*, of which the Bahādur Khāni, generally called *par excellence* Chitās, is the principal. Besides the *khālsa* and *jāgīr* villages, 4 villages in Ajmer proper are held by Kathāts on *istimrāri* tenure, *viz.*, Nausar, Rajosi, Ajaisar and Kharekhri. The villages were given them by the Mughal Emperors for protection of the city of Ajmer and the adjacent passes. The chief men of the Kathāts and Gorāts call themselves Thākurs, but in Beāwar, the chiefs of Hāthūn, Chāng and Jhāk, who are Kathāts, are called Khāns. Of the remaining sub-divisions of Chitās, the most important are the Laget, who hold 6 villages in Beāwar, and the Nanset, who own the villages of Bargāon, Pālrān, Phārkiā, Mānpura, and Hāthibata in Ajmer, besides portions of several others. Other *gōts* which may be mentioned are the Rajoriya and Bedariyat, the former holding 3 villages in Ajmer, and the Bajriyāt Borwāra. Bilādiya, Pithrot, Bālot and Nādot, who possess a village or parts of several. The other *gōts* live scattered throughout Merwāra.

Anup, the brother of Anhal, settled in Todgarh, and founded the Barār clan. His descendants, less enterprising than the Chitās, have remained in Merwāra, and are not to be found in Ajmer. They hold 11 villages in Beāwar, the most important of which are Kālikankar, Sendra, Bailān and Khera Sangnotān. They occupy the whole of the south of the Todgarh *tahsīl* and 48 entire villages. They are more unsophisticated, honest and straightforward than the Chitās. They call themselves Rāwat, a petty title of nobility, and do not like being called Mers. Their chief men are called Rāo, of whom the principal are the Rāo of Kūkra and the Rāo of Barār.

All these Chauhān Mīnas, with the exception of the Kathāts, are nominally Hindus. Formerly Kathāts and Gorāts ate together and nothing was forbidden food to either. But the tendency towards division is growing. Chitās and Barars used to intermarry, but a feeling has sprung up against it, and recently the Rāwats have agreed to forbid it. The Merāts of Ajmer have discarded the *dhotī*, although it is still worn by their brethren in Merwāra. Among all Merāts the Muhammadan *nikāh* form of marriage is now almost universal. The estrangement between them and the Rāwats appears destined to grow wider, but the customs of the two clans regarding inheritance, adoption, re-marriage of widows and similar matters are still identical.

Among the Merwāra tribes which boast other than a Chauhān Mina ancestor, the most important are the two which claim descent from Dhārānāth Powar or Pramar, who founded the city of Dharanagar in Mārwār before the Pramar Rājputs were obliged to give way before the Gehlots and Rāhtors. Tradition says that Rāo Bohar, a descendant of Dhārānāth, came and settled at Rudhāna, in the extreme south of the Beāwar *pargana*. From this place his descendants spread and founded the adjacent villages of Biliāwās, Jawāja Bihār, Barkochrān, Rāwatmāl, Lusāni in the Beāwar *tahsīl*, and Akhayjitgarh Naloi and others in the Todgarh *tahsīl*. The tribe is divided into six *gōts*—Delāt, Kallāt, Doding, Boya, Kheyāt, and Pokhariya. Of these, the Delat is the most numerous, and holds 14 whole villages in Beāwar and 5 in Todgarh. The Kallat clan hold only 1 village, Kalātankhera in Beāwar, while the others have no entire village in Merwāra. The Delāts appear to have pushed the other members of the tribe out of Merwāra, who thereupon settled near Ajmer, and specially in the *pargana* of Pushkar. There are 11 villages in Ajmer held by this tribe, and they hold parts of 8 others. The Dodings hold Barla, Madārpura and Gwārri; to the Boya clan belong the villages of Hokrān and Gudhli; Khwājpura and Kānākhera belong to the Kheyāts, and the Pokhariya clan hold the villages of Pushkar, Ganāhera, Naidla, and Naulakha. The men of this tribe affect the name Rāwats, and return themselves as such at the census. They are an industrious race, generally taller and better built than the Chauhān Mīnas. Kathāts will not give their daughters in marriage to this tribe, but will take wives from them, and they intermarry freely with Hindu Chitās and Barār and other Mer clans.

The second tribe which claims descent from Dhārānāth is that of the Moti Rāwats, who hold 14 villages in the *pargana* of Bhāilān. They own two villages, Fatahpur and Bhojpur in Beāwar, and only scattered representatives of the tribe are met with in Ajmer. The *pargana* of Bhāilān is supposed to have been originally inhabited by Brahmans. A descendant of Dhārānāth, Rohitas by name, came and lived at Bāghmāl as an ascetic in a cave in the hill now called Magatji. A Banjāra was passing near the hill with his wife, and deserted her at this spot; she lived for some time with the Jogi, and then descending the hill sought the protection of Khem Chand Brāhman in Bamanhera, and in his house was delivered of twin sons, of whom one remained in Bhāilān, and the other in Mārwār. In the fifth generation one Magat was born, who expelled the Brāhmans from Bhāilān. The hill, which was the cradle of the race, was named after him, and he is still venerated by the Motis. A fair is held on the hill in September, at which time the hero is believed to traverse the 12 villages of Bhāilān in the twinkling of an eye.

Gehlot. After the sack of Chitor by Ala-ud-dīn, two brothers, Rājputs of the Gehlot clan, fled to Bōrwa in the Sāroth *pargana*, where they intermarried with Mīnas. The tribe descended from them is divided into 16 clans, of which the most important are the Godāt, Medrat, Kāchi, Pinga, Baniyāt, Lahr, Bālot and Dhānkal. They hold 11 entire villages in all parts of Beāwar, 1 village, Kūkar Khera, in Todgarh, and are found in 23 other villages in Merwāra. In Ajmer they own 6 villages, Parbatpura, Ansari, Mayāpur, Lachmipur, Borāj, and Amba Masina. They consider themselves Surajbansi Rājputs, and call themselves Rāwat. Like the tribes of Puar origin, they intermarry with Hindu Chauhān Mīnas. Merāts will take wives from them but will not give them their daughters in marriage.

The Balāi caste holds 4 villages in Beāwar, Jāts and Gūjars hold 11, and Narsingpura and Dungar Khera belong to Mahājans. The remaining inhabitants of Merwāra belong to a few scattered clans who pass under the general designation of Mer, and who as usual claim to be descended from Rājputs, but have no clear history. The Pataliyāt clan claims to be of the stock of the Bhātti Rājputs of Jaisalmer, and hold one village, Bāriā Naga. The Chaurot claim the same descent and own one village, Kālikankar Kishanpura. They are also found in Mohanpura in Ajmer. The Bāch Mers inhabit Rājpur Būchān, and are found in a couple of villages in Ajmer. The Bharsal clan live in the village of Rāmkhera Dhanār, and are to be met with in Kotra, Sedaria, Bhawānikhera and Kishanpura in Ajmer. The Kharwāl Mers live in Nayānagar and Fatahpur 2nd, and the headman of the town of Beāwar is of this caste. Mamnots, Selots, Banats, and Bannas live scattered in a few villages. Other Tribes.

Of the other castes in Ajmer-Merwāra, the Mālis number 15,852. They are good cultivators and hold the greater part of *Kasbā* Ajmer. A peculiar caste, Kir, very few in number, devotes its attention to the cultivation of melons. The Rebāris, also few, breed camels and cultivate rice. The menial castes are Bhangīs, Balāis and Regars. Balāis are the most numerous, numbering 22,350, and consider themselves superior to the Regars, who correspond with the Chamārs of the United Provinces of Agra and Oudh. Minas, Sānsis and Bhils are the thievish classes, but none of them are numerous in the district. The names of the remaining castes point to the occupation of each— Kumhārs (potters) number 11,248; Khātis (carpenters) are 6,373; Chākars and Darogas (domestic servants), 6,933; Nāis (barbers), 6,846; and Chamārs (tanners), 19,350; Darzis (tailors), Dhobis (washermen), Kahārs (bearers), Lohārs (blacksmiths), Sunārs (goldsmiths), Telis (oilmen), are below 5,000; Bhāts (bards), Chippas (chintz printers), Khārols (salt workers), are below 2,000; Dholis (drummers), Gadaris (shepherds), Lakherās (varnishers), Rangrez (dyers), Tamoblis (pan sellers), are below 1,000; Beldārs (diggers), Bharbujās (grain parchers), Ghosis (milk and butter sellers), Halwāis (confectioners), Kalāls (liquor sellers), Silāvats (masons), Sikligars (steel sharpeners), and Thatherās (braziers), are under 500 in number.

Of the Muhammadans 31,972 are classed as Sheikhs; Sayyids are 5,703; Mughals 2,737; while Pathāns are numbered at 11,048. The latter two classes are scattered over the district, a large proportion being in the native army and the police. The remaining different classes number 20,571. Deswālis (1,442) hold two villages in the north of Ajmer and say they are Rājputs, who were converted in the time of Shahab-ud-dīn. One village, Muhammadgarh, belongs on *zamindari* tenure to a Pathān. The Banjāras, who live in Ghegal are Musalmāns, and were, they say, converted at the same time as the Deswālis. The Musalmāns in the districts are chiefly the attendants on the Muhammadan shrines, and most of them hold revenue-free land in the *jāgīr* villages attached to these institutions. They are generally poor and idle.

Religions. Hindus constitute the bulk (79·77 per cent.) of the population. These include the Mers, who return themselves as Hindus. The collective numbers of those who follow the Brahmanical faith has fallen from 4,36,831 in 1891 to 3,80,453 in 1901. The agricultural and labouring classes who suffered most in the famine come within the category. The Jains, who now number 19,922 have decreased by 7,017 since 1891, but the decrease is probably chiefly due to incorrect enumeration. The Muhammadan population numbers 72,031 or 15·1 per cent. of the whole. Residing chiefly within the urban areas, they were less affected by the famines than the Hindus. The Christians number 3,712. The Arya Samāj claims 366 members, and the district also contains 264 Sikhs and 164 Pārsis.

The principal sects of the Hindus are the Vaishnavas, or worshippers of Vishnu, the Shaivas, or worshippers of Shīva, and the Shāktas, or worshippers of the Shaktis, who are the female associates or active "Powers" of the members of the Hindu Trinity—Brahmā, Vishnu and Shīva. Manu's Code is taken as the theoretical standard of right and wrong, but is not strictly followed in all its applications. Life in this world is considered as being one of 84,00,000. But whether all are eventually absorbed in the supreme being, or whether some will gain *Vaikunth*(Heaven) and others be relegated to *Narak*(Hell), is doubtful. The Jāts worship a variety of Gods, including Māta and Mahādeo, but their chief object of veneration is Tejāji, whose legend is as follows:—Teja was a Jāt of Karnāla, near Nāgaur, who lived 890 years ago, and had been married at Rupnagar in Kishangarh. While grazing his cattle he observed that a cow belonging to a Brāhman was in the habit of going daily to a certain place in the jungle, where the milk dropped from her udder. Further observation showed that the milk fell into a hole inhabited by a snake. Teja agreed with the snake to supply him daily with milk, and so prevent the Brāhman suffering loss. Once, when preparing to visit his father-in-law he forgot the contract, and the snake appearing, declared that it was necessary he should bite Teja. The latter asked for permission to first visit his father-in-law, and the snake agreed. Teja went on his journey, and at Kishangarh rescued the village cattle from a band of robbers, but was desperately wounded in the encounter. Mindful of his promise to return, he, with difficulty, reached home and presented himself to the snake, who, however, could find no spot to bite, so badly had Teja been cut up by the robbers. Teja therefore put out his tongue which the snake bit, and so he died. The Jāts believe that if they are bitten by a snake and tie a thread round the right foot while repeating the name of Tejāji the poison will prove innocuous. Tejāji is represented as a man on horseback with a drawn sword, while a snake is biting his tongue. Nearly all Jāts wear an amulet of silver with this device round their necks. Colonel Dixon singled out Tejāji as the patron of the fair he established in his new town of Nayānagar or Beāwar.

Any remarks as to religious beliefs and standards are more applicable to the Hindus of Ajmer than to various clans of Merwāra. The latter do not trouble themselves much with the orthodox divinities of Brāhmanism. They worship incarnations of Shīva, under the names of **Bhairūnji** and Mātāji. *Sitla* stones daubed with red paint and consecrated to the latter are to be met with on all sides. Allahji is a common deity, and the deified heroes Deoji and Rām Deoji also find worshippers. The hills of Magatji and Goramji, the highest in Merwāra, share in the veneration of the people, and this is probably a relic of a pristine fetish worship, though now the hills have modern hero legends attached to them. But in truth the religion of these people is of a very undefined nature, and it is doubtful whether they go much beyond the observance of certain rites at marriages and funerals. Of recent years, however, there has been a growing tendency among the Mer population to split into two sections over religious customs and usages. The Kathāt Merāts, who have always eaten the flesh of cows and intermarried with Muhammadans, are tending to assimilate more and more with the orthodox followers of Islām. On the other hand the Hindu Merāts, or Rāwats of Todgarh as they are commonly called, are beginning to give a closer adherance to the social and religious rules of Brahmanism, as prevailing among surrounding Rājputs. In 1875 they had agreed to abstain from the flesh of kine and buffaloes, and to excommunicate all transgressors, and recently they have gone further and agreed no longer to eat or intermarry with Kathāt Merāts or Chitās. The origin of the recent movement, which began among the men serving in the Merwāra Battalion and other regiments, has been social rather than religious; but it is safe to predict that in course of time the whole of Merwāra will become Brahmanised or absorbed in the orthodox religion of Islām.

Of the total number of followers of the Arya Samāj, 331 belong to the towns. There was formerly only one Samāj, but it split into two over the question as to whether animal food was sanctioned by the Vedas or not.

All the Sikhs, numbering 264, are found in the Ajmer district. They are chiefly employed in the Railway workshops, in the Deoli Irregular Force and in the Police.

Of the Jains, 14,409 belong to Ajmer and 5,513 to Merwāra, 14,627 being numbered in rural and 5,295 in urban areas. Their standards of right and wrong and their ideas of ultimate reward and punishment are the same as those of the Hindus, but the Jains acknowledge no God, and substitute their *tirthankars*, or deified saints, 24 in number, for the Hindu *devatas*. They look forward to an unconscious, passionless, impersonal state, which they called *nirvāna*, and which can be reached only by liberality, forbearance, piety and remorse in this life. They are strongly averse to all forms of taking life. Like the

Hindus they burn their dead. Their temples, mostly of modern construction, are often graceful in design, but are overloaded with tawdry ornamentation. Plaster and stucco are too often preferred to solid stone. In the *Nasiyān* Jain temple at Ajmer there is an allegorical representation showing the progress of the *tirthankars* through life to *nirvāna.*

Of the Muhammadans 56,378 belong to Ajmer and 15,653 to Merwāra. Sheikhs predominate and Pathāns come next. The Muhammadans, as a whole, follow the Korān, supplemented by their *hadīs* or books of tradition. But in the case of the rustic Deswālis of Ajmer and Kathāt Merāts of Merwāra, circumcision of the living and burial of the dead is probably the sum total of religious observance.

Christian Missions.

The Christian community has increased by 1,029 since 1891, owing to conversions and to the natural growth among native Christians, who now number 2,362, as against 1,209 in 1891 and 799 in 1881. The principal and oldest Mission is the Rājputāna branch of the Scotch United Free Church Mission, which began work in Beāwar in A.D. 1860 as the "United Presbyterian Church Mission," but recently changed its designation upon the amalgamation of that Church with the Free Church of Scotland. A station at Nasīrābād was founded in the following year. The Ajmer station was established in 1862, that of Todgarh in 1863. Deoli received a missionary in 1871. There are now also stations at Jaipur, Udaipur, Alwar, Jodhpur and Kotah. The Mission has nine anglo-vernacular schools, six of which, including those at Ajmer, Beāwar and Nasīrābād, are High Schools, teaching up to the standard of the University Entrance Examination. Of these the Beāwar school is the largest with 389 pupils, Nasīrābād comes next with 302; Ajmer has 181. In addition, the Mission maintains 52 vernacular schools for boys and 37 vernacular schools for girls thoughout Rājputāna. Of these, 30 boys' schools and 18 girls' schools are within Ajmer-Merwāra, with an average number on the rolls of 2,851. With the exception of grants-in-aid to the Beāwar and Nasīrābād High Schools, the Mission bears the whole cost of these educational establishments. The Mission has also an orphanage for boys at Ashāpura, near Nasīrābād, in which there are nearly six hundred, and one for girls in Nasīrābād, containing nearly seven hundred. In connection with the former, workshops have been established for the training of boys as carpenters, blacksmiths, brick and tilemakers, leatherworkers, etc., under the management of a qualified man from the Technical School at Glasgow. A Mission training farm is also maintained in Kōtāh territory. The children in the orphanages are individually adopted by friends of the Mission at Home who pay an annual sum for their support. Government gave a grant-in-aid for children rescued in the famine of 1869, but no such grant is now made. A prominent feature of the Mission is its medical agency. There are five fully qualified practitioners (one of whom is a lady), five hospitals and dispensaries, where some 2,38,000 cases are attended to, and nearly 5,000 surgical operations are performed in the year.

Officially, the district lies within the diocese of the Bishop of Nāgpur. A Government Chaplain of the Church of England is stationed at Ajmer, and there are Church of England and Roman Catholic Military Chaplains at Nasīrābād. The Fordham Orphanage at Ajmer is managed by the local Chaplain.

As far as the Roman Catholic Church is concerned, Ajmer-Merwāra is considered to lie within the Prefecture of Rājputāna, which was created in 1892, and is administered by the Capuchin Fathers of Paris. The Prefect Apostolic has his head-quarters at Agra. Within the district it has established churches at Ajmer and Nasīrābād, and a native school at Jorepura near Akhri. At Ajmer the Convent of St. Mary Magdalen is a boarding and day school for European and Eurasian girls. It is managed by a Lady Superior, assisted by 12 Franciscan nuns.

The American Methodists established a Mission in Ajmer in 1882. They have now an orphanage in connection with it, which, with that of the Church of England and that of the Scotch Mission, took charge of Ajmer orphans during the famine. The boys' school contains 161 boarders and day pupils, and is graded to the lower middle standard. There is a similar school for girls, with an attendance of 180. The Mission work is carried on in the city and district by a staff of Native catechists, Bible readers and teachers, who did good work in relieving distress during recent famines.

It appears that all the Missions are making steady, if slow, progress.

Occupation.

The greater part of the population of Ajmer-Merwāra (54·81 per cent.) is agricultural. The industrial population amounts to 17·74 per cent. of the whole, and is chiefly engaged in cotton and leather industries, in the provision of food and drink and in the Railway workshops. General labour, as distinct from agriculture, supports 10·59 per cent. of the population. Personal service accounts for 5·91 per cent. and commerce for 4·21 per cent. The professions and Government service have 2·56 and 2·38 per cent. respectively. Persons of independent means without occupation number only 1·80 per cent. of the total population. To the famine is due an increase in the number of field labourers at the expense of the tenant class, and many occupations were severely affected; among others, many herdsmen, cotton weavers and dyers, cart owners and drivers and professional mendicants had to seek other means of livelihood.

The social characteristics of the people in the rural areas are very simple. The ordinary peasants may be described as generally docile and ignorant. Their wants are few and debts very often many. The cultivators as a class are suffering from the effects of recent famines. The condition of the landless labourers approaches the border of the subsistence minimum. They literally live from hand to mouth. In the urban areas the effects of the famine are less felt, and the trading classes are generally prosperous.

Food.

The higher classes of Hindus, with the exception of Rājputs and certain Brāhmans and Kāyasthas, are vegetarians. The staple food grains used are wheat, barley, gram, maize, *bājra* and *joār*, and various pulses. Wheat is generally used only by the richer classes of the community; the peasantry, except on special occasions, employ the coarser grains for their thick cakes or *rotīs*. These are eaten along with *dāl*, whey, uncooked onions or radishes, or with **chillies** They use only the cheapest kinds of vegetables. The wealthier people spread *ghī* upon their wheaten cakes or *chapāties*, and eat them with one or more cooked vegetables, *dāl* and pickles. Dairy produce is used by all classes. The Muhammadans, Rājputs, Merāts and other castes who eat flesh differ otherwise very little in their dietary from the Hindus. In the towns generally only two meals are taken daily, one between 9 and 10 A.M. and the other before 8 P.M. In rural areas the Jāts, Mālis, Gūjars and Mers eat three times a day. The early meal is called *sirāwan*, and consists of the food remaining over from the previous day. The mid-day meal is called *bhāt* or *rota*, and consist of barley or maize bread, with greens and buttermilk. All castes smoke tobacco and eat opium, and present them to friends and strangers coming to see them.

Dress. The ordinary dress of a male Hindu of the higher classes consists of a turban, which is generally a piece of silk or cotton cloth 30 to 40 feet long and 6 inches broad, with gold embroidered ends, a shirt (*kurtā*), a long coat (*angarkhā*) reaching nearly to the ankles, a loin cloth (*dhotī*) worn round the waist, and a scarf (*dupatta*.) The *kurtā* and *angarkhā* are usually made of a fine-textured material resembling muslin, and are generally white. Sometimes silk is used. The loin cloth is a long sheet of a coarser material. The Rājput *istimrārdārs* are fond of wearing embroidered garments, and multi-coloured turbans tied in narrow and picturesque folds, and have, especially on festive occasions, a martial appearance, which contrasts pleasantly with the silk and fine linens of other wealthy natives.

The dress of a Hindu female of the upper classes consists of a bodice (*kānchlī*), a sheet or veil (*orhnī*) as an upper garment, and a petticoat of chintz or coloured cloth. In the case of Mahājans and Rājput women the petticoat is very full, sixty yards of material being often employed in making it. From 15 to 20 yards of coarse cloth is sufficient for the petticoat of the lower classes. Agriculturists and labourers wear clothes made from a coarse fabric locally manufactured called *reza*. They consist of a turban (*pagri*,) a coat (*bakhtari*) extending to the waist, a loin cloth (*dhotī*,) and a sheet (*pacheora*). Some castes invariably carry a comb, a mirror, a pipe and a flint stone. The comb and mirror are kept in the turban, and the pipe and flint stone in the *dhotī*. The peasants in Ajmer are usually better dressed than those of Merwāra. In rural areas there is little difference in dress between Hindus and Muhammadans. The principal distinction is that Muhammadans wear trousers (*paijāmās*) and not *dhotīs*. Merāts and Chitas, however, though professing Muhammadans, retain the *dhotī*. Hindus, again, wear their coats with the opening on the right side of the chest, while the Muhammadans have it on the left side. In towns the latter can be distinguished by the buttoned-up coats of various lengths which they wear, together with trousers. A tendency to dress in European fashion, retaining the turban or a small round cap as head-dress, is apparent in the towns.

Dwellings.

The houses of the leading native bankers and traders in the towns, and in rural areas the residences of the leading *istimrārdārs* of the Ajmer district, are imposing buildings of masonry and stone, with roofs of the same material. As a rule they are two or more stories high, with one or more open courts to admit light and air. Every house has a *jharōka* or balcony, where the inmates can sit. The windows are small and the dwelling rooms often dark and ill ventilated. Though frequently covered with lavish and beautiful carving and ornamentation, these houses are generally built with little regard to ordinary rules of sanitation. In the reception rooms of the *istimrārdārs* the walls are often covered with paintings of their ancestors. In the villages the houses are small mud huts with tiled roofs. The entrance leads into a court-yard, round which are ranged the dwelling rooms of the family, according to its size and prosperity. Sometimes the cattle are kept in a shed in a corner of the court-yard, and sometimes in mud-fenced enclosures outside. The houses are generally clean. Signs, usually a square with the name of a deity entered in smaller squares within it, are painted at the entrance for good luck.

Disposal of the dead.

The Hindus burn their dead, with the exception of the Hindu worshippers of Rām Deoji in Merwāra, who bury them. Among Musalmāns burial is the rule. In the case of intermarriage between Hindu Mers (Rāwats) and Musalmān Mers (Kathāts), the wife is buried or burnt according to the religion of the husband. Gūjars and Jāts have a curious custom of shaving the corpses of male adults before burning them.

Games and Amusements.

Gymnastic exercises and athletics, sword and lance exercises are the principal games in the towns, apart from cricket, football and hockey, which are confined to the students in educational establishments. Chess, cards and a kind of draughts, known as *chopad*, are the indoor games. Hide-and-seek, kite flying, blind man's buff, a kind of touch in the ring, and a game called *ghota* (a kind of hockey), are played by children. In the village of Rāmsar a sort of organized fight with fists between two sections of the villagers takes place once a year. It is called *mukkirār*.

Among the lighter amusements, singing, playing on the fiddle (*sitār*) and flute (*bīn*) and drumbeating are extensively practised. A kind of rude opera, called the *Rai-kā-tamāshā*, in which the characters sing and dance all night long to the accompaniment of a drum only, is performed in the streets, and is much appreciated by the people. Among the lower classes in the towns, a circus is always popular. In rural areas the grown-up people have no games. Their ordinary amusement is to assemble in the evening at the village *hatāi*, or meeting house, and—sitting in the platform in front of it, usually built round a pipal or bar tree—to pass away a few hours talking and smoking. The village children play games similar to those in urban areas.

Festivals.

The principal festivals are the Holī, the Dewāli, the Gangor and the Tejā-ji-kā-melā (the fair of Tejāji) among Hindus, and the Moharram, the two Ids, and Urs Dargāh Khwāja Sāhib among Muhammadans. The Holī and the Dewāli are the two great festivals, held all over the country when the spring and autumn harvests are ripe. The Holī festival is attended with some local peculiarities of an interesting nature. The Oswāls of Ajmer have a procession, which they call *Rāo*: a man dressed as a bridegroom and seated on a cot is carried in procession through the Oswāl quarter. Men and women play on the *Rāo* with long syringes, in which they use water and the red powder (*gulāl*), which is the distinctive feature of the Holī. Women from the tops of houses use their syringes very effectively, while the *Rāo* carries an open umbrella to ward off the deluge. In Beāwar there is a procession of a much more dignified nature, known as *Bādshā*, in which a man dressed as a Rājā is carried through the streets, with people dancing and singing and occasionally throwing red powder. After passing through the town, the Rājā is taken to pay his respects to the Assistant Commissioner, Merwāra.

Another peculiarity of the local celebration of the Holī in Merwāra is the game called *ahera*, which is held on the first and last days of the festival. A whole village turns out into the jungle, each man armed with two sticks about a yard long, called *pokhri* or *kutka*. The people then form a line and beat for hares and deer, and, as they start up, knock them over with a general discharge of sticks. The village headmen provide opium and tobacco, and the bag is cooked and eaten at the feast which ends the day.

The festivals of Dewāli and Dasahra are the same as in other parts of the country. The Gangor festival, which is celebrated by Mahājans, begins a week after the Holī and lasts for 20 days. It is held in honour of the return of Pārvati, wife of Shīva, to the home of her parents, where she was entertained and worshipped by her female friends. Images of Shīva and Pārvati are paraded through the streets with music, and the places where thy are kept are illuminated at night and worshipped. The festival of Tejā-ji is confined to the Jāts. This fair is held about September. The Jāts, both men and women, keep awake the whole of the previous night, and worship the deity by singing songs and bringing offerings of cooked rice, barley and fruit.

The principal Muhammadan festivals of the Moharram and the two Ids are the same as elsewhere. But an exciting spectacle is added by the sword dance of the Indarkotīs, the inhabitants of the Indarkot *mohalla* of Ajmer city, in which 100 to 150 men, armed with sharp swords, dance and throw their weapons about in wild confusion. The Urs Khwāja Sāhib is a fair held at the Dargāh in the Muhammadan month of *Rajab*, and lasts for six days. Muhammadans came from all parts of the country to worship at the tomb of the saint, Muin-ud-dīn Chishti, and the yearly number of pilgrims approaches twenty-five thousand. The proceedings consist for the most part of recitations of Persian poetry of the Sufi School, at an assembly called the *mahfil.* The recitations are kept up until 3 o'clock in the morning, by which time many pilgrims are in the ecstatic devotional state technically known as *hāl.* One peculiar custom of this festival may be mentioned. There are two large cauldrons inside the Dargāh, one twice the size of the other, which are known as the great and little *deg.* Pilgrims to the shrine, according to their ability or generosity, propose to offer a *deg.* The smallest sum for which enough rice, butter, sugar almonds, raisins and spices can be bought to fill the large *deg* is Rs. 1,000. Besides this, the donor has to pay about Rs. 200 in presents to the officials of the shrine, and in offerings at the tomb. The small *deg* costs exactly half the large one.

When the gigantic rice pudding is cooked, it is looted boiling hot. Eight earthen pots of the mixture are first set apart for the foreign pilgrims, and it is the hereditary privilege of the people of Indrakot, and of the menials of the Dargāh, to empty the cauldron of the remainder of its contents. After the recitation of the *Fātiha*, one Indrakotī seizes a large iron ladle, and mounting the platform of the *deg* ladles away vigorously. All the men who take part in this hereditary privilege are swaddled up to the eyes in cloths to avoid the effects of the scalding fluid. When the cauldron is nearly empty all the Indrakotīs tumble in together and scrape it clean. There is no doubt that the custom of "looting the deg" is very ancient, though no account of its origin can be given. It is generally counted among the miracles of the saint that no lives have ever been lost on these occasions, though burns are frequent. The cooked rice is bought by Mahājans and others, and most castes will eat it.

Names and Titles.

Unlike the Madras and Bombay Presidencies, where three names are in general used for the identification of a male, the proper name, father's name, and family name, in Ajmer-Merwāra as in all northern India, the practice is to use one name only. Occasionally it happens that two persons with the same name but of different castes, add their fathers' names for distinctive purposes; but this is rare. Each person has his *zāt* or family name, which in rare instances is derived from the place of his ancestors, but it is not used in addressing him either by speech or by letter.

Every male of the "twice-born" classes has two names (*a*) the *janam-rāsi-nām,* only used at weddings, at death, and when the stars are consulted, and (*b*) the *bolta nām* by which he is generally known. The system of nomenclature is simple, and the names are generally of religious origin, or are given out of affection or fancy. Instances of the former are Har Lāl, Rām Singh, Shiv Charan, and of the latter Sundar Lāl, Gulzāri Lāl, and Pritam Chand. But there is an almost infinite variety of such names. Among the usual suffixes attached to names it may be remarked that Chand, Mal, Bhān, Pāl and Karan are principally used by Jains. On the other hand Datt (given) is exclusively a Brahman suffix.

Among the agricultural classes the males usually have one name only, which is a diminutive of a name of a higher class. For example, where a Mahājan or a Brāhman would call himself Birdhi Chand, Bherūn Rām or Udai Mal, the agriculturist, whether Jāt, Gūjar, Māli or Mer, would be known as Birdha, Bherūn or Uda. Except in rare instances the lower classes never use the suffixes Rām, Lāl, Chand and the like. Among them the name of the wife often corresponds with that of her husband, as Udi the wife of Uda.

Childrens' names take diminutive form in "u," as Moru, Phūlu. Occasionally Muhammadan names are used by Hindus and Jains, apparently out of reverence for the Muhammadan saint, whose Dargāh is at Ajmer. Or it may be a legacy of the conciliatory policy of Akbar. Some sections of Muhammadans, who were originally Hindus, have retained to this day their Hindu family names.

Among the names of places, Nasīrābād is the only instance of the suffix "ābād." Many villages have names ending "wās," meaning place of residence, and in "wāra," which means enclosure. Examples are Māngaliāwās and Bāndanwāra.

CHAPTER IV.

Agriculture.

General Conditions.

Ajmer and Merwāra are physically very distinct from each other. In Ajmer, plain country is the rule and hills the exception. There are several ranges of hills, but they spring more or less immediately from the plains, and there is little cultivation among them. The Pushkar *pargana*, cut off from the rest of the district by the Nāg-Pahār range, possesses a very peculiar character. It is entirely made up of hillocks of pure sand interspersed with depressions of rich soil. The sand hills absorb and retain the rainfall, prevent evaporation, and allow the water to percolate slowly to the lower ground. Here streams run but a short distance before they are finally absorbed. The soil is too sandy for irrigation tanks; but the hills contain the only two important natural lakes in the district. The Gangwāna *pargana* occupies the plain between the northern extension of Nāg-Pahār on the west, and the Srinagar and Kishangarh hills on the south. This plain drains to the north towards the Sāmbhar lake; the well land lies mostly along the main drainage channel, and, except under the hills to the south and west, there are few tanks. Along the lines where wells can be made, and under tanks there is much good cultivation, but in its general character the country is a broad unirrigated plain. East of the Srinagar hills and stretching south to Nasīrābād is the Rāmsar *pargana*. The broad shallow valleys or depressions in the plain offer better capabilities for irrigation than in Gangwāna. In some parts, especially towards Rāmsar, there is much salt in the soil, as the old salt mounds or *agars* scattered over the country show. In Rājgarh, south and west of Rāmsar, the villages under the hills have light and sandy soil, while in the plain there are some excellent tanks and good well cultivation. The plain of the Ajmer *pargana* is ill-adapted for tanks, but almost all the villages have wells dependent on the percolation of the Sāgarmati, in which the supply is constant and good.

In Merwāra, in contradistinction to Ajmer, the hill country is the rule and the plain the exception. The two ranges of the Aravalli which meet near Jawāja, enclose a valley which tapers from its extreme width on the north to a point at the south. In this valley, about two miles west of the main range of the Aravalli, runs a low range through which in former times the drainage had forced for itself numerous passages. By blocking these a line of magnificent tanks from Dilwāra on the north to Lusāni II, on the south, has been made. Below these tanks villages are numerous and the population is dense.

South of Jawāja, except the outlying villages of Jaitgarh and Bheron Khera in Mewār, for some 35 miles, until Gudha Lakha is reached, the whole breadth of the district is a confused mass of hills, and the cultivation is confined to the valleys and terraces made on the hill-sides. There are many tanks, but few of any size. For some ten miles south of Gudha Lakha there is a narrow plain on the Mewār border bounded still on the west by the Aravalli range. South of Barjāl again the whole district, including the outlying villages, is hill. Tanks in this part are rare, and well cultivation the rule. The ranges culminate in the peak of Goramji, south of Todgarh, which rises to more than 3,000 feet above the sea.

In general, the cultivated soil of both districts is composed of a mixture of stiff yellow loam and sand, in proportion of one to two. No superficial portion of soil is absolutely clayey, and alluvial soil is only found in the beds of artificial tanks. In tracts where euphorbia are common, carbonate of lime is found in large quantities. The richest soil in the province is among the sand hills of Pushkar, where sugarcane is grown without irrigation. But elsewhere all the most valuable cultivation is irrigated either from wells or tanks. The rainfall throughout is too precarious for the dry cultivation to be much considered by the people. Where it is carried out, the fields are sometimes surrounded by low embankments to retain the rain moisture as long as possible. All dry crop land is classed together as *bārāni*, and no sub-classification has so far been attempted. Irrigated lands are classed as *chāhi*, *talābī* and *abi*, according to the means of irrigation employed.

As the slope of the land is in every direction away from these districts, there is no permanent under-current of percolation to feed the supply in the wells. Both they and the tanks are dependent upon the rainfall. In Ajmer, where the beds of the *nallās* are sandy, a sufficient amount of water is absorbed during the rains to supply the wells on either bank; but wells can only profitably be made within a short distance of the stream. In Merwāra the beds of the drainage channels are rocky and the slope of the country greater. Tanks are essential to catch the rainfall, which would otherwise flow off rapidly into Mārwār and Mewār, and not give the wells any chance of filling by percolation. In many parts the soil is thin and the rock very near the surface.

Among the hills and valleys of Merwāra there is a system of *petite-culture*. Small fields have been made with great labour by terracing the hill sides and building up the lower end with stone walls to prevent the soil being washed away. Where the walls are sufficiently substantial to act as a dam and retain moisture, these fields, locally known as *paraband* are classed as *abi*. *Abi* strictly means land in the beds of tanks, which is everywhere cultivated after the tanks have dried up in the spring or hot weather.

Halsara.

In the dry crop lands in many villages of Ajmer there exists a system shifting cultivation called *halsara*, a survival of the original idea that the dry crop land was of little value and could be cultivated by any one. The custom is that a village sharer or cultivator takes a plough each year in the *halsara* area, for which he pays a sum fixed by village custom, ranging from Rs. 2 to Rs. 7. In exchange he is entitled to sow a certain area, which again varies by village custom, between 6 and 28 acres. The owner of the plough settles on the bit he fancies, and as long as he uses only one plough, no one enquires what area he occupies. When the land is broken up, *til* is sown, or if the season promises exceptionally well, gram, and after this the land remains for one year the private land of the sharer, in which he may grow *joār*. In the third year the cultivator abandons this, and goes to another spot, and the first piece lies fallow until someone else takes a fancy to the whole or part of it. Such a custom could not exist in a tract where rain is plentiful and dry crop land valuable. Even in Ajmer *halsara* possession is in many villages crystallizing into ownership.

Agricultural Implements.

As the soil is light and deep ploughing exceptional, a single pair of bullocks is generally sufficient for draught. The agricultural implements are similar to those used in the United Provinces, and have no distinctive features. No new appliances have been introduced into the districts. In the kharif season succeeding the great famine of 1899-1900 hand ploughs drawn by men were tried, to make up for the deficiency of cattle. Some land was brought under cultivation by their means, but they never became popular, and have now disappeared.

Agricultural Population.

According to the census of 1901 the agricultural population amounted to 2,54,763, as against 2,62,551 in 1891. The decrease was due to the disastrous famines of the decade. In Ajmer the agriculturists numbered 53·3 per cent. of the the total population. The percentages of actual workers and dependents were 63·5 and 36·5 in Ajmer, and 62·3 and 37·7 in Merwāra. The cultivators are principally Jāts, Gūjars, Mers, Merāts and Rāwats, whose numbers were returned in 1901 as 27,946, 36,248, 21,649, 8,554 and 32,209 respectively. The Jāts are the best cultivators, and the Gūjars come next in this respect.

Sowing.

In preparing for the *kharif* harvest, the land is ploughed up towards the end of April and beginning of May. It is then left till after the first rains have fallen, when it is re-ploughed and taken under various processes till it becomes ready for the sowing. For *rabi* the ploughing is generally done in September. The land thus ploughed is allowed to stand for a month, when it is ploughed a second time, and harrowed before the seed is sown.

Manure.

In dry crop areas manure is not used, but in the irrigated lands, owing to the general poorness of the soil, especially in Merwāra, heavy manuring is absolutely necessary. Much of such land in both districts is cropped twice in the year; there is little scientific rotation and no rest, so the necessity is sufficiently apparent. The salty soil of the Rāmsar *pargana* gives excellent crops when heavily manured, but without it is almost worthless. A full manuring of *chāhi* or *tālābi* lands is considered to be 360 maunds to the acre every third year, but this is a rate not often reached. The greater proportion of the cattle in the district are kept for purposes of manure. That of sheep and goats is more valuable, but their destructive habits made them unpopular until the heavy losses of cattle during the recent famine. Ashes, house sweepings and vegetable manures are also used to some extent. Nightsoil is in considerable demand as manure among the villages near the towns: it is not available elsewhere.

Principal Crops.

The principal crops, in order of extent of area cultivated, are maize, *joār,* or great Indian millet, barley, cotton, oilseeds, *bājra,* or bulrush millet and wheat. These occupied respectively 19·9, 18·4, 16·1, 10·1, 7·1, 6·5, and 3·5 per cent. of the average cultivated area during the ten years ending 1899-00. Maize is sown in June and July and is harvested in October and November. Where irrigation is available it is watered two to three times. Its average out-turn in cwts. per acre is 1·10 in *bārāni* land and 7·34 in irrigated land. It is rotated with barley and cotton, the land remaining fallow for the *rabi* harvest before the cotton is sown in *kharif.*

Barley is always a *rabi* crop. It is sown from 15th October to 15th November and is reaped in April. In irrigated lands it is watered from three to five times, and yields an average of 7·34 cwts. per acre. In dry crop lands the average out-turn is only 1·46 cwts. *Joār* is only grown as a dry crop; it is sown in June and July and harvested in October and November, and has an average yield of 1·73 cwts. per acre. *Bājra* is sown at the same season and also in dry lands only; its average yield is also 1·73 cwts. per acre.

Rotation of Crops.

Cotton, though not first in point of area, gives of all the crops the most valuable return to the cultivator. It is sown in June and July, and the seed is mixed with cowdung and ashes, with the idea of increasing its germinating power. The crop is picked in November and December, and gives an average yield of 3·11 cwts. per acre in irrigated and 1·10 cwts. per acre in unirrigated land. In the former it is watered from five to seven times during the season. After the cotton is reaped the land is always left fallow for one harvest before maize is sown on it, as already described. *Til* is sown in dry lands in July and August, and is reaped in November; its average yield is 1 cwt. per acre. Gram is a *rabi* crop, and is sown in dry crop lands in October and harvested in April, with an average out-turn of 1·73 cwts. per acre. Wheat, also *rabi,* is sown in late October and early November. In irrigated lands it is watered from three to five times before the harvest in April, when its yield averages 7·5 cwts. per acre. In *bārāni* land the average out-turn is only 1·73 cwts. It is rotated with maize and barley, after which, with one intervening *kharif* fallow, it is again sown.

The other crops (food as well as non-food) are very limited. Sugarcane cultivation is confined to the rich soil of the Pushkar valley, where it grows without irrigation, and gives an average return of 8·84 cwts. per acre. Poppy is cultivated in the Todgarh *tahsīl* as a *rabi* crop in irrigated lands, where it is watered from six to eight times. The average yield of poppy heads is 2·75 cwts. per acre.

Chillies are sown as *kharif* in wet crop lands. They require much irrigation, from 15 to 20 waterings, but the average out-turn of 2·19 cwts. per acre gives a good profit to the cultivator. The remaining crops deserve no special mention.

In all cases the cultivators endeavour to retain the best grain for seed. There is a prejudice in favour of local seed grains of all kinds as against foreign varieties. Seed of the previous year's crop is always used, as the local belief is that it loses some of its germinating properties if kept for longer. There are no model farms in the district, one started by Mr. Saunders having proved a failure; and it is feared that the influence of the Agricultural Department's publications has not done much towards the introduction of improved systems or new varieties.

Extension and Decrease of Cultivation.

Extension and decrease of cultivation is merely synchronous with good or bad seasons, so far as recent years are concerned. In the earlier history of the district, however, when tanks were being built and Merwāra was being surveyed, considerable extension took place. There were 58,079 acres under irrigation in 1884, as against 51,949 in 1874, and the unirrigated area cultivated had risen from 1,19,467 acres to 1,32,242 in the same period. But after the great famine the total irrigated area in 1902-03 had fallen to 37,046, and the unirrigated cropped area to 1,33,686 acres. The cultivation of poppy has decreased in Todgarh since the introduction of the Excise Rules, while the demand for raw cotton and its profitable return have caused its cultivation to increase steadily in popularity. Its average of 12,426 acres between 1881-1890 had risen to 21,011 acres in the next decade. Famine and scarcity, however, caused a fall of these latter figures to 12,756 acres in 1902-03. In this year, while in some cases the area under cultivation of a particular crop had increased, the production had decreased; this was markedly the case with wheat, barley and cotton.

Fruit and vegetable production is chiefly confined to a few gardens cultivated by mālis near Ajmer, although some vegetables are also grown in the municipal gardens at Beawar. The fruit is generally poor in quality, and no great variety of vegetables is obtainable. There are no model fruit or vegetable gardens in the province.

Land Improvement & Agriculturalists Loans Acts.

The introduction of the Land Improvements Act of 1883 and of the Agriculturists Loans Act of 1884 has, by making money available at a reasonable rate of interest, done much to modify the effects of recent famines. When the private lenders refused to advance money for seed and bullocks or for wells, and credit was severely contracted, the working of the two Acts was of the utmost value. Since they came into operation until 1902 Rs. 5,59,653 had been advanced under the Land Improvements Act, and Rs. 5,55,734 under the Agriculturists Loans Act. In good seasons punctual repayment of instalments is usual, but the famine, while making large advances necessary, made prompt repayment impossible, and at the end of September 1902

Rs. 2,04,106 were outstanding under the Act of 1883, and Rs. 2,08,131 under the Act of 1884. Under the former Act 917 new wells had been constructed at a cost of Rs. 74,984, which irrigated 1,951 acres; 4,230 old wells were deepened and repaired at a cost of Rs. 2,46,662, with an irrigable area of 9,328 acres; while 206 other irrigation works were constructed or repaired, costing Rs. 2,53,415 and irrigating 6,488 acres. The latter Act, supplying money for maintenance, seed and purchase of cattle, has formed one of the most valuable recuperative agencies after the ravages of famine.

Indebtedness. The amount of private indebtedness both in Ajmer and in Merwāra is enormous. Accurate statistics are not available, but, from inquiries made in Ajmer in 1900-1901, it is believed that the amount of private debt is over Rs. 10,00,000. That in Merwāra is probably no less. In 1885, at the time of the last settlement, it was calculated that 30,319 acres (including 19,778 acres of land mortgaged at the previous settlement) of land were mortgaged for Rs. 12,38,755 and 3,857 maunds of grain.

Recent calamities therefore, have increased the indebtedness by about two-fifths. The Rājput estate holders, who cannot encumber their estates beyond their own lives, have a large amount of private debt notwithstanding, and owed to Government for loans advanced in the famine the sum of Rs. 1,56,132, part of which has, however, been recently remitted. In 1872 a regulation was passed for their relief, and their debts, amounting to 7 lakhs, were taken over by Government at 5 per cent. interest. This debt to Government had been almost entirely liquidated before the recent famines made further loans necessary. The rates of interest on private debts vary from As. 8 to Rs. 2 per cent. a month. When given in kind it amounts to about one-third of the produce of the mortgaged lands. The large majority of money-lenders belong to the professional money-lending classes.

Years of famine give an opportunity to the grain-dealers to secure what would otherwise be bad debts. There is always a large amount of unsecured debt, which has descended from father to son, or consists of extortions of the grain-dealers which they could not recover in a civil court. A hungry man is not over-cautious as to what he puts his name to, and the grain-dealers find their opportunity in the necessity of the cultivators, who, if they require food, are obliged to sign bonds or mortgage their lands for the full amount which the grain-dealers state as due to them. Mortgage is generally of a usufructuary kind, and formerly the mortgagee only rarely took possession of the land. But of recent years it has become more common, the land being handed over to a third person for cultivation, owing to the difficulty found by the mortgagee in recovering his dues from the original mortgagor, who is protected by the courts from paying more than a certain amount of the produce by way of interest. Sales of land in execution of decrees are forbidden, except with the sanction of the Commissioner. In the present state of public credit, it is difficult to see how Agricultural Banks can succeed in the province. The question is, however, receiving attention.

Owing to the want of any large pastures and permanent water supply, the district is not well adapted for systematic cattle and horse breeding. Formerly large numbers were kept, and were grazed upon the hills and village pasture lands during good seasons, and were taken to Mālwa and more favoured districts when the rains failed. The enclosure of the forests, however, tended to reduce their number to what was actually required for agricultural purposes, as the village pastures became more limited. But on the other hand the opening of free grazing in the forests leaves a valuable resource to save what cattle there are in famine times. Of recent years restrictions have been put by many Native States upon cattle immigration for grazing purposes, and emigration when necessary is usually in the direction of the United Provinces. There is no indigenous breed of cattle deserving special mention, and the cultivators get their cows covered by bulls of various breeds. The cattle, as a rule, belong to four stocks, the Rendi Khān, Dhāora, Mārwāri and Mewāri. The first breed supplies the best milch cows, while the last three are stronger and are generally used for field work. The average price of a bullock is Rs. 30, of a cow Rs. 25, of a she buffalo Rs. 40 and of a calf of either species Rs. 15. A scheme for stationing Government bulls in central villages to improve the breeds of cattle is under contemplation. Cattle.

Horse breeding is rare, and more so since the recent famines. Until recently efforts were made to encourage it by keeping an Arab stallion at the Veterinary School at Ajmer, and by offering rewards at Pushkar fair for colts and fillies sired by him. The average value of the local pony is about about Rs. 50.

Sheep and goats are kept everywhere, especially since the want of cattle has increased the demand for other manure. They are very hardy and are little affected by famine. Their average value is Rs. 3 apiece.

The most important horse and cattle fair is held at Pushkar in November. Animals come from all parts, prizes are given by Government from the proceeds of the temporary tolls, and selling and buying are usually brisk. Two cattle fairs of minor importance are held at Beāwar and Kekri at the time of the Teja celebrations in early September.

Mention must here be made of the Rājputāna Veterinary School, which was established in Ajmer in 1894, with the idea of supplying veterinary assistants for Rājputāna. At the same time a Civil Veterinary Department was started with a view to improving the breeds of horses and cattle. A European officer holds the combined appointments of Principal of the Veterinary School and Superintendent, Civil Veterinary Department. He teaches medicine and surgery in the school, where he is assisted by three lecturers on bovine pathology, anatomy and physiology, and chemistry and materia medica, respectively. A hospital is attached to the school. Since 1894 131 veterinary assistants have been trained, and 4,774 animals have received treatment. A farrier teaches men who are sent from Native States to learn farriery. Under the Superintendent, Civil Veterinary Department, there are veterinary assistants attached to the Beāwar Municipality and the Ajmer District Board. The Superintendent goes on tour every year to inspect veterinary dispensaries, to visit horse and cattle fairs, and to give advice regarding horse and cattle breeding. He also investigates any cases of outbreak of contagious disease, and inspects the horse and cattle boxes and trucks on the railway. Government have recently decided to abolish the School, and place Rājputāna under the Civil Veterinary Department of Baluchistān and Sind.

Irrigation. It is unnecessary to recapitulate the various physical and meteorological conditions which make irrigation so important a factor in the agriculture of the province.

Tanks. The idea of tank embankments was one which early presented itself to the minds of those conversant with the district. The Bīsla tank was made by Bisal Deo Chauhān, about the year 1150 A.D.; his grandson, Ana, constructed the Anāsagar; the tank at Rāmsar was built by Rām Deo Pramar. In Merwāra the large tanks of Dilwāra, Kālinjar, Jawāja and Balād date from long before our rule. They have wide earthen embankments, generally faced on both sides with flat stones, and closing gorges in the hills. With ordinary care they will last as long as the hills which they unite, and their construction furnishes a substantial proof that before our rule the principles of subordination and co-operation were not unknown in Merwāra.

The tank embankments at present number 531, of which 377 are managed by Government, the remainder being in charge of the villages or the municipalities. There are 1,802 tanks in *istimrāri* and *jāgīr* lands, which are managed as part of the estates: a few tanks constructed within *jāgīr* and minor *istimrāri* lands by Government are managed by the Public Works Department and are included in the previous totals. The majority owe their existence to Colonel Dixon, who ruled Merwāra from 1836 to 1842 and the united districts from 1842 to 1857. He gives a very full account of them in his "Sketch of Merwāra," Chapter XII, *et seq*. The best site for an embankment is a narrow gorge, where, by uniting the hills on each side, the drainage of the valley above can be stopped and the water thrown back to form a lake, which will irrigate direct by a sluice, and feed the wells below by percolation. Such sites are, however, limited, and since the famine works of recent years nearly all of them have been utilized, though in many cases the embankment is capable of much improvement. In the open parts of the districts, where Colonel Dixon made a large number of tanks, the embankments run a considerable distance from one rising ground to the other. Some are nearly two miles in length. The centre portion of the dam arrests the flow of a drainage channel, and the water spreads on each side to the rising ground. Every tank is provided with an escape to prevent the water topping the embankment during floods. These tanks are generally very shallow, and seldom retain any water after the autumn harvest has been irrigated. Colonel Dixon attempted at first to form earthen embankments, but the soil is so devoid of tenacity that the plan was early abandoned.

There are four kinds of embankments in the districts. First, a wall of dry stone backed by an earthen embankment and faced with a coating of mortar, generally combined with a dry stone retaining wall; secondly, a masonry wall backed with earth, the masonry and embankment being of greater or less strength in proportion to the weight of water to be retained. Thirdly, an earthen embankment, with or without a masonry core wall. Fourthly, a wall of masonry without any embankment. This last is the best, and is adopted in the more hilly parts of the district, where the gorges do not exceed 100 yards in width. Similar to these are the small masonry weirs thrown across a *nalla* in its course through the hills, in order to ensure a supply to the wells on either bank.

The embankments of the Government tanks are in charge of the Public Works Department. They are inspected annually in December, when estimates for necessary repairs are submitted for sanction. It was noted at the last settlement that new sluices and new ducts were very necessary in many cases. Thus the ducts of the large Rāmsar tank were formerly laid out on no system; for long distances two and even three and four ducts were running side by side, owned by different interests, and each wasting water by overflow, evaporation and percolation. Of recent years this has been remedied. Ducts are fed in general by the gravitation flow of the water from the tank, but in cases of deficiency the water is often raised by lifts to the mouth of the sluice.

In the time of Colonel Dixon the water revenue was added to the ordinary assessment of the village, and both were paid together. The system was to fix 6 per cent. upon the cost of construction of any tank within the village and add the amount to the previous assessment.

Irrigation Revenue and Expenditure.

At the time of LaTouche's Settlement a change was introduced in the case of the first class tanks in Beāwar and Todgarh, and almost all the tank-irrigated villages in Ajmer. In their case the water revenue was entirely excluded from the *khewat*, and the villages were assessed at so much, *plus* a lump sum for water revenue. This lump sum was to be made good from the fields actually irrigated each year, unless its incidence on the irrigated area exceeded a certain fixed maximum, or fell below a certain fixed minimum. Out of a total of Rs. 55,432 water revenue, Rs. 37,172 was thus assessed. The balance, chiefly derived from smaller tanks, remained under the former fixed system, by which the water revenue, though separately recorded for the whole village and for each holding, was included in the *khewat*, or record of individual responsibility. In 1885 Government tank works were grouped into crop rate tanks, variably assessed tanks paying a fixed assessment maintained by Government, and tanks paying a fixed assessment and repaired by the villagers. There are now 45 crop rate tanks, 80 under variable assessment, 243 paying fixed revenue, and 9 paying on a combination of the variable and fixed systems. In crop rate tanks the area irrigated is recorded each year, and assessed to pay revenue at certain rates which vary as the crop grown. In the variable system there is a rate which varies between a certain maximum and a certain minimum according to the standard area, which is fixed. The assessment is based on the total tank area, whether irrigated or unirrigated in the autumn harvest. In the spring harvest the water revenue is assessed at full rates if the tank water is above sluice level on 15th February. If the water is below sluice level on that date the revenue is assessed on the number of irrigations given. In the fixed assessment a lump sum is taken irrespective of the area irrigated. Besides the land irrigated by flow from the tanks, called *tālābi*, there is also yearly cultivation in the dry beds of many tanks called *abi*. The assessment of this class of land is also both fixed and variable. At the last settlement 16,106 acres of *abi* land came under the former system and 7,176 under the latter.

The average annual receipts from water revenue during the ten years ending 1890, amounted to Rs. 58,170·5. In the next decade the average had, owing to suspensions and remissions on account of famine, fallen to Rs. 56,869·9. In 1902-03 Rs. 35,626 were collected, while Rs. 38,900 were outstanding as arrears. These figures include the water revenue from well-irrigated lands situated within the limit of the tank areas. Before 1880-81 the total capital expenditure on tanks in Ajmer-Merwāra amounted to Rs. 14,23,794. Between 1880-81 and 1889-90 Rs. 2,22,887 were spent. In the decade ending 1900 the expenditure, owing to the large construction works carried out during famine, rose to Rs. 11,78,529. In 1902-03 the capital expenditure on tanks was Rs. 89,439. Up to the 31st March 1903 the total capital outlay had been Rs. 30,89,122. Except in years of drought the works average a return of about 3 per cent. on their capital cost.

Wells. There are few permanent wells in the districts; in general they, like the tanks, depend upon the rainfall percolation for their water supply. In the Ajmer district the beds of the *nallās* are sandy, and a sufficient amount of water is absorbed during the rains to supply the wells on either side. In Merwāra, where the beds are rocky, the wells depend more upon the water which is retained in the tanks. Percolation tends to keep water in the wells as long as there is water in the tanks. When the water of a tank dries and the subsoil water sinks, the water level in the dependent wells sinks also. It is not, however, always the wells lying directly below a tank that benefit most from it. Percolation frequently, though by no means universally, shows itself along lines of natural drainage, but it always works along the line of least resistance, which may or may not be reflected on the surface. Instances of the latter frequently occur. In Bir there is some improvement to the wells for a short distance below the tank, but the same result shows itself ten miles away in Udaipur and Tikāorā in the Kishangarh State. In the British territory between there is no change, so that the water passes under Srinagar by a natural syphon. The effect of the Kālinjar tank is not felt so much in the wells below it to the west, but the wells in the village of Pālān in Mewār, which lies to the east and is separated from it by the main range of the Arāvallis, depend on it for their water supply. Other cases could be cited.

A few wells which may, perhaps, be called "permanent" exist in both districts. But the term is here merely relative. The springs from which they derive their water depend ultimately upon the infiltration of rain water, and as there is no supply from the outside, it only needs a long enough drought to dry up every well in Ajmer-Merwāra. These comparatively permanent wells are most common at the foot of hills, such as Rājgarh and Kothāj of Ajmer, or along stream beds draining from such hills as those near Beāwar. In no place are they numerous. Gopālpura in Beāwar with seven, and Chāpliān in Dawair with twenty, are the villages best off in this respect.

Where the water is plentiful the Persian wheel, or *dhimda*, is generally used to draw it from the well. In other cases the ordinary water lift by bullocks with the long pull rope and bucket, called *charas* is employed. There are two kinds of *charas* distinguished locally by the names *potliā* and *soondiā*. The former requires four bullocks and three or four men to work it, and can irrigate an acre of land in about six hours. The latter, with only two oxen and a single attendant, takes twice as long. Irrigated fields are divided into small beds, some 60 or 100 per *bigha*, in order to distribute the water. Some five years ago an attempt was made to introduce iron buckets in place of the *charas*, but they were not found satisfactory. A *kacha* well, without masonry, averages about Rs. 50 in cost. The price of a masonry well ranges from Rs. 200 to Rs. 700, according to its depth, diameter and the nature of the soil. At the last Settlement there were 2,879 wells dependant upon Government tanks, out of which 2,622 were assessed to water revenue.

In 1901, so far as can be ascertained, the total number of wells in use in Ajmer-Merwāra (*khālsa*) was 13,655, of which Ajmer had 6,511 and Merwāra 7,144. From these, 28,033 acres were irrigated, paying assessment to Government of Rs. 43,193. The average irrigated area per well was, therefore, 2·05 acres, with an average water rate of Rs. 1-8-7 per acre.

CHAPTER V.

RENTS, WAGES, AND PRICES.

Rents. The larger proportion of Ajmer-Merwāra, with the exception of the *istimrāri* areas, is cultivated by resident landlords. Where tenancy exists, it is generally that of tenants-at-will or of expropriétary tenants. The latter are those who have mortgaged their lands, but are continued in possession under the terms of the mortgage. In all *istimrāri* estates cultivators are considered to be tenants-at-will until the contrary is proved. They generally, however, hold under contract leases, and pay rent at fixed permanent rates, and are liable to ejectment only on breach of the terms of the contract. Rent is determined by agreement between landlord and tenant, and is usually paid in kind. The landlord's share varies from a half to a quarter of the produce of the land, according to the quality and capacity of the holding and the terms of the tenancy. So in the case of land irrigated from wells, where the landlord pays Government dues and supplies seed and manure, he gets half the produce. If he pays Government dues only, he gets one-third. If he pays nothing at all towards Government dues or expenses, his share will not exceed a quarter. In tank lands the landlord gets half produce where he pays Government revenue and half the expenses. If he pays the Government dues only he receives a third. In the case of dry crop land a third of the produce is the usual share of the landlord. Rent in kind is called *bānta.* Its actual quantity is decided either by appraising the standing crops, or by dividing the produce after the grain has been threshed out. The former system is known as *kūnta* and the latter as *latāi.* On certain crops, however, rents are paid in cash. In cases of cash rents the standing crop is measured at each harvest, and the rents are calculated either at fixed rates mentioned in the Record of Rights at the Settlement, or according to special rates agreed upon between landlord and tenant. The cash rents vary from Rs. 2-8 to Rs. 8 per acre according to the crop. In Ajmer among the *kharif* crops cotton, maize and sugar-cane in well lands usually give rent in cash. In the *rabi* season, cash rents are only paid for lands which grow melons, vegetables, garden produce and lucerne. In the case of opium the rents are paid partly in cash and partly in kind, and vary from Rs. 10 to Rs. 20 per acre. In Merwāra rents paid in kind are almost universal; cash rents are rare.

The only local legislation regarding rents refers to expropriétary tenants. By a regulation passed in 1877, their rents are fixed at one-third less than the ordinary rents for similar lands in the vicinity. These rents are, however, usually fixed so as to bring to the mortgagee landlord interest at a specified rate on the money advanced by him, and are independent of the total produce of the land. They are locally called *ghūgri*, and are due even if the lands remain uncultivated. Expropriетary tenants cannot be ejected for non-payment even by decree of a Civil Court, without the sanction of the Commissioner. Owing to consequent difficulties in recovering their dues, the tendency is becoming more and more for money-lenders to advance money only on terms of mortgage with possession. They then employ third persons to cultivate the land as tenants. In the Settlements a half of the gross produce is calculated as cost of production, one-sixth as Government revenue, and the remaining one-third as the landlord's profits. There is no tendency visible for cash rents to displace rents in kind. In the present circumstances the latter system seems both to tenants and landlords to possess the greater advantages. Under it, enhancements and abatements due to changes in area, to improvement and deterioration, or the rise and fall of prices, are adjusted automatically.

Wages.

The average daily wage of an unskilled labourer is 2 annas in rural areas and between 2 and 4 annas in urban areas. The wages of unskilled labour have not changed since 1881. They are usually paid in cash, but agricultural labourers are sometimes paid in kind, receiving grain of the equivalent value of the cash payment. During the three famine years ending in 1901, the dominating money wage has been that paid on the Government relief works, which is scientifically calculated and gives the worker enough to live on, and probably, when a family is on the works, a margin for saving. In the towns, masons, blacksmiths and carpenters get an average wage of 4 to 8 annas a day, as against $5\frac{1}{3}$ to $10\frac{2}{3}$ and $5\frac{1}{3}$ to 8 annas in 1881 and 1891 respectively. The Railway Locomotive and Carriage and Waggon Shops in Ajmer give employment to a large number of skilled hands. In the Locomotive Shops the maximum rates of their wages vary from Rs. 7-8 per day, in the case of European fitters to 5 annas a day in the case of strikers, the minimum varying from Rs. 2 to 2 annas. In the Carriage and Waggon Shops the daily wage varies from a maximum of Rs. 2-12 to 3 annas a day, the minimum being from Re. 1 to 2 annas according to the class of labour. The maximum daily wage paid in the Krishna Cotton Mills at Beāwar is Rs. 1-4, and the minimum is $1\frac{1}{2}$ annas. In rural areas carpenters, blacksmiths, leather makers and other village servants get allowances of grain from the villagers in return for their services. Thus, carpenters, potters and blacksmiths are given 15 seers of grain per plough at each harvest. If a cultivator owns a well with a Persian wheel he has to give then 30 seers, owing to the greater amount of labour required for repairs. At the reaping time they are given in addition by each cultivator a sheaf of corn weighing about 5 seers. When the seed is being sown they receive a contribution of 2 seers of seed grain from each cultivator. If, however, a carpenter prepares a new plough for a landholder, he is given 2 annas extra for his labour. If he makes a new cart he is paid separately for it, or is fed for a time in lieu of payment. Tanners or *balāis*, for repairing shoes and assisting in the storage of manure, get from 5 seers to 20 seers of grain per harvest from each household. If they have to supply new shoes and other small leather articles, the allowance per harvest is from

20 seers to a maund. If a new leather bucket is prepared, the cultivator has to feed the tanner in addition. The food allowance, consisting of a mixture of wheat, *ghī* and *gur* is called *lash.* Barbers are given 10 seers of grain per harvest for every adult male in the village. Drummers (*dholis*) get a share of grain per house per harvest, and the priests receive a smaller allowance. In addition, all are given something at the *Holī* and *Dewāli* festivals and upon marriage occasions.

As wages in rural areas are to so large an extent paid in kind, they have not been much affected by the price of food grains. There has been no extension of the railway system since 1879, nor have factory and mining industries developed so as to affect wages. Times of scarcity and consequent temporary rises in prices have not resulted generally in increase of wages. The ordinary work available decreases, while the demand for it increases. The labourer is willing to accept his normal or even a decreased money wage in order to secure employment at all. As already noticed, in such times the price paid for labour on Government relief works, as representing the subsistence minimum, becomes the dominating wage. Only the wages of domestic servants in towns have risen considerably of late years.

Prices.

The prices of the staple food grains in 1902-03 at Ajmer, Beāwar and Todgarh respectively were in quantity per rupee :—wheat, 12 seers 11 chittāks, 13 seers 3 chittāks and 12 seers ½ chittāk; barley, 16 seers 11⅔ chittāks, 17 seers 8½ chittāks and 16 seers 2½ chittāks; *joār,* 17 seers 13 chittāks, 18 seers and 19 seers 7 chittāks; *bājra,* 16 seers 6 chittāks, 15 seers 8⅔ chittāks and 16 seers 3¼ chittāks; and maize, 18 seers 7½ chittāks, 18 seers 12 chittāks and 18 seers 11 chittāks. In this year deficient rainfall had produced famine conditions in Merwāra, and prices on the whole were higher than in the previous decade. It is noteworthy, however, that the absence of octroi and the prevalence of the *sauda* system of contracts among the merchants of Beāwar made the grain prices in Merwāra generally lower than those in Ajmer. Taking maize as a representative food grain of a large bulk of the population, we find that during the last three decades its average prices at Ajmer, Beāwar and Todgarh respectively varied as below :—between 1873 and 1880 they were 21 seers 12 chittāks, 23 seers 1 chittāk and 24 seers 15 chittāks respectively; between 1881-1890 they where 23 seers 3 chittāks, 25 seers 9 chittāks and 28 seers 12 chittāks. Betweeen 1891-1900 the average price rose considerably, being 18 seers 12 chittāks, 20 seers 11 chittāks and 22 seers 10 chittāks respectively. From 1871 to 1890 there had been a long series of prosperous years, the railway had given improved communication, and cultivation had extended, so prices ruled easy. But the natural calamities of the following decade more than counteracted the improvements in transport, and prices were bound to rise. In 1891-92 the rise was inconsiderable, as the scarcity was purely local, and imports promptly arrived to meet the demand. In all seasons a certain amount of importation is necessary, as the districts do not produce sufficient for their own consumption. Imports come mainly from the United Provinces and the Punjāb, and famine in those provinces in

1896-97 raised prices in Ajmer-Merwāra. In the famine of 1899-00 grain was always procurable in the most distant part of the districts at a price which nowhere exceeded 7 seers to the rupee. The extraordinary prices of the 1869 famine, due to imperfect means of communication, can hardly be seen again.

Material condition of the People.

The material condition of the urban population is generally satisfactory. That it has been so little affected by the recent famine is due to the railway. The standard of comfort among the well-to-do has been gradually rising and European articles such as mineral waters and ice are widely used. Among the richer classes an increased use of articles of dress of European fashion is also to be observed. If a middle-class clerk be taken as an example, it is seen that he has sufficient income to enable him to live with comfort in a town. If he is in the service of Government he has a pension to look forward to, and if in that of the Railway, his Provident Fund savings. He can afford to dress well, to diet himself liberally, and generally to give his sons an English education. In rural areas, on the other hand, the effects of the famine are shown in a perceptible falling-off in the standard of living. The quantity of the daily food has diminished, the stores of ornaments and household vessels are depleted, and smaller amounts are spent on clothing. The less initial cost has caused many to clothe themselves in the cheap and flimsy foreign cottons rather than in the stronger *reza* cloths of local manufacture. Little margin is left for luxuries such as liquor and opium. Expenses on social ceremonies have been curtailed considerably, rather from stern necessity than from natural habits of thrift. On the other hand many conveniences are available which were unknown to previous generations, and matches, kerosine oil and cheap cloths from Lancashire or Bombay mills are procurable in every substantial village. Indebtedness has increased largely among the cultivators, but the difficulty of recovering debt on the part of the money-lenders has recently led to a contraction of credit. Liberal grants of *takāvi* by Government have tended to rectify the situation; much revenue has been suspended and much remitted.

The labouring classes have been the most affected by recent famines, and since 1870 their position has probably never been worse. They are living upon the border line of the subsistence minimum, and any failure in their usual employments makes it necessary for Government to go at once to their relief. The recognition of this fact has had a bad effect upon their moral though adding to the security of their material condition. During the famine the *istimrārdārs* incurred considerable debts to Government, but their existence was not allowed to interfere with their standard of living, and in general their material condition is unchanged.

CHAPTER VI.

FORESTS.

History. The history of the forest administration in Ajmer-Merwāra deserves notice, as it explains the peculiarities which distinguish some of its rules from those of ordinary British districts. In ancient times the hills about Ajmer were probably covered with scrub jungle, but they were denuded of trees long before the commencement of British rule. The Marāthās are generally given the credit of the denudation. Merwāra, described as "impenetrable jungle" in 1819, had, after 50 years of peaceful Government, reached a condition not much better than that of Ajmer. The demands of the town of Beāwar, of the cantonment of Nasīrābād, and for wood to burn lime for the tank embankments, joined to the absence of all attempts at replacing what was destroyed, left but few trees in any accessible part of the district, and by 1870 wood of all kinds had become exceedingly scarce and dear. Colonel Dixon alone, in the intervening period, paid any attention to the planting of trees, and the gardens of Ajmer and the *nīm* trees of Beāwar owe their existence to him. After his death, no attempt was made either to plant in the plains or to re-forest the hills as they rapidly became bare. But in 1871 Government sanctioned the proposal to appoint an Assistant Conservator and Sub-Assistant Conservator of Forests, more for the purpose of creating than of conserving forests. The operations were not intended as directly profitable speculations on the part of Government; their principal aim and object was an indirect and climatic advantage, to prevent the rainfall rushing down the bare hillside carrying in its course what little soil remained, and to cause it to penetrate into the crevices of the rocks and fill the springs. It was hoped that the roots of the trees and the vegetation would retain and create soil on the steep slopes, and, by lowering the temperature of the hills, cause the clouds passing over the district to part with their moisture within its boundaries.

Apart, however, from the intrinsic difficulty of re-foresting the arid hills, it was not easy to obtain the land. The waste land had been made over to the village communities by the Settlement of 1850, and it had of old been made use of by them for grazing purposes, and as a support to fall back upon in years of distress by the sale of wood. And it was naturally the hills where there was most wood that the Forest Officer was most anxious to take up, and the people most loth to part with. It was therefore determined to resume the management of certain chosen tracts, and to take up the land under an ordinance of the Governor-General in Council. This was done under Regulation No. VII. of 1874, by which the proprietary right vests in Government as long as the land is required for forest purposes. To compensate them for the deprivation, certain rights in these lands are secured to the villagers. They are allowed to cut grass within the forests, and such wood as is reasonably necessary for their household requirements and agricultural implements, and their rights of way previously existing, are maintained for them. It was further stipulated that two-thirds of the net profits from the management of the forests should be distributed among those persons who, previous to the taking up of the land, were interested therein. As a matter of fact the revenue of these reserves has yet been insufficient to cover the expenses, so no profits have been distributed. Only in two years (1890-91 and 1891-92) has the revenue exceeded the working expenses. All other years have shown deficits. But the supply of grass and wood available for the right-holders has increased to such an extent that the people have in reality profited by the protection of these areas, and the benefits of the measure are beginning to be recognized by the more intelligent among them.

The forests, as at present existing, consist of three clsses—State Forests taken up under the above-mentioned Regulation and covering an area of 142 square miles, Protected Forests, covering 101 acres, and Village Estate Commons. The last are insignificant in area (6 acres), and are voluntarily placed under local conservancy by their proprietors. Formerly they amounted to 10 square miles, but in 1900-01 the greater proportion was, at the request of the owners, withdrawn from the management of the Forest Department. Nine hundred and forty-seven acres are appropriated for nurseries and plantation operations. Of the reserved forests by far the larger proportion (90,747 acres) is in Merwāra, Ajmer having 17,974 acres. The forests are either fenced or efficiently demarcated by masonry pillars or by stone slabs at suitable distances. The culture operations are of two kinds, sowing during the rains and transplanting of young trees from the nurseries.

Trees.

The principal trees found in the forests are the dhokra (*anogeissus pendula*), the sālar (*boswellia thurifera*), the kumpta (*acacia rupestris*), the babul (*acacia arabica*), the khair (*acacia catechu*), the orinja (*acacia leucophlœa*), the khejra (*prosopis spicifera*), the gol (*odina wodier*), the nīm (*azadirachta indica*), the dāsan (*rhus mysorensis*), the farangan (*grewia pilosa*), and the gangan (*grewia populifolia*). These indigenous trees grow easily from seed, and, if the rainfall is favorable, require no irrigation. The babul is the only tree which furnishes wood useful for any other purposes than fuel. The chief exotic trees, the acclimatisation of which is attempted, are the pīpal (*ficus religiosa*), bar (*ficus bengalensis*), farās (*tamarix orientalis*), siris (*acacia speciosa*), mango (*mangifera indica*), jāman (*eugenia jambolana*), shisham (*dalbergia sissoo*), and the cork tree (*millingtonia hortensis*). They are difficult to rear, as the young plants require much watering; none of them will grow on the hillsides, and they only thrive in good soil.

Management and Control.

The Forest administration is under the control of the Commissioner and the District Officers. The former exercises the powers of a Conservator of Forests, while the latter have those of Deputy Conservators. The District Officers are assisted by an officer of the Provincial Forest Service of the United Provinces, who is responsible for the technical part of the duties and for general supervision over the works. He exercises the powers of a Divisional Forest Officer. The forests are worked under a system of coppice fellings, with standards. The coupes are either sold in a lump sum to a purchaser, or the produce is removed at a fixed rate per cart, camel, or donkey load. The standards are marked by the Departmental subordinates, and fellings are conducted under the supervision of the foresters or range officers. As, under the Regulation of 1874, the local villagers have considerable rights over the grass and timber in the forests, the produce available for sale to outsiders is correspondingly diminished. Unfortunately the relations of the people with the Department are far from satisfactory. This is due largely to discontent on the part of the villagers with the restrictions imposed on indiscriminate fellings and grazing. The latter especially was a serious complaint of the villagers, but steps have been taken to remove it by opening the forests to the grazing from March to June yearly, a period in which fodder on village lands becomes scarce.

Disposal of Produce.

In general the local demand for fuel is amply met by the State forests. But the large towns of Ajmer, Beāwar and Nasirābād create demands which the limited and right-burdened forest areas in their vicinity are inadequate to supply. There are no separate sub-divisions for fuel and fodder reserves: both are produced under the same treatment and within the same areas. In times of famine the reserved tracts are thrown open to the villagers for grazing, and for the removal of dry wood for fuel at nominal rates. The restrictions even upon lopping and felling for fuel have been removed in time of severe scarcity. Forest fires occur occasionally in the hot weather. The villagers generally furnish ready help in extinguishing them and in burning and clearing the preventive fire lines.

Forest Revenue and Expenditure.

During the ten years ending in 1890, the average annual revenue was Rs. 9,141, and the average annual expenditure Rs. 15,159. The average deficit was therefore Rs. 6,018. During the next decade the average annual revenue was Rs. 14,719, and expenditure Rs. 16,077, showing an average annual deficit of Rs. 1,358. In 1902-03 the figures of revenue and expenditure were Rs. 10,973 and Rs. 15,520, respectively, with a deficit of Rs. 4,547. The continued deficit is largely due to the amount of fodder, fuel and timber given away free to the right-holders every year, and the provision of which is the main object of the forest management in Ajmer-Merwāra. But for this, the results would show a surplus.

Mines and Minerals.

Traces of many minerals are to be found among the hills of Ajmer-Merwāra.

Lead.

The Tārāgarh hill at Ajmer is rich in lead, and iron and copper mines have been worked, but did not pay their expenses. The lead mines of Tārāgarh were farmed by the Marāthās for Rs. 5,000 yearly, the custom being for the miners to receive three-fourths of the value of the metal as the wages of their labour, and to cover their expenses in sinking shafts. Mr. Wilder, the first Superintendent of Ajmer, took the mines under direct management, and they produced annually from 10,000 to 12,000 maunds of lead, which was sold at Rs. 11 per maund. The Ajmer magazine was the chief customer, and on its ceasing to take the metal in 1846, the mines were closed. The lead is admitted to be purer and of a better quality than European piglead, and it is chiefly owing to the want of fuel and of cheap transport that it has been driven from the market. There is no longer the same demand for the metal as in the troubled times at the beginning of the last century.

Mica.

Since 1899 progress has been made in developing the mining industries in other directions, mica and asbestos especially receiving attention. Of recent years the demand for the former metal has increased enormously, owing to its valuable properties as an insulating medium for electricity. New sources of supply are being sought for everywhere, and as mica occurs very abundantly throughout the district, Ajmer-Merwāra is being exploited by prospectors. The deposits consist mainly of muscovite of a similar quality to the Bengal ruby mica. Other qualities are, however, frequently to be met with, including biotite and phlogopite. Of these, the former is quite useless from a commercial point of view, while the latter, although of sound quality, appears to occur only in crystals of too small a size to be of much value. The same remark applies to the deposits of muscovite, the majority of which are too small to be worked with profit. Some specimens of larger crystals have, however, been found, and it is possible that more may follow. The value of two of the known deposits is considerably depreciated on account of all the crystals being densely stained by interlaminar inclusions of a ferruginous substance.

At present thorough prospecting work is being undertaken at some seven or eight different areas in the district, but it is thought probable that none of the deposits extend to a greater depth than 30 or 40 feet. In these circumstances, the work is carried on in the form of open quarries, which can hardly attain to the dignity of "mines."

At the moment of writing, about 400 labourers, men and women, are employed on mining operations within the district. They are mostly of the agricultural class, and come from the villages nearest to the deposit that is being worked at the time. The men earn on an average from 1½ to 2 annas per day, and the women 1 anna.

Asbestos and other Minerals.

Asbestos occurs in some three or four deposits round Sendra, in Merwāra, and is now being mined in small quantities. The quality is, however, poor, and apparently the mineral is wanting in those textile characteristics which are so necessary for most of the uses to which asbestos is put. Most of these mining operations are carried on by two Companies, who have been granted licenses.

Hæmatite exists in considerable quantities in some of the hills, especially near Sāroth in Merwāra, but on account of the absence of coal it has not been considered worth working. Traces of copper are also to be met with, and lead is said to exist in the south of Merwāra as well as at Tārāgarh. Garnets and aquamarines have been found in the Ajmer district.

Stone.

Good building materials are abundant, and stone is largely used for purposes for which wood is employed elsewhere in India. Door frames are often made of stone, and the best roofing is formed of slabstones resting on arches or on stone beams, while thin slabs are sometimes used as slates. The best quarries in the Ajmer district are at Srinagar, where slabs 12 or 14 feet long by 3 or 4 feet in width can be obtained. Near Beāwar, slabs not quite so large, and generally too hard to be dressed with a chisel, are quarried at Atitmand. At Khetra Khera, about 6 miles north-east of Beāwar, limestone slabs are found which can be dressed. Near Todgarh good slabs have not been found, but beams 10 or 12 feet long and uneven in thickness are procurable.

For rubble masonry stone is everywhere to be met with. The best quarries are in the hills running between Ajmer and Nasīrābād, and down the east side of Merwāra. The stone here is found in slabs of almost any size, both sides perfectly parallel: and if it is carefully quarried one smooth face can generally be obtained. For ashlar work limestone and granite are procurable. Marbles of various colours are quarried in the vicinity of Ajmer.

Lime.

Lime is burnt from *kankar* and from limestone, and the latter kind is preferred by the natives. The limestone generally used in the city of Ajmer is a gray stone obtained near the village of Nāralli, about 6 miles from the city. The lime obtained from it is not very pure, but is tenacious, and bears a large admixture of sand. At Mākhopura, Kālesra Konlāi and other villages, a pure white limestone is found, but the stone is hard and difficult to burn. Limestone is also found in abundance near Beāwar. *Kankar* is to be met with in all parts of the district, but varies considerably in quality as a carbonate of lime. That which breaks with a blue fracture, and which when breathed on causes the moisture to adhere, is considered fit for lime burning. *Kankar* lime has higher hydraulic properties than stone lime, and is generally used by the Public Works Department. No material, however, producing good hydraulic lime has as yet been discovered in the district.

Road Metals.

Materials for road-making are everywhere abundant. For heavy traffic, broken limestone, the refuse of the slabstone quarries, or granite are found more suitable than *kankar*, which, though it makes a smooth even road, will not stand heavy traffic. For the district roads any coarse, brittle stone if not too micaceous, or an inferior kind of gravel called *barha* is often substituted for stone or *kankar*. They are everywhere found, are easily dug, and answer the purpose very well where the traffic is light.

CHAPTER VII.

Arts and Manufactures.

Ajmer is not remarkable for arts and manufuctures, while Merwāra is even less so. Indian art has always required the stimulus of wealthy patronage, and such no longer exists in the province. It has been remarked that, as a rule, the accident of patronage has alone determined the home of artistic industries. The Mughal Emperors no longer rule in Ajmer, and the wealthy Seths are but indifferent supporters of art. The best artificers of Rājputāna are to be looked for in Jaipur, Jodhpur, Alwar, Bikāner, and other Native States, where patronage is still available. The industries of Ajmer are similar, but inferior.

The Hand Industries.

There is no silk weaving, and hand industries are limited. The cotton hand-looms in Ajmer and the larger villages turn out cloths known as *reza, khes, dhotī, susi*, and *chārkhāna*, for local use. *Reza* is a stiff white cloth made from native thread, used largely for garments by the peasantry. It is also the favourite medium for the dyers, who print designs upon it with wooden stamps, which are cut in Mārwār. The local industry is, however, perishing in the face of foreign competition, and cannot revive. *Khes* cloth has a diagonal pattern, owing to the threads of the weft being twined alternately with those of the warp. It is used for sheets and *chādars* by the lower classes. *Susi* is a narrow cotton fabric, used only by Muhammadan women for trousers: it has stripes lengthwise down the piece of a different colour from the groundwork. *Chārkhāna* is a sort of superior *susi* with a check pattern. Towels, table-linens and other cloths are made in the Ajmer Jail. Fabrics made there of country *reza* cloth, dyed red with *al* root, and stamped with patterns in black, are very popular in the rural areas. The cotton bed-covers and printed floor-cloths of Beāwar are the best in the district. Carpets and rugs are manufactured in the Ajmer Jail only. Considerable trouble has been taken to secure attractive designs, and the old Indian patterns, as well as those of Kashmir and of Persia, are reproduced here. There is nothing noteworthy or distinctive about the jewellery, most of its forms being well known in the adjacent Native States, such as Jaipur; and those of Ajmer are generally inferior. The Mers wear rough ornaments of silver or of base metal which sometimes preserve old forms, while ornaments bearing the figure of their hero, Tejāji, are common among the Jāts. None of them deserve special mention.

Of artistic metal vessels there is practically no manufacture. The village blacksmith's art is limited to implements of husbandry of the roughest description. Gadulia lohārs of the wandering castes supply rough locks, knives, spoons, etc. The brass and copper vessels made in the towns are plain and without special characteristics. Artistic pottery is unknown. Though some of the houses of the wealthier citizens of Ajmer are adorned with rich carvings in wood and stone, the best workmen have to be obtained from outside the district. The turners of Ajmer are chiefly employed in making rosaries, combs, etc., of sandal wood, which are purchased by the pilgrims who resort to the Dargāh. They also turn bangles of ivory, the only description of ivory work known in the district. Bangles of lacquer work are also made, but are inferior to those of Delhi. Many of the carpenter class have obtained employment in the workshops of the Rājputāna-Mālwā Railway.

Cotton Mills.

The Krishna Cotton Mill at Beāwar is the only factory. The concern was floated as a Joint Stock Company in 1889, with a capital of Rs. 7,00,000, and the mill started working on 1st June 1891. In 1897 there were 250 looms and 12,312 spindles working, and 542 hands were employed. The out-turn was 13,81,080 lbs. of yarn, and 5,18,252 lbs. of cloth, of the total value of Rs. 6,58,323. In 1902 the number of spindles was the same, but the looms were 252, and the number of hands employed had risen to 606. The total value of the out-turn was Rs. 7,31,803, consisting of 13,91,290 lbs. of yarn and 7,78,292 lbs. of cloth. The yarn is spun in combs of from eights to twenties, and cloth of coarse quality is made from the local thread for use as *dhotīs*, shirtings, *chādars*, and *khadis*. A small quantity of fine cloth is made from warp and weft imported from England. Such cloth and yarn as are not used locally are exported to Agra and Cawnpore. The rates of daily wages paid vary from 2½ annas to 20 annas in the case of men, from 2 annas to 5½ annas for women, and from 1½ annas to 2½ annas for children.

Cotton Presses.

There are six hydraulic cotton presses at Beāwar, three at Kekri, and one at Nasīrābād. The annual profits on each of those at Beāwar vary from about Rs. 2,000 to Rs. 8,000. The three presses at Kekri are said to clear about Rs. 10,000 each every year, and the one at Nasīrābād about Rs. 2,000. There is also a ginning factory at Kekri, with an annual profit of Rs. 3,000. Cotton from the States of Mewār, Kishangarh, Tonk, Kōtāh, and Bundi is brought to the presses at Kekri and Nasīrābād. The Beāwar market draws its supplies principally from Mewār, though some of the cotton used in the Krishna Mills is imported from Berār. According to the census figures of 1901, 13,908 persons were supported by the various branches of the cotton industry. There are no other factory industries in the districts besides those mentioned. As their range is so restricted, their influence upon internal migration is insignificant. The permanent employees in the mills and presses are few in number, and the supply is adequate. Their material condition is generally good. In the spring and summer large numbers of women come into the presses for employment as cotton pickers. With the first fall of the rains they return again to their villages. The temporary occupation is of valuable assistance to the labouring classes in the season when agricultural operations are at a standstill.

CHAPTER VIII.

COMMERCE AND TRADE.

General Character.

In ancient times Ajmer was an entrepôt for the trade between Bombay and upper India. As early as A.D. 1614 an agency was established there for the East India Company by Mr. Edwards of the Surat factory, and for many years the city was the principal mart for the exchange of European goods and the products of Rājputāna and northern India. But the dimensions of the trade are not known. It appears to have been at all times hampered by vexatious customs and duties, and many of these were continued until after the British occupation of the districts.

Before 1879 the trade of Ajmer city had fallen off considerably, owing to the competition of the growing towns of Beāwar and Nasīrābād, but it has revived with the establishment of the railway. Whereas the transit trade of the district was formerly entirely carried by camels and *banjāra* bullocks, it is now mostly railborne. There is, however, still a certain amount of conveyance by camels and bullocks into Mārwār on the north, and to the south down the main road to Deoli and the Native States beyond Deoli. Similarly the Merwāra district is fed chiefly from Beāwar, the grain being carried up the tract by road in carts. By the same agency the cotton from Mewār and the south arrives in the market at Beāwar. This is clearly shown by the export and import figures. In 1891 only 1,075 tons of raw cotton were imported by rail to Beāwar, while 8,471 tons were exported. The difference between these figures must have come into the market by road. Ajmer, Beāwar, and, in a lesser degree, Nasīrābād are the three chief centres of trade. Kekri, which in the early days of British rule bade fair to rival Ajmer as a trading mart, has been long in a declining state. It is still, however, a considerable cotton mart, and its exports of that commodity amount to about half those of Beāwar. As the province has but few manufactures, and produces but little in excess of its own requirements, the import and export trade in ordinary times is entirely one of transit. An import trade can only exist in proportion as the province has something to offer in exchange. Times of famine are of course exceptional, for in these years the enormous grain imports are paid for with the money spent by Government on works and other forms of relief.

Exports and Imports.

Grain and pulses, followed at a distance by sugar and *jagri*, salt, metals and piece-goods form the chief imports of Ajmer. In 1881 the total imports were 7,138 tons, of which grain amounted to 1,971 tons, and sugar and *jagri* to 2,931 tons. Most of the grain comes from the Punjab and the United Provinces of Agra and Oudh, the sugar and *jagri* from Bhiwāni in Hissār and from the province of Agra. Pachbhadra and Sāmbhar in Mārwār supply the bulk of the salt. Metals, seeds and piece-goods come from the surrounding Native States, Calcutta, and Bombay. Much of the sugar is re-exported to Mewār. The export trade for the same year amounted to 601 tons, of which grain formed the largest item. In 1891 the imports had gone up to 22,945 tons, chiefly owing to the increase in grain and pulses. Local crop failure was met by large consignments from outside, and 18,355 tons were imported into Ajmer city. Exports were again out of all proportion to imports, being 1,737 tons only. The year 1902, following the great famine of 1899-1900, found grain imports still at a high level, 18,022 tons. Sugar and *jagri* maintained their average with 2,184 tons. The total imports were 22,196 tons, and exports only 1,340 tons. It may be noted that in the famine of 1898-1900, 61,972 tons of grain were imported into Ajmer, and 53,539 into Merwāra. All these figures refer to railborne trade only.

The most valuable export of the district is raw cotton, and of this trade Beāwar is the almost exclusive entrepôt. Besides the local product, much of the cotton from Mewār and other southern Rājputāna States is brought to Beāwar, where it is pressed before export to Bombay. Messrs. Ralli Brothers, Volkart Brothers and many native firms have agencies in Beāwar. The export of raw cotton rose from 3,561 tons in 1881 to 8,471 tons in 1891. In 1900 difficulties connected with the Mewar border threatened the trade with extinction, and only 592 tons were exported, as against 8,424 tons in the preceding year. They were, however, surmounted, and in 1902 the figure rose again to 4,683 tons. The grain imports to Beāwar in 1891 and 1902 show the same features as have already been remarked in the case of Ajmer, and were due to the same causes. The total figures of railborne import to Beāwar in 1881, 1891 and 1902 were 16,015 tons, 31,011 tons and 25,032 tons respectively. The total export figures for the same years were 11,930 tons, 15,350 tons and 8,711 tons respectively.

It is difficult to form even an approximate estimate of the total exports from the whole province. The *istīmrāri* estates, with the exception of Junia, Pisāngan, Sathāna, Keybāniā, Prānhera, Kādhera, Goella, Shokla and Keronj, have never been measured, and there are no satisfactory returns of the crops grown in this portion of the Ajmer district. Their exports consist of grain, cotton and opium. Without reliable returns of the area under grain crops in these estates, which in area exceed one-half of the Ajmer district, it is impossible to calculate how much more grain is produced in an average year than is necessary to supply local consumption. Cotton is largely grown in the *istīmrāri* estates, but most of it finds export *via* Ajmer or Beāwar

Trading Classes. The Mahājans or Baniās are by far the most important trading class in the province. There are a few Pārsi shopkeepers in Ajmer and Nasīrābād.

CHAPTER IX.

COMMUNICATIONS.

Railways.

The main line of the Rājputāna-Mālwā Railway, from Ahmadābād to Delhi, passes through Ajmer and the north of Merwāra from west to east for a length of 59 miles. The Ajmer-Khandwa branch of the same railway runs through the Ajmer district due south of Ajmer for 41½ miles. The portion of the line north of Ajmer and the portion towards Nasīrābād were surveyed in 1869, and that south of Ajmer towards Ahmadābād in 1872. The construction was commenced in 1873 and completed in 1876. The portion connecting Nasīrābād with Chitorgarh was finished in 1881. The latter is constructed for a single metre-gauge track, but sufficient land has been taken up to admit of another track being laid, if necessary, hereafter. The line was constructed by Government, by whom it was worked until 1st January 1885. It was then taken over on lease by the Bombay, Baroda and Central India Railway and worked as part of that Company's system. The head-quarters of the railway have been located at Ajmer, and handsome offices and extensive locomotive and carriage and waggon shops have been constructed there in connection with the line. Ajmer city is 275 miles from Delhi, the terminus of the main line on the north, and 305 miles from Ahmadābād, the southern terminus.

The total mileage of railway in the district being 100½, the number of square miles of country per mile of railway is 26·97. The average cost of construction per mile came to Rs. 81,551.

The local traffic has steadily increased since the line was opened. During the Pushkar and the Ajmer "Urs" annual fairs, there is a heavy pilgrim traffic in the direction of Ajmer. *Via* Beāwar it carries much of the cotton of Mārwār and Mewār to upper India and Bombay.

The opening of the line has conferred great benefits on the district. The population of the towns of Ajmer, Beāwar and Nasīrābād has increased steadily since 1881; the railway workshops at Ajmer give employment to several thousands of hands; and the increased facilities for transport have resulted in the general cheapening of commodities. The recent famines were so widespread throughout India that prices of food grains were bound to rise high, but the railway has made it possible for local scarcity and even total crop failure to exist without an appreciable rise in the price of food. This phenomenon was a noteworthy feature of the famine of 1891-92. The value of the railway in thus preventing sudden and acute distress in any local area can hardly be over-estimated. A railway line is now projected from Bārān to Mārwār junction, and will pass through the Merwāra district at Pipli. The earthwork of this section was constructed in 1900. In the same year the earthwork of a projected line from Nasīrābād to

Deoli was undertaken, and completed to a point fifty-five miles south, east of Ajmer.

Roads. Most of the roads in the district have been constructed or metalled during years of famine. Prior to 1869 the only metalled roads were 14 miles between Ajmer and Nasirābād, and 7 miles between Ajmer and Gangwāna on the Agra road. But the famine of that year gave a great stimulus to their construction, and before 1875 the Agra-Ahmadābād road had been metalled throughout from the borders of Mārwār 44½ miles to the west of Ajmer, to the boundaries of Jaipur State, 30 miles to the east. From Nasīrābād a metalled road was made to the cantonment of Deoli, 57 miles, another in the direction of Nimach and Mhow, extending to Barl on the Khāri river, 28 miles, and a third from Nasīrābād to Māngaliāwās, 14 miles. The road to Nimach, beyond Barl, though once metalled is now falling into disrepair. No addition to the metalled roads has since been made in Ajmer. These roads are maintained from Imperial funds.

Merwāra was a country without roads before 1869, but during the famine a tolerable road to Todgarh, and fair roads over the Pakheriāwās and Sheopura passes into Masūda and Mewār were constructed. All of them are now metalled and in good order.

In 1891 the total mileage of roads maintained from Imperial funds was 187, costing Rs. 27,495 for maintenance. Maintained from District Funds were 304½ miles of road, costing Rs. 9,495 for upkeep. Of this total only the Ajmer-Pushkar road, 8 miles, was fully metalled. Municipal roads extended to 26⅔ miles and cost Rs. 3,035.

In 1901 the mileage of Imperial fund roads was unchanged, but that of Local fund roads had increased to 308¼ miles, of which 33 miles were fully metalled. Their cost of maintenance was Rs. 47,914 and Rs. 3,264 respectively. The large increase in the former and decrease in the latter is explained by the fact that 1901 was a famine year, and famine labour paid from Imperial funds was employed in repairing the Local fund roads. In 1902, with the same mileage, Rs. 18,112 was spent on maintaining Imperial roads, Rs. 13,191 upon Local fund roads and Rs. 2,712 on Municipal roads. Owing to the necessity for providing work for famine labourers, the roads, especially in Merwāra, have tended to increase beyond the power of the District funds to maintain them, and some of them are falling into disrepair.

In addition to the roads, the district is served by a network of country-cart tracks, the quality of which varies according to the nature of the ground over which they pass. The country-carts are similar to those used in other parts of Rājputāna. They are smaller than those of the United Provinces of Agra and Oudh. Springed and tyred conveyances are little met with outside the towns.

Post Offices. Ajmer is the head-quarters station of the Rājputāna Postal Circle, which is controlled by a Deputy Post Master-General, and is divided into 4 divisional charges.

In the Ajmer and Merwāra districts there are at present 39 Imperial and 11 District Dâk post offices. The combined offices at

Beāwar, Deoli, Kekri and Pipli also perform telegraph work ; all other head and sub-offices and certain selected branch offices are empowered to receive telegrams for transmission to the nearest telegraph office. The District Post is maintained by funds derived partly from a local cess and partly from a grant from Imperial revenues. It has 11 branch post offices, and there are 193 miles of District Post mail line. The offices are all worked by extraneous agents, who receive small stipends as remuneration for this service. As each District Post office becomes self-supporting it is taken over by the Imperial Post, and with the funds thus set free another District office is opened.

Telegraphs.

Besides the Rājputāna-Mālwā Railway telegraph offices at all stations on the line, there are telegraph offices at five places in the districts. Of these, Beāwar has a first class office, Ajmer, Nasirābād and Deoli second class offices, and Kekri a third class office. A telegraph office was also opened at Pipli for famine relief purposes on the 10th May 1900, and it is kept open pending the settlement of the question of the railway from Mārwār junction to Lāmbia, which will pass through Merwāra at this point. Proposals have been made to open an office at Todgarh, but the idea was abandoned, as it did not appear likely to be a financial success. Taking the four years before 1901 at the five district telegraph offices we find that 29,746 telegrams were sent and 36,294 were received in 1897-98. In 1898-99 the numbers rose to 33,031 and 39,405 respectively. In 1899-00 there was a large increase, due probably to the necessities both of traders and of officials in a famine year. The number of telegrams sent was 45,088, and 46,380 were received. In the following year 1900-1901, under more normal conditions the figures were 40,230 and 46,143. The popularity of this means of communication is evidently advancing. Much use of the telegraphic system is made by the native merchants of Ajmer and Beāwar, where a great deal of opium and cotton speculation goes on, necessitating the use of urgent wires.

CHAPTER X.

FAMINES.

What has already been written regarding the position, physical characteristics and rainfall of Ajmer-Merwāra is sufficient to explain why the province has always been peculiarly exposed to recurring periods of scarcity, and occasionally to the ravages of famine in its worst form. As the debateable land between the two monsoons, and beyond the full influence of either, it is apt to fall a victim to the worst eccentricities of even an Indian rainfall. Deficiency in quantity and irregularity of distribution are both to be feared, as either may produce crop failure. Although Colonel Dixon has given it as his opinion that 12 inches of rain properly distributed in any village is sufficient to secure the payment of the assigned rent, the history of the province shows how hard it has been for nature to maintain that seemingly moderate standard. Scarcity is seldom absent from some part of the country. Formerly in such years the people in the afflicted tracts, taught patience by constant adversity, used to emigrate with their families and cattle to more favoured regions, and return to their homes in time for the sowings of the succeeding year. Modern measures of relief, promptly undertaken, have somewhat checked the tendency in Ajmer-Merwāra, but in Native States it still continues, and the province, lying as an island among them, is on the high road of the yearly migration.

The fickle nature of the rainfall throughout the tract makes it difficult to distinguish any special part as peculiarly liable to scarcity; even history points to no definite conclusion. The monsoon is generally supposed to break at the end of June or the beginning of July, but a late commencement is less to be dreaded than a premature withdrawal. A heavy rainfall in September may, by filling the tanks and assuring the *rabi* harvest, save a situation which appears hopeless, but the bulk of the population depends on the autumn harvest for their food supply, and both this and the grass for fodder are imperilled by non-arrival of the early rains. When both the south-western and north-eastern monsoons fail, the province is destined to the miseries of a famine of the three great necessaries of lifeg—rain, grass and water—called in the country a *trikāl* or treble famine.

Of recent years the opening of the railways and improved facilities for import of grain have counteracted the tendency to a rapid rise in prices in the case of local famines. Only a widespread scarcity over India, as in 1899, can lead to the sudden heightening in the price of grain, which does so much to intensify acute distress and precipitate the crisis. Transport of fodder is, however, more difficult, and migration of the cattle-owning classes is one of the earliest warnings of the commencement of scarcity. It is often accompanied by an increase of crime against person and property. But much experience may be said to have given the people a knowledge of the requirements of the Famine Code, and loudly-expressed demands for the opening of local works can now be added to the list of famine warnings.

Earlier Famines.

The first famine in Rājputāna of which we have written record occurred in A.D. 1661. A memorial of it is preserved in the beautiful marble *band* erected at Kānkraoli in Mewār at the cost of a million sterling by Maharāna Rāj Singh of Udaipur, to save his people during the dire calamity. Other famines occurred in 1746 and in 1789, the latter of which is supposed to have exceeded in intensity even the terrible one of 1812, which is said to have lasted five years and has gained the name of *panch-kāl* Three-fourths of the cattle died, and, as stated also in the record of the famine of 1661, man ate man. Traces of the devastation caused by this famine were visible in Ajmer at the beginning of British rule.

Between 1812 and 1869 there was no general famine in Rājputāna, but in 1819, in 1824, in 1833 and 1848 there was severe scarcity in Ajmer.

Famine of 1868-69.

For some years previous to 1868 the seasons had been irregular and the crop deficient in Ajmer-Merwāra. Stocks of grain had been depleted, and there was no surplus with which to face the approaching crisis. The rainfall of 1868 was unfavourable from the commencement; the early rains were insufficient for sowing; from the 1st June 1868 to the 1st June 1869 the average fall from all the stations of Ajmer-Merwāra was only 7·4 inches, or about one-third of an average fall. The state of Jaipur and Jodhpur was as bad or worse. The south-west monsoon failed entirely west of the Aravallis. East of the range Indore alone got rain, and the starving population of Central India and Bundelkhund flocked into Mālwā. In Gujarāt a terrible flood in August swept away cattle and crops and destroyed the stores of grain below the ground. The north-eastern monsoon had equally failed, and great scarcity overshadowed the North-Western Provinces (now the United Provinces of Agra and Oudh.) Ajmer-Merwāra was thus isolated in the midst of a famine tract. It had no supplies of its own, and, owing to want of fodder, the ordinary transport by bullock-cart utterly broke down. Camel transport was not available in the rains, and even when available was insufficient to cope with the demands of the situation.

Emigration began towards the end of August. Wheat was then selling in Ajmer at 10 seers; barley, *jowār* and grass were 12 seers per rupee. Such was the scarcity of fodder that cows were offered for sale at Re. 1 each, and good plough cattle at Rs. 10 a pair. Relief works were commenced, but by November the condition of the country was sufficiently deplorable. The *kharif* had failed entirely; half the cattle had been driven into Mālwā; water in the wells was scanty and brackish, and the tanks were empty. As the season advanced, the situation grew worse. The few irrigated crops were destroyed by mildew and hail storms; the people were apathetic, and the money-lenders would make no advances. The distress was intensified by enormous immigration from surrounding Native States. People were reduced to the necessity of mixing bark and roots with the grain which they ground up to make bread.

Poor-houses were established in April 1869. The rains did not set in until July, and were then insufficient; hope of the *kharif* failed, even roots and bark became scarce, and the mortality was frightful. Copious rain in September was discounted by a plague of locusts, which destroyed from 50 to 85 per cent. of the standing crops. Prices touched their highest point in September, when barley was sold for 3 seers per rupee in Ajmer city, but at times even men with money in their hands were unable to get food. This was the crisis. Thereafter, importation of grain commenced from Bhīwāni and Rewāri, and the tension gradually slackened until the rains of the following year brought relief. The losses were calculated at 25 per cent. of the population of 4,26,000, at 33 per cent. of the cattle, and 50 per cent. of the plough and milch cattle. Government spent altogether Rs. 15,20,074, out of which Rs. 2,30,000 were given in gratuitous relief.

As a direct result of these lamentable experiences, the system of famine relief had been considerably improved before the province had again to face severe scarcity in 1890-92. The Land Improvement Loans Act of 1883 and the Agriculturist Loans Act of 1884 had provided the cultivators with new sources of capital, and, unlike the operations of the native money-lender, these sources were allowed to flow more freely, according to the severity of local scarcity. The railways, too, had been opened, and importation of grain could be prompt and effective. In the local famine of 1891, grain prices rose very little. But the railway could do little to import fodder for cattle; this was the greatest difficulty of all, and large mortality among such as were not removed abroad for pasturage was inevitable.

Famine of 1890-92. Twenty years of comparative prosperity had followed the disastrous season of 1869. But in 1890, although the monsoon opened auspiciously throughout the district, it stopped abruptly in the early part of August, the crops withered and indications of scarcity began to show themselves. It commenced as a fodder famine, and the emigration which started in October was confined to the owners of cattle. As regards the condition of the people themselves the period from October 1890 to August 1891 is more properly described as one of scarcity. The Famine Code was not applied. Relief by means of works was found sufficient. In Merwāra the first was opened in October 1890, but in Ajmer *takāvi* loans to the *istimrārdārs* and cultivators adequately met the situation up to January 1891. Until after the month of August the average number of labourers on the works never amounted to more than 6,700. By the failure of the monsoon of 1891, which gave an average rainfall of only 8·50 inches to

Ajmer and of 10·24 inches to Merwāra, the scarcity deepened into famine. The drought continued throughout September and October; the winter rains were also unfavourable, and the autumn crops of 1891 and the spring crops of 1892 both failed. More extended relief and the application of the Ajmer Famine Code became necessary. The numbers on relief works, which were 3,623 at the end of September, rose to 14,914 by the end of October, and reached their maximum (29,471) in the following May. In this month some 10,000 persons were in receipt of gratuitous relief. The works were closed in October 1892, when copious rains had fallen. The relief works in both districts were almost entirely managed by the Public Works Department. As a rule they were small and numerous, owing to the deficiency of large works in the sanctioned programme. Relief other than that on the works was distributed by the civil officers. There were only three poor-houses, and these proved unpopular. A system of home labour for the assistance of *parda nashin* women was tried in Ajmer city.

The total cost to Government of the relief operations amounted to over 21 lakhs of rupees.

This famine had certain characteristics which distinguish it both from the preceding and subsequent famines. The comparatively stationary condition of food-grain prices, and the reasons for the phenomenon have already been noted. A curious outbreak in the shape of grain riots in many villages of Ajmer took place in September 1891. The village traders, who had stopped giving credit in August, were the victims, and the Mers are believed to have been the principal instigators of the disturbances. For a short time things looked serious, and the aid of cavalry from Deoli and Erinpura was called in to assist the police patrols. But a show of force was sufficient, and the lawlessness soon subsided. Again very few labourers from *istimrāri* estates came upon the relief works, and, compared with previous famines, the emigration into Ajmer-Merwāra from adjoining Native States equally affected by scarcity was very restricted. This was due partly to improved systems of relief available in those States, and still more to extensive emigration to Mālwā.

The water level in the wells also fell to an unprecedented extent. Many dried up, and the want of drinking water was a constant anxiety, which even threatened at one time to render it impossible for the people to live in Ajmer city. An epidemic of fever followed this famine and caused great mortality.

The country was given but little breathing space before the next disaster came upon it. The seasons of 1892-93 and of 1894-95 were very fair, but that of 1895-96 was indifferent. The recuperative capacity of the districts was shown by the fact that at the end of the latter year the suspensions of Land Revenue given during the famine (Rs. 1,03,714) had been practically cleared off, and of the *takāvi* loans (Rs. 6,08,854) only Rs. 1,43,951 remained outstanding.

Famine of 1898-1900.

But thereafter the situation gradually deteriorated until it culminated in the great famine of 1899-1900. A partial failure of the *kharif* in 1896-97 was followed by indifferent *rabi* in 1897-98. In 1898-99 there was a deficiency of rainfall, especially in Merwāra, and in this tract relief measures began to be undertaken in November 1898. Until September 1899 these were comparatively restricted; village relief was not found necessary until May of that year, and the total numbers in receipt of relief did not rise above 9,000 until the end of July. But by that time fears regarding the rains, only too well justified by results, intensified the general anxiety. Prices, which had shown an upward tendency since May, began to rise rapidly, and by the end of August the relief figures in Merwāra had been more than trebled.

September saw the rains ended in almost complete failure. Ajmer received 8 inches and Merwāra only 5. The tanks were empty, wells were drying up, and a total loss of both crops was seen to be inevitable. Nor was the disaster merely local. All western and central Rājputāna was similarly affected. Central India was declaring famine, and Gujarāt, where crop failure was hitherto almost unknown, was entering upon the most calamitous period in its history. Bombay was preparing for famine in all its districts south of Sind. The prices of food grains mounted steadily. They reached their highest point in October, when barley was at about 9 seers to the rupee. This, though high, is in striking contrast to the level reached in the 1869 famine, and shows the great prophylactic value of the extended railway systems.

Test works were opened in Ajmer in September 1899, and the numbers rose rapidly in October. Thereafter, until the cold weather of 1900, both districts were under the operation of the Famine Code. The numbers reached their highest point in June 1900, when 68,728 persons, or 16 per cent. of the population, were receiving relief in Ajmer. In Merwāra the pressure was even more severe, and at one time 72 per cent. of the whole, or the entire rural population, was in receipt of Government relief, and the percentage was over 70 for a considerable period. The figures began to fall after the setting-in of the rains in July 1900, and thereafter declined until relief measures were stopped in November. The relief works undertaken consisted chiefly of the construction of new and the repair of old tanks, the making of new roads and collection of metal for existing ones. They were under the management of the Public Works Department. The civil officials arranged for the poor-houses, civil kitchens and distribution of gratuitous relief in the villages. Both departments were considerably strengthened for the purpose, as it is now recognized that ordinary district staffs cannot cope unaided with the special circumstances of severe famine. As compared with the famine of 1892, crime statistics were light, and the public peace was well maintained throughout.

A notable feature of the famine was the enormous immigration of famine-stricken wanderers from Native States. In the beginning of the scarcity, thousands had passed through the districts on the way to their usual migration grounds of Mālwā and Gujarāt. But they found famine there also, their cattle died, and as they struggled homewards they helped to swell the death rate and tax the resources of Merwāra and Ajmer. It is estimated that half the inmates of the poor-houses in the districts were foreigners.

The mortality during the famine itself was dwarfed by that of a terrible fever epidemic which followed, and in the autumn of 1900 caused the deaths of 44,236 persons. During the whole year a death-rate of 150 per 1,000 was reached in Merwāra and one of 112 in Ajmer. Infant mortality was especially high. Great numbers of cattle died in both districts, and it is calculated that Merwāra lost a half, including many of the more valuable animals. The Government forests were thrown open to grazing, but the grass was scanty and of little assistance. State importation of hay was also attempted, but private enterprise on the same lines proved more successful. When the rains came in 1900 liberal grants of *takāvi* and of money from the Indian Famine Charitable Relief Fund were made, and did much towards replenishing the stock of cattle from outside the province, and giving the people a fresh start. The cost of the famine was Rs. 47,64,866.

Famine of 1901-02.

The great famine ended in the cold season of 1900. The rains had been plentiful, and both autumn and spring crops were fair. But in 1901, although the rains began well in July and August and secured the grass crop, they failed later, giving Merwāra an average of only 10·81 inches and Ajmer 12·91 inches. The result was a recurrence of scarcity in the latter and of famine in the former district.

Test works were opened in Merwāra in January 1902 and were converted into regular relief works in the succeeding months. They were kept open until October of the same year, when relief of all kind was discontinued. They consisted of three tank works, at Kūkarkhera, Asan and Makrera, while 5 sections of roads were also improved and repaired. The number of persons upon relief touched its highest point (30,446), in the month of August.

In addition to the works under the Public Works Department, civil agency works were opened between May and July. Gratuitous relief was confined to doles distributed in cash in the villages: it was found unnecessary to open kitchens or poor-houses. Hospitals were maintained in connection with all the relief works.

No difficulty was felt regarding fodder for the cattle, and there was very little emigration. As the famine was entirely local, prices ruled low throughout. The public peace was well maintained, and there was no appreciable increase of crime.

The scarcity in Ajmer was of so mild a nature that very limited relief measures were sufficient. Only two test works were opened, and the workers never numbered more than 860. Gratuitous relief on a limited scale was given in certain villages.

The cost of relief during the famine, including the grants of *takāvi* to cultivators up to the end of September 1902, was Rs. 2,49,311.

The effects of the calamities of the past decade upon the numbers of the people have already been detailed in the chapter on Population. Between 1891 and 1901 the population of the province has declined 12 per cent. In the last two famines active measures of relief have largely reduced the deaths from actual privation, but epidemics of disease and especially the autumn fevers proved excessively fatal. The effects upon the social condition of the survivors have been equally apparent, and it will be long before the previous standard of comfort is attained by the cultivating classes. A tendency towards loss of self-respect and reliance has also been remarked, and each succeeding famine finds the poorer classes more ready to clamour for and accept relief from Government. During the famine a loosening of family ties was sometimes evident; children were found showing greater signs of privation than their parents, while child desertion was a deplorably common feature among the wanderers from Native States.

Protective Measures.

Protective measures, properly so called, are extremely hard to find in Ajmer-Merwāra. Irrigation can only be perfectly protective where the water supply is beyond being effected by the vicissitudes of rainfall. But the province has no large perennial rivers, and natural springs are rare. Increase of tanks and wells may do something, but most of them are dependent upon the monsoon for their water, and where that fails, remain dry and useless. What can be done, however, in this direction is being effected by loans under the Land Improvement Act of 1883. An attempt is being made to store grass in the forests as a provision against famine, and each villager contributes a head-load yearly. Such measures, however, can be only palliative in the face of severe scarcity. Fortunately the province is now well served by railways, and will shortly be even better. Importation of grain to meet local scarcity is easy, and unless famine is wide-spread throughout India, prices need hardly be affected. When the crops have failed, the further measures for protection of the people are prescribed in the Ajmer-Merwāra Famine Code, now revised and improved according to the teachings of past experience. If the local officials are watchful and energetic they can hardly fail to be successful.

Ordinary private charity in times of famine cannot be much counted upon to supplement Government aid. This is due not so much to deficiency in quantity as to complete want of organization in distribution.

Langar-khāna of Dargāh Khwāja Sāhib.

An exception is, perhaps, the institution attached to the Dargāh Khwāja Sāhib at Ajmer, known as the *Langar-khāna*, the only permanent poor-house in the district. Two maunds and six seers of grain with six seers of salt are cooked and distributed to all comers before day-break in the morning, and the same quantity before 5 o'clock in the evening. The average daily attendance is about 900: no enquiry is made as to recipients. The expenses of the morning distribution are chargeable to the income from the Dargāh *jāgīr* villages, while those of the evening meal are met from a jāgīr given by the Nizām of Hyderābād. Besides the 1,570 maunds of grain which are thus yearly consumed, 644 maunds are annually distributed to infirm women, widows and other deserving persons at their own houses. During the last famine an extra amount of grain was added at each distribution, both morning and evening. Rs. 1,644 per year are spent in fees to *hakims* and doctors for attendance upon the poor sick. The normal cost of the charity is about Rs. 5,000 per annum. It is controlled by two *dārogās*, under a manager appointed by the Dargāh committee. They receive their pay from the funds of the Dargāh. The cost of supervision is a somewhat high percentage of the total expenses.

The Indian Charitable Relief Fund, supplemented by local subscriptions and distributed by Goverment officers, did much to relieve distress during the recent famines.

CHAPTER XI.

GOVERNMENT.

General Administration.

The two tracts of Ajmer and Merwāra were originally distinct districts. After the British occupation they were administered by two Superintendents until 1842, when they were united under one officer bearing the title. Ajmer in 1832, and Merwāra in 1846, had been placed under the administration of the Government of the North-Western Provinces (now the United Provinces of Agra and Oudh), and in 1853 Colonel Dixon, who then had charge of them was appointed a Commissioner, and corresponded direct with that Government. From 1858 the united districts remained a Deputy Commissionership under the Agent to the Governor-General in Rājputāna and Chief Commissioner, Ajmer-Mewāra, who in his latter capacity was subordinate to the Government of the North-Western Provinces. In 1871 the province was taken under the direct administration of the Foreign Department of the Government of India and the arrangements then made still continue.

The Hon'ble the Agent to the Governor-General for Rājputāna is *ex-officio* Chief Commissioner, and performs the functions of chief revenue authority and the Local Administration, being also the highest court of appeal, both civil and criminal. In subordination to the Chief Commissioner, a Commissioner, whose head-quarters are at Ajmer, has direct charge of the districts. He has the powers of a Civil and Sessions Judge, and has the direct management of the Police, Forest, Jail and Education Departments. Beneath him are two Assistant Commissioners and District Magistrates, with head-quarters at Ajmer and Beāwar, and in charge of Ajmer and Merwāra respectively. Besides the Chief Commissioner, the administration is carried on by 36 officers, invested with various magisterial powers, while 23 are invested with various civil and revenue powers.

Sub-divisions.

Ajmer and Merwāra are further sub-divided into *tahsīls*, each in charge of a *tahsīldār*, who is assisted by a *nāib tahsīldār*. Ajmer proper has now only one *tahsīl* at head-quarters. Its area is 560·6 square miles; it contains 195 villages, with a population of 1,27,320. Formerly it had three *tahsīls* (Ajmer, Rāmsar and Rājgarh), which were established in order to provide constant supervision of the tanks. The Rājgarh *tahsīl* was abolished in 1858, and the Rāmsar *tahsīl* on the re-organization of the district in 1871. The owners of *istimrār* estates, which in area are more than double the *khālsa*, pay their revenue direct into the Ajmer Treasury without the intervention of a Sub-Collector. Under Ajmer is the sub-division of Kekri which is administered by an Extra Assistant Commissioner.

The urban area is 3·07 square miles and the population 7,053. It consists of one *khālsa* town, Kekri. The remaining *parganās*, Bhinai, Masūda, Sāwar, Pisāngan, Kharwa and Baghera, are held by *istimrārdārs.* The military cantonment of Nasīrābād with its surrounding hamlets also forms a civil sub-division measuring 8·58 miles, and with a population of 22,494. The *parganās* of Ajmer proper, or, as they are now called, *chaklās*, are five in number, Ajmer, Rāmsar, Gangwāna, Pushkar and Rājgarh. But for executive work the *tahsīl* is divided into five circles, Jethāna, Derānthu, Gangwāna, Srinagar and Rāmsar, each under a circle officer, called *girdāwar.*

Merwāra is divided into two *tahsīls*, that of Beāwar and that of Todgarh. A third *tahsīl*, Sāroth, was after Colonel Dixon's death amalgamated with Beāwar. The Beāwar *tahsīl* formerly contained four *parganās, viz.*, Beāwar, Jhāk Chāng and Sāroth. Of these Beāwar was sub-divided again into Beāwar, Jawāja, Lotāna and Barkochrān. These names have now only a historical interest, and the term *parganā* is never used. Instead there are the three *chaklās* of Beāwar, Chāng and Shāmgarh, or for executive purposes the four circles of Beāwar, Shāmgarh, Kālinjar and Kotra. Each of these circles is under a *girdāwar.* The *tahsīl* has an area of 317·2 square miles comprising 228 villages, with a population of 49,132. The Todgarh *tahsīl* used to contain four *parganās*, of which Bhāilān was British territory, Kotkirāna belonged to Mārwār and Dewair and Todgarh to Mewār. It is now divided into the three circles of Todgarh, Bhāilān and Dewair, each with its own *girdāwar.* All revenue papers, registers and returns are prepared according to these circles. The Todgarh *tahsīl* contains 87 villages, has an area of 269·9 square miles and a population of 38,399.

Both in Ajmer and Merwāra all the purely revenue work is in the charge of an officer called the Revenue Extra Assistant Commissioner, who has his head-quarters at Ajmer. All the registers and files relating to revenue matters are kept by him, but in each district he acts under the control of the Assistant Commissioner. **Revenue Officers.**

Beneath the *tahsīldārs*, who have general revenue executive powers within the limits of their *tahsīls*, come the *girdāwars*, whose duty is to supervise, verify and correct the working of the various village officers within their circles. Of these the *patwāris* are the village accountants. As a rule each has two or more villages in his charge, and is sometimes helped by an assistant *patwāri.* Except that they do not collect the revenue, their duties do not differ from those of the *patwāri* in ordinary British districts. They maintain the village accounts and registers, and watch the interests of Government within their limits.

Patels and *lambardārs*, with functions almost identical, are the representatives of the village communities. Their chief duty is that of collecting and paying the Government revenue and cesses. There may be one or two or more to every village, according to its size and the amount of revenue due from it. Their numbers were fixed at the time of the last Settlement according to this standard, and they are paid five per cent. on the revenue collected by them. *Patels* pay ¼ less than the ordinary rate on their holdings, and are further remunerated by Rs. 3-2-0 per cent. allowance on the crop-rate tank water revenue collected by them. They defray the village expenses in the first instance, supervise the accounts of the village common lands, and represent the community in all their dealings with Government.

The village autonomy of former times has almost entirely passed away. Perhaps the only existing survival is the management of the *shāmlāt*, or village common lands. This is carried on by the *lambardārs*, who render accounts to the villagers of all receipts, payments and sources of income. In a few places, such as Rāmsar, Kekri and Ajmer *shāmlāt* committees are appointed for a similar purpose. In other matters the intervention of the revenue officials or of the civil courts has superseded the village council.

CHAPTER XII.

LEGISLATION AND JUSTICE.

Legislation.

Ajmer-Merwāra has no local Legislative Council. Local rules and orders are framed by the Chief Commissioner, either under General Acts of the Governor-General in Council or under Local Regulations made under the statute 33 Victoria Cap 3. Among the more important of the former, since 1880, may be mentioned the Vaccination Act, the Land Improvement Loans Act of 1883, the Agriculturalists' Loans Act of 1884, the Excise Act of 1896, and the Epidemic Disease Act of 1897; and among the latter the Ajmer Municipalities Regulation of 1886 and the Ajmer Rural Boards Regulation of the same year.

Civil and Criminal Justice.

The system of administration of civil and criminal justice is the same as in force in other non-regulation British Provinces. On the side of civil justice the lowest courts are those of the Munsiffs, with civil powers up to Rs. 100. They are exercised by the *tahsīldārs* of Ajmer, Beāwar and Todgarh, and by the *nāib tahsīldārs* of the same places. The *istimrārdārs* of Bhinai, Pisāngan, Sāwar, Kharwa, Bāndanwāra and Deoliā have also these powers. Appeals from the Munsiffs' Courts lie to the Sub-Judge, 1st class, within whose jurisdiction they are, and from them to the court of the Commissioner as District Judge. The Chief Commissioner is the High Court for appeals from decisions of the Commissioner. Civil powers up to Rs. 500 are exercised by the Cantonment Magistrate, Deoli, and the Revenue Extra Assistant Commissioner, Ajmer-Merwāra. Their appeals lie to the Sub-Judge, 1st class, entrusted with appellate powers.

The following officers have powers as Subordinate Judges of the 1st class in all suits up to Rs. 10,000: the Assistant Commissioners of Ajmer and Merwāra; the Cantonment Magistrate, Nasīrābād; the Judicial Assistant Commissioner, Ajmer; the two Extra Assistant Commissioners, Ajmer; the Extra Assistant Commissioner, Kekri; and the Deputy Magistrate, Beāwar. Of these only the Assistant Commissioners of Ajmer and Merwāra and the Judicial Assistant Commissioner, Ajmer, have appellate powers. Appeals lie from their courts to the Commissioner as District Judge, and thence to the Chief Commissioner as High Court. Small Cause Court powers up to Rs. 500 are also exercised by the Assistant Commissioner, Merwāra; the Cantonment Magistrate, Nasirābād; the Extra Assistant Commissioner, 2nd grade, Ajmer; and the Deputy Magistrate, Beāwar; and up to Rs. 20 by the Registrar Small Cause Court, Ajmer. The applications for revision in Small Cause Court cases lie only to the Chief Commissioner.

Civil Justice.

During the ten years ending in 1890, the number of suits for money or moveable property instituted annually in the subordinate civil and revenue courts averaged 2,675·2. In the next decade the average rose to 2,936·2, while in 1902, 3,190 were instituted. The steady rise may be ascribed to the increase in private indebtedness due to the famine. On the other hand the average number of suits for title fell from 376·4 to 264·4 in the last decade. In times of famine such suits in which both parties are usually of the cultivating classes, must diminish from want of means to pay the fees. A reviving prosperity is shown by an increase in these suits to 317 in 1902. Rent suits were similarly affected, and the average fell from 557·9 in 1880-90 to 461·7 in 1890-1900. In 1902, 451 were instituted. Litigation in Small Cause Courts also shows a steady fall. The average number instituted annually was 5,672 between 1880-90, 4,888 between 1890-1900 and 4,790 in 1902.

Criminal Justice.

The Chief Commissioner acts as a High Court for the purpose of appeals from the Commissioner, who exercises the powers of a Sessions Judge for Ajmer-Merwāra. Below him the Assistant Commissioners of Ajmer and Merwāra are District Magistrates within their respective charges. The Cantonment Magistrate, Nasīrābād; the Judicial Assistant Commissioner, Ajmer; the two Extra Assistant Commissioners, Ajmer; the Extra Assistant Commissioner, Kekri; the Deputy Magistrate, Beāwar; and the Assistant Commissioner of Didwāna are Magistrates 1st class. Their appeals lie direct to the Sessions. The Cantonment Magistrate, Deoli; the *tahsīldārs* of Ajmer, Beāwar and Todgarh; and the Honorary Magistrates, Ajmer and Beāwar, have 2nd class powers, from which appeals lie to the District Magistrates.

The *nāib tahsīldārs* have 3rd class powers, as have also the Honorary Magistrates of Bhināi, Pisāngan, Sāwar, Kharwa, Bāndanwāra and Deoliā. With the exception of Bhinai, of which the *istimrārdār* is a minor, the local *istimrārdārs* are Honorary Magistrates. During the ten years ending 1890 the annual averages of persons tried for offences against the Indian Penal Code and for offences against local and special laws were 6,218·7 and 2,782·8 respectively. In the next decade the figures were 4,227·1 and 4,074·9. In 1902 they were 3,356 and 3,997 respectively. It is a notable fact that, though the decade ending in 1900 included several years of famine and scarcity, the average annual number of trials for offences against persons and property had fallen as compared with the figures for the preceding 10 years of comparative prosperity. They were 3,866·7 as against 5,519·7 for the previous decade. In 1902, 3,086 such cases were tried. Offences against special and local laws, however, rose from an average of 2,782·8 between 1880-90 to 4,074·9 for the next ten years. Taking all offences, the average annual number of persons tried and percentage of convictions were 9,001·5 and 42·6 for 1880-90, 8,302·0 and 65·0 for 1890-1900 and 7,353 and 68·1 for 1902. The steady decrease in cases and increase in percentage of convictions point to the growing efficiency of the police force.

There are seven Registration offices in Ajmer-Merwāra, the number remaining unchanged since 1881. The Commissioner is the Inspector-General of Registration, while the Assistant Commissioner of Ajmer is the Registrar of Assurances in Ajmer-Merwāra. The average number of documents registered annually between 1881-90 was 1,360·5 and in the next decade 1,681·6. In 1902, 1,711 documents were registered. Registration.

CHAPTER XIII.

FINANCE.

Finance in former times.

Little can be said regarding the finance of the native rulers of Ajmer-Merwāra before the British occupation. In Merwāra, with its wild tribes and jungles, such record is of course blank. Even of Ajmer we have little information on the point before the time of the Marāthā invasions, and how much of the immense revenues of the "Great Mughal" came from that province, it is difficult to say. In the treaty of cession with Sindhia the revenue of Ajmer was valued at 5,05,484 Srishāhi, or 4,50,986 Farukhābād rupees. But this was admittedly a considerable exaggeration. Neither Tāntia nor Bāpu Sindhia had ever collected more than Rs. 3,76,740 from the district, and of this sum Rs. 31,000 was the amount at which the customs had been farmed, the remainder being land revenue. Of this land revenue the assessment of the *istimrāri* area was Rs. 2,16,762, that of the *khālsa* Rs. 1,28,978. The system of Marāthā financial administration was practically to exact all that could be paid, but about nine years before the cession a kind of settlement had been concluded in the *istimrār* and *khālsa* areas, in accordance with which it had been arranged that instead of recent arbitrary enhancements of the *istimrār* revenue, all future augmentations should take the form of taxes or levies, and the land revenue of the *khālsa* was shown as a fixed sum, Rs. 87,639, while the remainder was to be collected in the shape of a number of extra cesses. The object of this arrangement was two-fold. The *istimrārdārs* were anxious that the arbitrary exactions should not be consolidated with the original revenue, lest on a change of rulers it might be difficult to obtain their remission, and the Governor of Ajmer only sent to Gwalior the land revenue proper, and appropriated to himself the extra collections. The *khālsa* villages were farmed for the amount of the *aen*, and the extra cesses were levied under 44 heads. Of these, a tax called *nandrak*, equal to 2 per cent. over and above the *aen*, was the perquisite of Sindhia's wives. A similar tax was denominated *Bhet Bāi Sāhiba*, and was an offering to his sister; and his daughter and his *Pīr* (spiritual director) received respectively Rs. 2 and Re. 1 from each village. The produce of these four cesses was sent to Gwalior and the Governor appropriated the produce of the remaining 40 exactions. The chief was *Fauj kharch*, levied on account of the expenses of maintaining troops for the protection of the villages. This was uncertain in amount, and varied with the ability of the people to pay and the power of the Governor to compel payment. *Patel bāb* and *bhūm bāb* were percentages levied from *patels* and *bhūmiās*. There were numerous offerings at all the Hindu festivals. There were charges on account of every act of civil government and sundry arbitrary cesses uncertain in amount. The actual collections from the *khālsa* area in 1818, the year before the cession, amounted to Rs. 1,15,060.

Currency.

The question of the currency caused considerable difficulty to the first British Superintendent of Ajmer. None of the East India Company's coins were current further south than Jaipur, but there were six principal mints, of which coin was current in Ajmer. The Ajmer mint had been established since the time of the Emperor Akbar, and turned out yearly about a lakh and a half of rupees called Srishāhi. The Kishangarh rupee was struck at Kishangarh, and the mint had been established about 50 years, although frequently suppressed by the rulers of Ajmer. The Kuchāwan rupee was struck by the Thākur of Kuchāwan in Mārwār without the permission of the Mahārāja, who was too weak to assert his rights. The Shāhpura mint had been established for some 60 years, in spite of the attempts of the Rāna of Udaipur to suppress it. The Chitori and Udaipuri rupees were the standard coins of Mewār, and the Jhārshāhi rupee was struck at Jaipur. Mr. Wilder cut the knot of the coinage difficulty by concluding all transactions on the part of Government in Farukhābād rupees, and receiving only these in payment of Government revenue. The fixed revenue of the *istimrāri* estates he converted from Srishāhi into Farukhābād currency, and it is on this account that the *istimrāri* revenue payable by each Thākur consists of rupees, annas and pies.

Early Taxation.

The first few years of the British occupation saw few improvements in financial administration, and many old abuses, both in the customs and revenue departments, were continued merely because they brought in money. The Marāthā taxes were at first retained in their integrity. *Māpa* was the most vexatious, being a duty levied on the sale of every article in every village. Originally it was levied at the rate of Rs. 1-6 per cent. from persons not residing in the place in which the articles were sold, so that the every-day transactions between the inhabitants of the same place were exempt, and the burden fell on what may be called the external trade of the village. Mr. Wilder levied the transit duty on the maund instead of on the bullock or camel load as had before been customary; but his successor, Mr. Cavendish, introduced other provisions which still further fettered trade. He extended the *māpa* tax to all towns as well as villages, and to the transactions between the inhabitants of the same place, and raised the rate to Rs. 2-6-0 per cent. He established a new duty in the towns of Ajmer and Kekri on the sale of sugar, tobacco, rice and *ghī*, and for the transit trade introduced a system of *rawānas,* which fell with unmitigated severity on all but the richer merchants. No goods were allowed to enter the district without a pass, and all merchants were required to file a petition to take out a pass, and again on the arrival of the goods within the precincts of the district, or at the city of Ajmer, to subject them to examination and weighment, and thus prove their exact identity with the species and quantity mentioned in the *rawāna*. In order to prevent their goods being stopped on the frontier, the mercantile firms at Ajmer were obliged to obtain from their correspondents previous information of any despatches of goods, particularizing every article, and then a pass had to be procured and sent to meet the goods on the frontier. On the recommendation of a Committee in 1836, Government abolished this system, and restricted the customs taxes to a transit duty to be levied once for all on the import of foreign goods into the district, whether intended for domestic consumption or for re-exportation. To avoid vexatious enquiries, the tax was directed to be taken on the bullock or camel load at a fixed sum.

These orders do not appear to have been acted on, for many of the old abuses seem to have been as rife as ever in 1859, when the Deputy Commissioner complained that if a cultivator in a village a mile from Ajmer wished to sell a seer of *ghī* in the city, he had to procure a pass from the customs agent in his village, stating his name and abode, and specifying the goods taken for sale. On arrival at the town he was obliged to have his goods examined again to see if they agreed with the pass, and export duty was still levied. In 1860 Government sanctioned other reforms, all in the direction of the orders of 1836. Export duties were abolished and the customs tax remitted on 18 articles, while the duty on 17 articles was considerably reduced. The whole district was consolidated into one circle, whereby the separate duties formerly levied in Merwāra and the *pargana* of Sāwar ceased. By these reforms the dutiable articles were reduced to 37, of which the duties on cotton, *ghī*, salt, tobacco, cloths, blankets and opium chiefly affected the produce of the district. The revenue from these customs before 1860 averaged about one lakh, and from that year till 1868 about Rs. 1,12,000.

In 1869 customs were entirely abolished and trade became free as far as Ajmer was concerned, excise being levied once for all on the North-Western Customs line.

Between 1868 and 1871; while Ajmer-Merwāra was subordinate to the Government of the North-Western Provinces, the revenues of the districts were part of the financial system of that Government. But in 1871 the province was formed into a Chief Commissionership under the Foreign Department of the Government of India, and was given a Commissioner of its own, and since then, as it is directly administered by the Government of India, no financial contract applies to its revenue and expenditure.

The revenues are divided into Imperial revenue and Local receipts. The latter include the incorporated and excluded Local funds and Municipal funds.

During the decade ending in 1890, Imperial revenues averaged Rs. 11,10,405, and Local receipts Rs. 2,87,674, while Imperial expenditure averaged Rs. 5,00,230, and Local Rs. 2,83,264. In the next ten years the average of Imperial and Local revenues had increased. They were Rs. 11,56,278, and Rs. 3,53,565 respectively. In the Imperial receipts a reduction in the land revenue and one or two other items due to the famines of the decade, was to some extent counterbalanced by a large increase in receipts from assessed taxes. In the Local receipts the advance was principally in the Municipal funds, which showed an increase of about Rs. 50,000. Expenditure had, however, risen also, and the average under the head Imperial stood at Rs. 9,91,990, under Local at Rs. 3,55,578. The former was due to the enormous expenditure on famine relief and public works rendered necessary by the calamities of the decade. In 1902-03, Imperial receipts stood at Rs. 11,86,187, while Local receipts rose to Rs. 4,13,012, Municipal funds again claiming the lion's share of the increase. Imperial expenditure in this year reached a total of Rs. 9,49,882. Local expenditure is shown as Rs. 3,64,073 of which Municipal expenditure amounted to Rs. 2,17,208. Much of the Municipal finance consists of book transactions, octroi being paid on import, and refunded upon re-export of the scheduled commodities.

In 1902-03, the *khālsa* land revenue, including water revenue in the Ajmer *tahsīl*, amounted to Rs. 1,04,957, the revenue from stamps to Rs. 1,47,774, from income-tax Rs. 64,589, and from local cesses Rs. 20,240. Opium and excise gave Rs. 1,16,322. In the Beāwar *tahsīl* for the same year the land revenue—including water-revenue—came to Rs. 25,525 ; Rs. 31,997 were derived from the sale of stamps, Rs. 7,899 from income-tax. and Rs. 1,852 from local cesses. Miscellaneous receipts amounted to Rs. 1,115. Owing to bad harvests in the *tahsīl* much of the land revenue and local cesses had to be suspended. In the Todgarh *tahsīl* the land revenue for the year was Rs. 33,402 ; Rs. 2,501 were received from the sale of stamps and Rs. 4,888 from excise. Income-tax gave Rs. 1,246 and local cesses Rs. 10,322. Rs. 565 were derived from other sources of general revenue.

CHAPTER XIV.

LAND REVENUE AND TENURES.

Tenures.

The land tenures of Ajmer are, as might be expected, entirely analogous to those prevailing in the adjacent Native States, and though they have been often misunderstood, yet the *vis inertiæ* of the province has sufficed to prevent their being interfered with, except in the one instance of the *mauzāhwār* settlement of 1850. The soil is broadly divided into two classes: *khālsa*, or the private domain of the crown; and *zamīndāri*, or land held in estates or baronies by feudal chiefs who were originally under an obligation of military service, but who now hold on *istimrār* tenure. *Khālsa* land again might be alienated by the Crown, either as an endowment of a religious institution, or as a reward for service to an individual and his heirs. Such grants, when they comprised a whole village or half a village, are termed *jāgīrs*, and fifty-one whole villages and three half villages have been alienated in this way.

Khālsa.

The basis of the land system is, that the State is in its *khālsa* lands the immediate and actual proprietor, standing in the same relation to the cultivators of the soil as the feudal chiefs do to the tenants on their estates. The *jāgīrdārs*, who are assignees of the rights of the State, have the same rights as the State itself.

From ancient times, however, it has been the custom in the *khālsa* land of Ajmer that those who permanently improved land by sinking wells and constructing embankments for the storage of water, acquired thereby certain rights in the soil so improved. These rights are summed up and contained in the term *biswāhdāri*, a name which is synonymous with the term *bāpota* in Mewār and Mārwār, and with the term *mirās* in Southern India, both of the latter words signifying "heritable land." A cultivator who had thus expended capital was considered protected from ejectment as long as he paid the customary share of the produce of the improved land, and he had a right to sell, mortgage, or make gifts of the well or embankment which had been created by his capital or labour. The transfer of the well or the embankment carried with it the transfer of the improved land. These privileges were hereditary, and the sum of them practically constitutes proprietary right. Hence the term *biswāhdār* came to mean owner, and a right of ownership gradually grew up in permanently-improved land.

In a district like Ajmer, where the rainfall is so precarious, unirrigated land was hardly regarded as of any value. The State was considered owner of this as well as of the waste. A cultivator without a well, or at any rate an embankment, was looked on as, and must always be, a waif with no tie to bind him to the village where he may reside. No man, in fact, cultivated the same unirrigated fields continuously, the village boundaries were undefined, there was always more unirrigated land round a village than could be cultivated by the number of ploughs, the State exercised the right of locating new hamlets and new tenants, of giving leases to strangers who were willing to improve the land, and of collecting dues for the privilege of grazing over the waste from all tenants, whether *biswāhdārs* or not.

The first two Superintendents of Ajmer were of opinion that waste lands were the property of the State. Their successor, whose experience was gained in the North-West Provinces, considered them to belong to the village community. Mr. Edmonstone, who made a ten years' settlement in 1835, investigated the question, and was clearly of opinion that the State was the owner.

When Colonel Dixon commenced the construction of his tank embankments in 1842, he acted as steward to a great estate. He founded hamlets where he thought fit, he gave leases at privileged rates to those who were willing to dig wells, and distributed the lands under the new tanks to strangers whom he located in hamlets in the waste. In no instance did the old *biswāhdārs* imagine that their rights were being invaded, nor did they consider themselves entitled to any rent from the new-comers. The latter had the same rights as to sale and mortgage of improved land as the old *biswāhdārs*.

Such was the tenure of the *khālsa* land of Ajmer till the year 1849, when the village boundaries were for the first time demarcated, and under the orders of Mr. Thomason a village settlement was introduced. This settlement effected a radical change in the tenure. It transformed the cultivating communities of the *khālsa*, each member of which had certain rights in improved land, but who, as a community, possessed no rights at all, into *bhyāchāra* proprietary bodies. The essence of the *mauzāwār* system is, that a defined area of land—that, namely, which is enclosed within the village boundaries—is declared to be the property of the village community, and the community consists of all those who are recorded as owners of land in the village. The change, however, was unmarked at the time, and was only slowly appreciated by the people. In many cases where Colonel Dixon established a new hamlet, he assessed it separately from the parent village, *i.e.*, the revenue assessed on each resident of the hamlet was added up and announced to the headman of the hamlet. The waste remained the common property of the parent village and of the hamlets. In 1867 these hamlets were formed into distinct villages, the waste adjacent to the hamlet being attached to it. The *biswāhdārs* of the parent village retained no right over this land, nor do they imagine that they possess any. In this way there are now 195 *khālsa* villages in Ajmer, against 85 at the time of Colonel Dixon's settlement.

Until the *mauzāwār* system of 1850, the tenure in the *khālsa* was *ryotwāri*. The State owned the land, but allowed certain rights to tenants who had spent capital on permanent improvements in the land so improved. This collection of rights gradually came to be considered proprietary right, and since 1850 the State has abandoned its exclusive and undisputed right of ownership over unimproved land.

Istimrār. The tenure of the feudal chiefs was originally identical with that of the Chiefs in the Native States of Rājputāna. The estates were *jāgīrs* held on condition of military service, and liable to various feudal incidents. Colonel Tod, in his Rājasthān, Volume I, page 167, thus sums up the result of his enquiries into the tenure :—" A grant of an estate is for the life of the holder, with inheritance for his offspring in lineal descent or adoption, with the sanction of the Prince, and resumable for crime or incapacity; this reversion and power of resumption being marked by the usual ceremonies on each lapse of the grantee, of sequestration (*zabti*), of relief (*nazarānā*) of homage and investiture of the heir."

The original tenure of the mass of the *istimrār* estates in Ajmer is exactly described in the above quotation. The grants were life-grants, but like all similar tenures they tended to become hereditary.

None of these estates ever paid revenue till the time of the Marāthās in 1755 A.D., but were held on condition of military service. The Marāthās, however, wanted money more than service, and assessed a sum upon each estate, presumably bearing some relation to the number of horse and foot soldiers which the Chief had been liable to furnish. Naturally, however, the assessment was very unequal, as a much larger proportion of their income was taken from the weaker Chiefs than from the more powerful thākurs, whom it might have been difficult to coerce. On the cession of the district in 1818 A.D. the tālukdārs were found paying a certain sum under the denomination of *māmla* or *āen,* and a number of extra cesses, which amounted on the whole to half as much again as the *māmla.* These extra cesses were collected till the year 1841, when, on the representation of Col. Sutherland, Commissioner of Ajmer, they were abandoned. In 1830, 1839, and 1841 the Government of India had declared that the estates were liable to re-assessment, and had given explicit orders for their re-assessment, but these orders were not acted on, nor apparently communicated to those concerned. The Chiefs who at a very early period of our rule, perhaps even before it, had acquired the title of *istimrārdārs,* no doubt considered themselves as holders at a fixed and permanent quit-rent. This belief of theirs was strengthened by the action of Government in 1841, when all extra cesses were remitted avowedly on the ground that they were "unhallowed Marāthā exactions," and the demand of the State was limited to the amount which had been assessed by the Marāthās nearly a century before. Finally, in 1873, Government consented to waive its right in the matter of re-assessment, and to declare the present assessments of the Chiefs to be fixed in perpetuity. This concession was accompanied by declaration of the liability of the estates to pay *nazarānā* on successions, and the conditions on which the *istimrārdārs* now hold have been incorporated in the *sanad* which was granted to each of them.

There are in all 66 estates, containing 230 villages, with an area of 8,19,523 acres. The *istimrār* revenue is Rs. 1,14,734-9-11, and the estimated rent roll of the *istimrārdārs* is Rs. 5,59,198. In 60 estates, all held by Rājputs, the custom of primogeniture now prevails. Of these, however, 11 only are original fiefs, the remainder having been formed by sub-division in accordance with the rules of inheritance. Originally all the sons divided the estate, although the elder got a larger share than the others. In the next stage the eldest son succeeded to the estate as well as to the *gādi*, while provision was made for the younger sons by alienation to them of villages on *grās* tenure. The last instance of such alienation occurred in 1823. In the third stage the provision of the cadets of the house is limited to grant of a well and a few bighās of land for life. But nowadays the younger tend to become mere hangers-on at the elder brother's table. Some provision for them is considered imperative on every *istimrārdār*.

There are six estates, each of a single village, the tenure of which differs from that above described. Five of these are held by co-parcenary bodies, succession is regulated by ancestral shares, and both land and revenue are minutely divided. In one village, Karel, belonging to a community of Rāhtors, the property of the two chief men of the village is distributed on their death into one share more than there are sons, and the eldest son takes a double share. Rājosi stands apart from all other *istimrār* estates. It belongs to a Chita, who is sole *istimrārdār*, but the land is owned not by him but by the actual cultivators from whom he collects a fixed share of the produce, and himself pays a fixed revenue to Government. One of these villages, Kotri, belongs to Chārans or Bhāts, and was originally separated from the *istimrār* estate of Bhinai. The other five were stated by the *kānūngos* in the time of Mr. Cavendish to be *khālsa* villages, and they probably should not have been included in the *istimrār* list.

The subordinate rights in the *istimrār* area have never formed the subject of judicial investigation, nor with the exception of six small estates, have settlement operations been extended to the *istimrār* area. The principle followed under our rule has been to leave the *istimrārdārs* to manage their own affairs, and to interfere with them as little as possible. It is well known, however, that in most of the larger estates there are villages held by Chārans, Jogis, and others, and villages held by sub-tālukdārs, relations of the *istimrārdār*, who generally pay an unvarying amount of revenue to the head of the family, and who are succeeded in the sub-talukās by their eldest sons. As a general rule *jāgir* villages are not resumable, nor can the sub-tālukās be resumed except for valid cause assigned.

The *istimrārdārs* have always claimed to be owners of the soil, and their claim has been allowed. The prevailing opinion is that all cultivators are tenants at will, but there are good grounds for hesitating to adopt this opinion. Mr. Cavendish's enquiries extended to 296 villages, and in 158 villages the thākurs disclaimed the right of ouster of cultivators from irrigated and improved lands where the means of irrigation or the improvement had been provided by the labour or capital of the cultivators. In 161 villages were found hereditary cultivators whose rights were the same as those of the owners of wells. Unirrigated and unimproved land was universally admitted to be held on a tenure at will from the *istimrārdār*. Disputes between an *istimrārdār* and his tenants seldom come before our courts. Whatever rights of ouster the former possesses are rarely put in practice by him.

Jāgīr. The subject of *jāgīr* estates was investigated by a mixed committee of Government officials and *jāgīrdārs* in 1874, and their report contains a history of each estate. Out of a total area of 1,50,838 acres, yielding an average rental of Rs. 91,000, 65,472 acres belong to the endowments of shrines and sacred institutions. The remaining *jāgīrs* are enjoyed by individuals and certain classes specially designated in the grants. No conditions of military or other service are attached to the tenure of any *jāgīr*.

In all *jāgīr* estates the revenue is collected by an estimate of the produce, and money assessments are unknown. As was the case in the *khālsa* before Colonel Dixon's settlement, the ideas of rent and revenue are confounded under the ambiguous term *hāsil*, and until the year 1872 the relative status of the *jāgīrdārs* and cultivators as regards the ownership of the soil was quite undefined. In that year it was decided that all those found in possession of land irrigated or irrigable from wells or tanks, which wells or tanks were not proved to be constructed by the *jāgīrdār*, were owners of such land. The *jāgīrdār* was declared owner of irrigated land in which the means of irrigation had been provided by him, of unirrigated land, and of the waste.

Bhūm. The tenure known as *bhūm* is peculiar to Rājputs. The word itself means "the soil," and the name *bhūmiā* properly signifies "the allodial proprietor," as distinguished from the feudal Chiefs and the tenant of crown lands. According to Colonel Tod's Rājasthān, Vol. I, page 168, the *bhūmiās* in Mārwār are the descendants of the earlier princes who, on the predominance of new clans, ceased to come to court and to hold the higher grades of ranks. They continued, however, to hold their land, and became an armed husbandry, nominally paying a small quit-rent to the crown, but practically exempt. In course of time the various kinds of *bhūm* grew up, which, unlike the original allodial holding, were founded on grants, but had this apparently in common, that a hereditary, non-resumable, and inalienable property in the soil was inseparably bound up with a revenue-free title. *Bhūm* was given as *mundkati*, or compensation for bloodshed, in order to quell a feud, for distinguished services in the field, for protection of a border, or for watch and ward of a village. Whatever the origin of a *bhūm* holding, however, the tenure was identical, and so cherished is the title of *bhūmiā* that the greatest Chiefs are solicitous to obtain it even in villages entirely dependent on their authority. The Mahārāja of Kishangarh, the Thākur of Fatehgarh, the Thākur of Jūnia, the Thākur of Bāndanwāra, and the Thākur of Tāntoti are among the *bhūmiās* of Ajmer.

There are in Ajmer 109 *bhūm* holdings, and except in those cases where a Rājā or *istimrārdār* is also a *bhūmiā*, the property passes to all the children equally. It is probable that none of these holdings are original allods, but belong to the class of assimilated allods. These *bhūmiās* are nearly all Rāhtors, descendants of younger branches of *istimrār* families, and cannot claim an origin higher than that of the estates from which they sprang. Whatever the origin of the holdings, however, the rights and duties of all *bhūmiās* came in course of time to be identical. At first the land was revenue-free, subsequently a quit-rent was imposed but irregularly collected, and this quit-rent was abolished in 1841 along with the extra cesses from the *istimrārdārs.* The duties of the *bhūmiās* were three in number: first, to protect the village, in which the *bhūm* is, and the village cattle from dacoits; secondly, to protect the property of travellers within their village from theft and robbery; and thirdly, pecuniarily to indemnify sufferers from a crime which they ought to have prevented.

This last incident is a peculiar feature of the Ajmer tenure, and grew out of the custom of Rājputāna that the Rāj should compensate losses of travellers by theft or robbery committed in its territory. This custom is still carried out by the inter-statal Court of Vakils. Where the theft or robbery has occurred in a village belonging to a fief, the chieftain to whom the village belongs is called on to indemnify the sufferers; and the *istimrārdārs* of Ajmer have always been compelled to indemnify sufferers from thefts and robberies committed on their estates. Similarly a *jāgīrdār*, to whom the State had transferred its rights and duties, was pecuniarily liable. In case of theft in a *khālsa* village the State was called on to pay compensation. In Ajmer, the State finding this responsibility inconvenient, transferred it to a *bhūmiā* as a condition of the tenure; but in *khālsa* villages, where there were no *bhūmiās*, the State remained responsible.

However useful the system of pecuniary indemnification may have been, and, however well adapted it was to the times of anarchy in which it had its birth, there is no doubt that in Ajmer it had long been moribund. When the average rental enjoyed by a *bhūmiā* is only Rs. 17 a year, it is hopeless to expect that more than a very few *bhūmiās* could compensate even a moderate loss. As soon as the Native States adopted a system of regular police, this distinctive feature of the *bhūm* tenure vanished, and Government in 1874 sanctioned a proposal to abolish the pecuniary responsibility, and to revert to what seemed to be the original incidents of the tenure, to hold the *bhūmiās* liable as an armed militia, to be called out to put down riots and to pursue dacoits and rebels, and to take from them a yearly quit-rent under the name of *nazarānā*.

The above sketch shows that in *khālsa* villages the State still possesses considerable proprietary rights. In *istimrār* estates, on the other hand, it has few or no rights beyond that of taking a fixed revenue and of a royalty on minerals. In *jāgīr* villages it has assigned its rights to others. To the State belong in sole proprietary right all mines of metals in *khālsa* villages, while for its own purposes it can quarry free of payment where and to what extent it pleases. Two ranges of hills near Ajmer, that of Tārāgarh and that of Nāgpahār, have been declared to be the property of Government. The tank embankments of Ajmer have nearly all been made by the State, and Government is the owner of the embankments, and all that grows thereon. Under the forest ordinance the State has reserved to itself the right to resume from the village communities the management of any tract of waste or hilly land, the proprietary right subject to certain conditions being vested absolutely in Government as long as the land is required for forest purposes.

Tenures in Merwāra.

Merwāra possessed no settled Government till 1822, when it came under British management. The people found the occupation of plunder more profitable and congenial than that of agriculture. No crops were sown except wha was actually necessary for the scanty population. The tanks were constructed and used solely for the purpose of providing water for the cattle. No revenue nor rent was paid. The Rājputs were never able to get a firm footing in the country. Whatever small revenue they could get from it was obtained at a cost both of life and money far exceeding its value. In such circumstances tenures could not spring up. Colonels Hall and Dixon, to whom the civilization of the Mers is due, treated Merwāra as a great *zamīndāri*, of which they were the managers and Government the owner. Their word was law, they founded hamlets, gave leases, built tanks and collected one-third of the produce of the soil as revenue. At the settlement of 1851 all cultivators who had recently been settled in the villages were recorded as owners of the land in their possession equally with the old inhabitants.

Non-proprietary cultivators.

At the settlement of 1875 nearly all cultivators were recorded as proprietors, and a non-proprietary cultivating class hardly exists in the *khālsa* of either Ajmer or Merwāra. When they are tenants they pay generally the same share of the produce as the proprietors themselves paid before the regular settlement. Custom and not competition regulates the rate of rent. The *istimrārdārs* and *jāgīrdārs* collect their rents without the intervention of the Courts, and in these estates there is still more land to be brought under cultivation than there are cultivators for. The population has been periodically decimated by famine; and as no Rājput will, if he can possibly avoid the necessity, ever touch a plough, cultivators are still at a premium.

Revenue in former times.

Figures are not available to show what tribute Ajmer paid to the Mughal Emperors. The Marāthās never collected more than Rs. 3,76,740 from the district, and of this sum Rs. 31,000 was the amount at which the customs had been farmed; the remainder was land revenue. Of the land revenue amounting to Rs. 3,45,740, the assessment of the *istimrār* was Rs. 2,16,762, that of the *khālsa* Rs. 1,28,978. Under British rule the administration of the *istimrār* estates in Ajmer has been confined to collecting from them a fixed assessment, the thākurs and *jāgīrdārs* being left to manage their own affairs. The following retrospect therefore will be restricted to the administration of the *khālsa* or Government villages in the province.

Mr. Wilder's administration.

The actual collections from the *khālsa* in the year before the cession of Ajmer to the British on the 26th July 1818, amounted to Rs. 1,15,060. Mr. Wilder, Assistant to the Resident at Delhi, was the first Superintendent appointed to Ajmer. In the first year of his administration he decided to take the revenue in the *khālsa* at the rate of one-half the estimated out-turn of the crop. The collections for the year were Rs. 1,59,746, and Mr. Wilder writes that the measure of an equal division of the crop had been productive of all the benefits he had anticipated. The people had acquired confidence in the moderation and justice of their new government, and though it would not be advisable for the next two years to demand any great addition to the increase that had already taken place, yet he was confident that on the third year the *jama* might be raised to double what it had reached under any preceding government without at all pressing on the inhabitants. He accordingly proposed a three years' progressive settlement—in the first year Rs. 1,79,437, in the second year Rs. 2,01,691, in the third year Rs. 2,49,303. His dominant if not sole anxiety appears to have been to increase the Government revenue. He furnished no information of the principle on which the demand had been fixed, nor of the grounds on which a progressive assessment had been resolved, and the settlement was confirmed with some hesitation by Government, who remarked on the proved disadvantages of an assessment framed on anticipated improvement, which checks the rising spirit of industry and the accumulation of capital.

Owing to two bad harvests the settlement broke down the first year. Mr. Wilder proposed to relinquish the balance and to make a settlement on a fixed annual *jama* of Rs. 1,64,700. Both proposals were sanctioned by Government, the term of the settlement being fixed for five years. The assessment was fairly collected for the first four years, though in the last year the people were obliged to borrow to pay their revenue; but the fifth year was one of famine. Recourse was had to collecting one-half the produce, and the amount realized was Rs. 31,920. The next year was a good one, but the people objected to pay according to Mr Wilder's settlement, and the revenue was again collected *khām*. Mr. Wilder had been transferred in December 1824, the middle of the famine year His six years' administration had not been productive of any great results. He took little pains to ascertain the value of the land he assessed, or the condition of the people, and the era of material improvement had not yet dawned. His administration was rather starved: the whole cost of the revenue and police establishment of the district was Rs. 1,374 a month, or less than half his own salary of Rs. 3,000.

Re-adjustments between 1818 and 1841.

Mr. Henry Middleton, also a North-West civilian, succeeded Mr. Wilder in December 1824. He was of opinion that monetary assessments of any kind were unpalatable to the people, and if confidence could be reposed in the subordinate officers, the system of taking in kind would be best. The experience, however, of the year 1825-26 rendered Mr. Middleton loth to adopt this system. Accordingly he proposed a five years' settlement, and reported its completion on the 26th November 1826. He had rough measurement rolls prepared, but he chiefly relied on the collections of the previous year as a criterion of resources. He remarks on the poverty of the people and the extortions of the money-lenders. Many cultivators who had come to the district in the first years of the British rule had been driven away again by bad harvests and high assessment. The wells had fallen into disrepair, and the people had no money to repair them. Mr. Middleton's settlement was sanctioned at Rs. 1,44,072 for five years.

The assessment, however, was only collected in the first of the years the settlement had to run, and that with considerable difficulty. Mr. Middleton did not remain long enough in the district to collect the next year's revenue, and made over charge to Mr. Cavendish in October 1827. He cannot be said to have initiated any useful measures.

Mr. Cavendish, his successor, was a great reformer, and left the impress of his energy on every department of administration. To him the district is indebted for a very valuable collection of statistics regarding *istimrār, bhūm* and *jāgīr* tenures. He carried out, however, little of what he put his hand to, and the sanction which had been accorded to Mr. Middleton's settlement prevented his interference in the assessment of the *khālsa*. Mr. Cavendish considered that Mr. Middleton's assessment was too high for several reasons: "because the cultivated area has remained stationary since the time of the Marāthās, who only collected Rs. 87,689; because the rate of assessment exceeds half the produce; because no cultivator in the soil of Ajmer, which requires much trouble and expense, can afford to pay one-half the produce; because the assessment is collected not from the produce of the soil, but by a fluctuating and arbitrary tax; and because the assessment has been made on the basis of a favourable year's collections when corn was dear." Mr. Cavendish applied the rates to which he had been accustomed in Sahāranpur to Mr. Middleton's areas, and calculated that the assessment ought to be Rs. 87,645 instead of Rs. 1,44,072.

Along with other reasons, he gives what seems to be the real key to the over-assessment of the district, *viz.*, that 1818-19 was a very good year in Ajmer, while, owing to the devastations of Amir Khān in the territory of Mewār and Mārwār, there was a large demand on all sides for grain, and prices were very high. Indeed, the first assessments of British revenue officers in newly-acquired districts almost invariably broke down through the error of over-estimating corn prices. They used to take the old war prices that prevailed during the anarchy preceding annexation, and they forgot that with peace and order came plenty and open markets. Mr. Cavendish recommended that people should not be pressed for their revenue in bad seasons. He also partially introduced an assessment of individual holding, a measure unknown to Mr. Middleton's settlement. He lays stress on the point that remissions granted in a lump sum benefit not the real sufferers, but the *tahsīldārs, kānūngos, patwārīs* and *patels.* He introduced for the first time *patwārīs'* accounts, appointed them for many villages where there were none, and directed every *patwārī* to give a receipt. Although Governmeut refused to revise the assessment, they directed that diligent enquiry as to the resources of each village should be made during the unexpired period of the settlement. Under Mr. Cavendish, however, remissions were regularly applied for and granted where there was a difficulty in paying, and the settlement was not worked up to in any year. He left the district at the end of 1831, the year of the expiry of the settlement. He writes that he had intended to make the settlement with *patels,* and to give to each tenant a statement showing the amount for which he should be individually responsible.

His successor collected on the principle established by Mr. Cavendish. Major Speirs did not attempt a settlement. He collected all he could, and the remainder was remitted by Government. In 1833-34, however, even the pretence of working on the settlement was abandoned. The season was a disastrous one. The *kharīf* instalments were collected by an equal division of the scanty produce, and it was proposed to allow the people to keep the *rabi* revenue. In December 1833 charge was made over to Mr. Edmonstone, who in the following year made a summary settlement with reference to the deteriorated state of the country owing to drought, the demand of which was Rs. 1,19,302. If the villagers did not consent to his terms the revenue was collected *khām* at half produce.

In the cold weather of 1835-36, Mr. Edmonstone proceeded to make a regular settlement, which, as it was subsequently sanctioned for ten years, is generally known by the name of the decennial settlement, and which was reported on the 26th May 1836. He was of opinion that the district had receded rather than advanced under the previous administration, and he adopted a method of his own for assessment. The villages were measured, and the cultivated area, amounting in all to 36,257 acres, classed into: *chāhī* (well land), 8,989 acres; *tālābī* (tank land), 2,180 acres; and *bārāni* (dry land), 25,088 acres. He then assessed the cash-paying produce (Indian corn and cotton) area at the current money rates at the central market, and estimated the average produce per bigha of other crops. The Government share of one half, except in the case of *patels* and Mahājans, he converted into money by the average price current of the previous five years. He thus obtained a rough *jamābandi* amounting to Rs. 1,57,151, and then visited each village and fixed his demand with reference to the past fiscal history, present circumstances, and future capabilities of each estate. No villages were given in farm. Two small ones were held on the system of half produce, as they could not be brought up to his standard; the rest accepted his terms. The amount finally assessed was Rs. 1,27,525, or adding the *khām* villages Rs. 1,29,872.

Mr. Edmonstone describes the people as reckless, improvident, poverty-stricken, and much in debt. They were entirely in the power of the Bohrās who furnished no accounts, and the debt to whom ran on from generation to generation. The settlement was made with the headman of each village in the belief that he generally acted in accordance with the wishes of the village community. The incidence of the assessment was Rs. 3-9 an acre, while the unirrigated area was nearly 69 per cent. of the cultivated. The settlement returns show 5,621 cultivators, 2,675 non-cultivators, 3,185 ploughs, and 1,575 wells.

Although the assessment of individual villages appears to have been fair and judicious, the great defect of the settlement was the very imperfect and inequitable manner in which the village assesssment was distributed over the holdings. Mr. Edmonstone introduced for the first time the principle of joint responsibility of all cultivators. It is evident that a cultivator who is assessed at half his produce in good and bad years alike cannot afford to pay for others who have migrated or given up agriculture. In the first year of the settlement the distribution over the holdings was proved to be quite inequitable, and the people began to clamour for a return to collections from the actual produce. Mr. Edmonstone had left Ajmer at the end of 1836, and his successor proposed to make a fresh distribution of the revenue, and to give each cultivator a separate lease specifying what rent he had to pay. As this was tantamount to changing the settlement from *mauzāwār* to *ryotwār*, Government would not sanction the proposal. But the villages were offered the option of returning to direct management, and 41 out of 81 villages accepted it.

In the meantime Colonel Sutherland became Commissioner. He took great pains to make himself acquainted with everything concerning Ajmer, and his reports on the *khālsa* administration and on the *istimrārdārs* are standard papers of reference. He strongly condemned the village assessment system as inapplicable to Ajmer, and looked to the repair and construction of tanks for a remedy. He advocated the mode of assessment which had been carried out by Captain Dixon in Merwāra as that suited to the country, and consonant with the wishes of the people. Under this system lands under cotton, maize, sugar-cane and opium were charged with a money rate. Other *rabi* and *kharif* crops were estimated and measured, and one-third of the produce was taken as the Government share by a money assessment fixed according to the average yearly value of produce in the principal neighbouring markets. Land newly broken up paid one-sixth of the produce for the first year, one-fifth for the second, and one-fourth for the third and fourth years, after which the full rate of one-third was charged. A remission in the amount of the share was given to those who constructed embankments and dug new wells.

It was evident that some remedial measures were necessary. The four years from 1837 to 1841 were years of severe distress, and at the time of Colonel Sutherland's report, 26th January 1841, the *khālsa* villages had reached the lowest depths of poverty. Many families had left the district owing to the pressure of revenue which they were unable to pay. The tanks were broken, the wells out of repair, and the people were thoroughly demoralized. They preferred paying half the produce to accepting the reduced assessment of Mr. Edmonstone. For these deplorable results the previous settlements were largely responsible. The last and highest of them had an incidence per acre about twice as heavy as that made in the North-West Provinces. With the experience gained in these settlements the Government of the North-West might have concluded that its "trust that the settlement would prove moderate and be realized without distress to the people" was fallacious.

The success of Major Dixon's administration of Merwāra had for some time attracted the attention of Government and the Commissioner, and in February 1842 he was appointed Superintendent of Ajmer, in addition to his other duties as Superintendent of Merwāra and Commandant of the Merwāra Battalion.

From the date of his assuming charge a new era commences in the history of the administration of the country. Within the next six years Rs. 4,52,707 were expended on the construction and repair of embankments. Advances were made for agricultural improvements, and the Superintendent succeeded in infusing a good deal of his personal energy into the people. To enable Government to reap a benefit from the new works, sanction was procured to allow such villages as desired it to abandon their engagements. All were invited to return to *khām* management, and when a tank was made or repaired in one of the few villages which insisted on retaining their leases, a percentage of the cost was levied in addition to the assessment. The rate of collection at the same time was reduced from one-half to two-fifths, and the cash rates were also lowered. On the expiry of the ten years' settlement, the whole district was held *khām*, and managed as Major Dixon had managed Merwāra.

The system, however, depended for its success largely upon the energy and experience of one man, and was unsuited for general adoption. It was considered expedient to return to the system of village settlements, as the people had learned to recognize the principle of joint responsibility, and their land, from the means of irrigation with which it had been provided, possessed a higher and more uniform value than was previously the case. Arrangements were therefore made for a revenue survey, and instructions were issued to Major Dixon for the formation of a village settlement. Moderation was inculcated, and the standard to be aimed at was the punctual realisation of a *jama* equal to Mr. Edmonstone's assessment, and yielding over and above that amount a moderate profit on the money invested in tanks and reservoirs. This moderate profit was afterwards put at 5 or 6 per cent. These orders were followed by a year of severe scarcity, and at one time it was doubtful whether engagements for a fixed period could be entered into. The succeeding year, however, was a favourable one, and the settlement commenced from the *kharīf* harvest of 1849.

Col. Dixon's Settlement.

In making his assessment Colonel Dixon was guided chiefly by the experience he had gained of the capabilities of each village while it was held under direct management. His method of assessment was as follows:—

He took Mr. Edmonstone's assessment and added to it 6 per cent. of the sum expended on tanks in that village. This was the standard. If the past history of the village warranted Colonel Dixon in believing that it could be paid, he assessed the village at this amount. If he thought it could pay more he assessed it at more; if he thought that it could by no possibility pay this amount, he reduced the standard. No rates were worked out till after the assessment, nor was any attempt made to compare the incidence of the revenue in different villages, or to explain its variations. The inequality of the assessment was no doubt tempered by Colonel Dixon's intimate knowledge of the district, but the system necessarily produced inequality. For all practical purposes of assessment the measurement of the villages in Colonel Dixon's time was superfluous. If 6 per cent. of the outlay on the tanks were added to the assessment of Mr. Edmonstone, the amount would be Rs. 1,58,273, and this was the amount proposed as a fair amount to distribute. The highest amount which had ever been collected was in 1847-48, when, at two-thirds the produce, the revenue stood at Rs. 1,67,237, and this included all the cesses. Colonel Dixon's actual assessment, excluding the 1 per cent. road cess, but inclusive of the tank cess of 1 per cent., which was merely a deduction from the Government revenue set apart for a particular purpose, was Rs. 1,75,756, or, adding the assessment which was subsequently made on Neārān and Karānipura, Rs. 1,85,161. The assessment was lighter than Mr. Edmonstone's, but the unirrigated area had increased in greater proportion than the irrigated, and the average rate of assessment on a total area, including 28 per cent. of irrigation, was Rs. 2-0-3 per acre.

The best description of the settlement is that given by Colonel Dixon himself in a demi-official letter to Sir Henry Lawrence, dated 25th January 1856:—"If the season be moderately favourable and the *talāos* be replenished, the rent will be paid with ease and cheerfulness by the people. If drought ensues, we have been prepared to make such a remission that distress in paying the revenue shall not reach the people. It is necessary to bear in mind that we have given the profits to the people, ourselves bearing the onus of loss. In a country like Ajmer-Merwāra, where the seasons are so extremely irregular, to burden the *zamīndārs* with arrears of rent on account of what was not produced would check the energies of the people, and render them less industrious than they now are, when they know we shall only claim the rent or a portion of it, when it has been assured to them by Providence. To have made the *jama* less would have been to have left the *zamīndārs* only partially employed, while in a season of scarcity we must still have relaxed the demand." This extract clearly sets forth the nature of the settlement. It was not intended to be an equal annual *jama* to be collected in all years, except what in other parts of India would be called famine years, but the assessment was pitched at the highest amount that Colonel

Dixon believed should be collected in good years, and he was prepared to apply for remissions whenever they were required.

The people accepted the settlement with reluctance, but as proposed, it was sanctioned for 21 years. The Lieutenant-Governor, however, desired it to be understood "that except after report to Government and special sanction, no other penalty was to be attached to the non-fulfilment of the settlement contract than annulment of the lease and return to *khām* management." The settlement thus sanctioned was a *mauzāwār* settlement only in name, and the system of collection adopted by Colonel Dixon rendered it practically a *ryotwāri* one. Before the instalments were due the villages were divided into circles and a *chaprāsi* was appointed for each circle. It was the duty of this official, in company with the *patel* and *patwāri*, to collect from each individual tenant the sum recorded against his name in the *patwāri's* register. If the cultivator himself could not pay, the *bania* with whom he kept his accounts was called up and the money generally produced. When the revenue could not be collected, Colonel Dixon made up his mind as to how much should be remitted about the month of May, and applied for sanction for the remission of the amount proposed. It was a matter of common tradition in the district that when the revenue of any village was found to come in with difficulty, the Deputy Collector was sent out and arranged for a re-distribution of the assessment. Such a mode of administration, though the best suited to the district and perfectly consonant with the wishes of the people, differs very considerably from the *mauzāwār* system, and could only succeed where the Collector was intimately acquainted with the resource of each village.

Having completed the settlement of Ajmer, Colonel Dixon took up the assessment of Merwāra. He was embarrassed with no instructions, as he was rightly considered the best judge of what should be done. He went into Merwāra in the cold weather of 1849-50 and reported his settlement of the district on the 27th September 1850. It was sanctioned for 20 years at a net demand of Rs. 1,81,751 and a gross demand of Rs. 1,88,742. The incidence of the assessment was Rs. 2-11-2 per acre on an area which included 38 per cent. of irrigation.

For several years after the settlement there was a sucesssion of favourable seasons, and remissions for which Colonel Dixon had to apply were but small in amount. Many tanks and wells were made by the people themselves, and the country was prosperous and contented. With Colonel Dixon's death, however, in 1857, the era of material improvement may be said to close, and the era of inflexible realization of revenue commenced. The principle of his settlement was forgotten, and the idea gradually gained ground that the assessment was an equal annual demand to be collected in full each year.

An account of the further progress of the settlement is given by Captain J. C. Brooke, the first Deputy Commissioner of Ajmer, in his report of the 24th July 1858. He found that there had been no *bānchh* or distribution of deficiencies caused by defaulters over the village community since the settlement. No account has been kept of the profits of common land, and any remissions received from the State were appropriated by the whole village, giving a very small modicum of relief to those really requiring it. The *patwārīs* were miserably paid, and generally acted as money-lenders to the people. Captain Brooke revised the *patwārīs'* establishment, and doubled up the smaller villages so as to enable a more fitting remuneration to be given to those who undertook the duties. He called attention to the manner in which land submerged in the beds of tanks had been assessed at high rates, and proposed to strike out of the settlement all lands liable to constant submersion, and to take revenue from them only when they should be cultivated. He was of opinion that the settlement had pressed heavily, and showed that the price of wheat and barley had fallen 50 per cent. below what they were for the three years preceding the settlement. Many of his suggestions were valuable, but nothing was done.

Major Lloyd, Deputy Commissioner in 1860, was struck by signs of growing prosperity, but it is significant that five villages had come under *khām* management in Ajmer and seven in Beāwar. Major Lloyd arranged for a systematic revision of the settlement records and a fresh distribution of the revenue. But the season of 1860 was a bad one, and remissions and suspensions were necessary in most estates. The work of re-distribution of the revenue was held in abeyance and never recommenced. Thereafter until 1867 the revenue was collected in full. In 1866 an important change was introduced into the system of collecting the revenue. The whole revenue was ordered to be collected from the headmen alone, and the system initiated by Colonel Dixon was abolished.

In 1868-69 came the great famine, the most disastrous since the one of 1812. In 1869 the Deputy Commissioner reported that the state of apathy and demoralization of the people was such that nothing availed for the collection of revenue save active coercive measures. In Merwāra it was found utterly impossible to collect the revenue during the famine years, and eventually the arrears were remitted. A summary settlement was made for Merwāra from the year 1872-73, which was at a reduction of 32 per cent. on the settlement demand.

Mr. La Touche's Settlement.

In 1871, as the existing settlements were nearing their term of expiry, Mr. J. D. LaTouche was appointed to make a new settlement of the districts. Operations began with a complete village survey of the three *tahsīls* of Ajmer, Beāwar and Todgarh, which was finally completed in 1873. Various improvements were introduced into the settlement registers, one of the most notable being that the fields were numbered in the *khasra* so as to show the various holdings as recorded in the *khatūnī*. The system of assessment also had distinctive features, as compared with those of previous settlements. Up to that time the assessments had never been founded on or checked by rates, but had been exclusively based on the history of past collection. Rates for the various kinds of land had never been worked out from the total assessment on a tract, nor had the assessment on a village been decided by inductive process from the rates decided for lands. The assessment of each individual village had been a deductive guess on the part of the assessing officer.

The principle now to be followed was laid down in the instructions from Government. The Settlement Officer was first to divide the villages to be assessed into groups, so as to avoid applying a uniform rate to those of which the characteristics were markedly different. In every group he was then to select some specimen villages, in which the records of the Deputy Commissioner's Office and local enquiry would show him that the revenue had been paid with a fair amount of ease. From the statistics of these specimen villages he was then to work out fair rates for the different kinds of soil. These soil rates were then to be applied to the remaining villages, after carefully examining the accounts of past collections and remissions in the villages to see if the amount indicated by the soil rates could fairly be paid. In deciding thus, he was not to consider years of exceptional drought, extraordinary bad seasons being left to be dealt with by the application of extraordinary remedies. In order partly to surmount the difficulty of an equal annual demand being assessed in a tract where the seasons are so irregular, water revenue was assessed separately from the land revenue on the irrigated aspect. The assessment on the dry area included the full assessment on well land, but in each village where the tanks failed to fill, the water revenue was to be proportionately remitted each year.

Tanks were divided into classes according to their irrigating capacity, and a lump sum was fixed as the assessment of each tank. This was to be made good from the fields actually irrigated in each year, unless its incidence on the irrigated area exceeded a certain fixed maximum or fell below a certain fixed minimum. When the incidence maximum per acre was exceeded, only the maximum was charged and the balance remitted; when the incidence per acre fell below the minimum, the minimum rate was charged and the excess over the total lump sum was credited to Government. A certain amount of stability was thus secured for the water revenue. Extended irrigation was also encouraged, as within the minimum the more the water was economized and spread, the less per acre each cultivator had to pay. The total revenue thus fixed in Ajmer-Merwāra amounted to Rs. 55,432. Lands were divided into *tālābi*—irrigated from tanks and *abi* land in the dry beds of tanks. The maximum, minimum and average rates for *tālābi* land per acre at this settlement were Rs. 5-5, Rs. 1-9, and Rs. 3-8 respectively. For *abi* lands the figures were Rs. 1-14, Rs. 1-4, and Rs. 1-9.

Including the water rates the total net land revenue demand amounted to Rs. 2,61,557, of which Ajmer contributed Rs. 1,42,896 and Merwāra Rs. 1,18,661. Owing to a new arrangement for the collection of cesses, this net amount cannot be compared with the previous demand of Colonel Dixon. By the new system six per cent. was deducted from the Government demand, 5 per cent. being allowed as the pay of *lambardārs* and 1 per cent. as the pay of *zaildārs* or circle headmen, the remainder constituting the net Government demand. To this was added 10 per cent, $3\frac{1}{8}$ per cent. belonging to the District Funds, and $6\frac{7}{8}$ per cent. belonging to the *Patwārī* Funds. The gross demand exclusive of this 10 per cent. addition may be compared with with Colonel Dixon's figures. Doing so, we find that in Ajmer the assessment was a reduction of 14 per cent. on Colonel Dixon's settlement, and in Merwāra of 25 per cent. For Ajmer-Merwāra the total demand of Colonel Dixon was Rs. 3,56,231, as compared to Rs. 2,86,548 under Mr. LaTouche's settlement. The total assessable area was 311,314 acres and the average holding 5·32 acres.

The principle of joint responsibility was not formally abolished, but one of the main objects of the settlement was to reduce its evils to a minimum. All well-known and recognized divisions of a village were allowed to choose a headman, and each cultivator was permitted the option of deciding through which headman he would pay his revenue. The total amount payable through each *patel* was added up, and a list of each headman's constituents given to the headman and filed with the settlement record. In this way the headmen become the strictly representative body that they ought to be.

The settlement was sanctioned for ten years and expired in 1884. The period, though marked by severe droughts in 1877 and 1878, was on the whole a series of average years, and under the moderate assessment of the settlement, the district made substantial progress. In 1877 the rainfall did not come up to 12 inches, and yet the revenue was paid without any difficulty. All but Rs. 5,857 were collected within the year, and Rs. 1,117 only remitted. Between 1880 and 1884 only Rs. 655 had to be remitted in Ajmer and Rs. 591 in Merwāra. Combined with the progress and prosperity of the district, these figures give ample proof of the general success of the settlement.

Mr. Whiteway's settlement.

That Government were of this opinion is evident from the instructions issued to Mr. Whiteway upon his undertaking the work of re-settling the districts in 1883. In view of the precarious condition of the climate they considered that it would be unwise and dangerous to venture upon any material enhancements of a permanent character. In the circumstances a revision of assessment might not have been necessary at all, had not Government been anxious to take the opportunity of placing the assessment of the province upon such a footing that any future revisions that might be required might be effected on the basis of existing records, upon known principles, and without any addition to the existing establishments of the districts. To secure these objects thoroughly, correct maps and records were to be prepared, and a proper system of maintaining up to date such records established. It was further desired to introduce into the revenue system the principles of suspensions and remissions as approved by Government.

An account of the methods by which the maps were completed and the records framed will be found under the chapter on surveys.

Whether permanent correctness can be claimed for these maps may be doubted. No survey of unculturable ground and topographical features was attempted, and hillsides which were classed as unculturable may in course of time become cultivated by a system of terraces.

The chief innovation in the new settlement was the division of the districts into fluctuating and non-fluctuating areas. It was an extension of the principle already introduced by the previous settlement in the case of the water rate on tank irrigated areas, and its object was the same, to surmount the difficulty of assessing an equal annual demand upon tracts liable to the constant vicissitudes of indifferent seasons. The arrangement, as sanctioned, refers the revenue to a dry rate which can at a future time, should the rise in prices warrant the change, be raised; while, whenever a revision of the revenue is decided on, such revision will merely consist in raising the standard cultivated area, and consequently the standard revenue. On the basis of the assessment rates of the other classes of soil, which are multiples of the assessment dry rate, the areas irrigated from wells or tanks can be expressed in terms of the dry rate. That is to say, if the well rate be ten times the dry rate, then a well-irrigated acre is worth ten dry acres. The total cultivated area of a village, referred by these means to the dry rate, is called the dry unit area. The dry rate to which the revenue is referred is not fixed, but varies within certain limits, and the rate of the year is determined by the standard revenue divided by the dry unit area. When the rate exceeds the maximum, only the maximum is taken and the balance of the revenue is remitted, while when the rate falls below the minimum the mininum is taken and the balance credited to Government. The advantages of the system are that Government and the *zamindār* share equally in the prosperity of good years and losses of calamitous ones. The fluctuating system was applied only to the villages considered most liable to scarcity. In a tract like Ajmer-Merwāra such a distinction was difficult to make. According to the final result of the settlement there are no fluctuating villages in Merwārā. In the Ajmer *tahsīl* out of 142 villages, 61 were assessed as fluctuating. Of these 26 were situated in the Gangwāna circle and 23 in the Rāmsar circle. The system required constant supervision on the part of superior officers, and to it was largely due the appointment of a Revenue Extra Assistant Commissioner sometime later.

In the non-fluctuating villages all increase of cultivation was assessed at the dry rates of the previous settlement, and no increase of irrigated area under wells was to be assessed at well rates. All increase of irrigation from Government tanks, or cultivation in the bed of such tanks, was assessed at tank and *ābi* rates respectively. But the rates paid for irrigation from such tanks and those paid for bed cultivation were revised and raised where necessary. The Settlement Officer also went into the question of tank improvement, and suggested rules for their better management.

The final result of the settlement showed a total assessment of Rs. 2,98,927, as compared with Rs. 2,78,281 of Mr. LaTouche's settlement. The percentage of increase was 8·9 in Ajmer, 4·8 in Beāwar, and 6·9 in Todgarh, without considering the fact that areas in the bed of tanks amounting to 7,176 acres were excluded from the fixed assessed area, and made variable to pay a certain rate on the yearly cultivation. Out of the total assessment, Rs. 61,147 represented the share from the variable villages in Ajmer.

The cultivated area showed a satisfactory advance upon the figures of the previous settlement. Land under well irrigation had increased by 6,304 acres, or 18·9 per cent. In dry cultivation the increase was 12,270 acres, or 11·9 per cent. The total increase of cultivation over the area assessed at Mr. LaTouche's assessment was 10·7 per cent. The number of proprietors had increased by 12 per cent. and that of cultivators decreased by 42 per cent. Taking only the cultivated and fallow land and omitting waste, the average holding was, in Ajmer 7·9 acres, in Beāwar 3·1 acres, and in Todgarh 1·6 acres.

Throughout the district the maximum assessment per acre on land irrigated from wells (*chāhi*) is Rs. 8-2 and the minimum Re. 1-8. In tanks land (*tālābi*) the maximum is Rs. 6 per acre and the minimum Re. 1. In tank bed land (*ābi*) the minimum is As. 8, but the maximum rises to Rs. 6-12 per acre. In dry crop land (*bārāni*) the assessment varies from a maximum of Rs. 1-4 to a minimum of 3 annas 9 pies per acre. As a rule the rates are highest in the Ajmer and Todgarh *tahsīls*.

The settlement was sanctioned for 20 years, and is still in force, although with certain modifications in the case of the variably-assessed villages. In the opinion of the local authorities, this system has proved a failure in practice, in spite of its excellence in theory. It has been unpopular with the people, and Government has at various times consented to allow a fixed assessment to be substituted for the variable system in certain villages. The number of those variably assessed is now only 37.

Suspensions and Remissions of Revenue.

According to the Government order at the time of the 1874 settlement, extraordinary bad seasons were not to be considered in deciding the ordinary assessment; they were to be left to be dealt with by the application of extraordinary remedies, and it has only been by means of generous suspensions and remissions that this settlement has come successfully through the recent famines. In 1895 special rules were introduced for the suspensions and remissions of land revenue. They had previously been granted, but under no well-defined system. By the new rules such a system was initiated, and proposals to suspend or remit now follow promptly upon the occurrence of any local calamity, scarcity, or famine.

Between 1884 and 1890 only Rs. 785 were remitted in Ajmer and Rs. 3,718 in Merwāra. But the next decade tells a different story. During the 10 years in Ajmer Rs. 40,041 were remitted and the collection of Rs. 2,09,694 temporarily suspended. Of the latter amount Rs 46,045, Rs. 67,378 and Rs. 75,838 were suspended in the famine years of 1891-92, 1892-93 and 1899-1900 respectively.

In Merwāra during the same period Rs. 6,769 were remitted, and the large amount of Rs. 4,29,701 was suspended. In 1891-92 Rs. 53,526, in 1892-93 Rs. 88,492, in 1893-94 Rs. 61,881, in 1894-95 Rs. 36,993, in 1898-99 Rs. 37,389 and in 1899-1900 Rs. 1,37,319 remained uncollected at the end of each year respectively. At the end of 1902-03 the outstanding balances of revenue stood at Rs. 1,34,389 in Merwāra and Rs. 89,219 in Ajmer, although remissions to the extent of Rs. 2,55,000 were granted over the two districts on 1st April 1902.

The figures quoted above bear eloquent testimony to the difficulty of assessing an annual demand from a tract like Ajmer-Merwāra to be recovered in good and bad years alike. A general recognition of the principle of suspensions and remissions in famine years, combined with a settlement based on the results of average harvests, is now agreed to be the best form of revenue administration for the districts.

CHAPTER XV.

Miscellaneous Revenue.

Opium.

The Opium revenue is obtained from the duty on opium exported. Ajmer-Merwāra is an opium-growing tract on a small scale, the cultivation being almost entirely restricted to the hilly tracts of Merwāra. Ajmer is nominally a supply centre for the Bombay Presidency, *via* Indore, but no opium has been exported in that direction for some years. Large quantities are still exported to the Panjāb. The import and export of opium to and from Ajmer-Mewāra is regulated under passes, import by rail being permitted only to prescribed railway stations, and export by rail being allowed from the Ajmer railway station only. The levy of an import duty and of a corresponding excise duty upon locally produced opium has recently been sanctioned with effect from the 1st April 1904 and 1st April 1905 respectively.

During the 10 years ending in 1890, the average number of acres under opium cultivation in the *khālsā* area was 2,683. During the next decade the average fell to 1,351 acres. In 1902-03 only 852 acres were so cultivated, the decrease being partly due to more stringent measures for prevention of opium smuggling. During the same period the average numbers of chests exported were 181 and 463 respectively, while 466 were exported in 1902-03. The average Imperial opium receipts, *viz.*, the duty on opium exported during the decade ending in 1890 came to 1·15 lakhs. In the next ten years they were 1·03 lakhs, and 1·31 lakhs in 1902-03. In 1903-04 the duty on opium exported amounted to Rs. 1,01,220.

Salt.

The salt consumed in the province comes from the Government works at Sāmbhar and Pachbhādrā in Rājputāna, and pays revenue there.

Excise.

By rules introduced in 1901 the cultivation of poppy is permitted only under a license to be obtained from the Collector. The licensee may possess crude opium and poppy-heads produced from his land, and dispose of them wholesale to a farmer or licensed vendor or to a person authorized by order in writing of the Collector. The possession of opium, other than preparations used for smoking, in quantities exceeding 5 tolās, and of preparations used for smoking in quantities exceeding one tola, is prohibited throughout the area except to licensed vendors. The right of retail vend is farmed in the four urban areas of Ajmer, Beāwar, Kekri and Nasīrābād, and in the rural areas. In 1900-01 there were ten shops in the urban areas, and the vend fees amounted to Rs. 6,983. In 1903-04 there were 47 shops throughout all Ajmer-Merwāra, and the receipts from farm and vend fees amounted to Rs. 16,079. The quantity of opium issued from the shops was 115 maunds 27 seers 2 chittāks, the incidence of taxation being Rs. 3·75 per seer. As already stated, an excise duty on locally-produced opium will come into force on 1st April 1905.

The arrangements for the control of the spirits resembles the district monopoly system of Bombay. The privilege of manufacturing liquor is leased for a number of years to a contractor, who must have the liquor distilled at the central distillery near Ajmer city. He issues the liquor from the distillery on payment of still-head duty, and removes it to a main depôt, whence it is supplied to the various depôts and shops in the districts. The distillery premises and fittings are the property of the contractor for the time being, but a new contractor is bound to purchase them at a valuation, to be fixed by the local authorities. The distillation is carried on under the supervision of a Government excise inspector. The materials used for distillation are mahua, molasses and toddy. The liquor is either 15°, 25°, or 50° under proof, the duty on which is Rs. 2-4, Rs. 2 and Rs. 1-4 per gallon respectively.

There is a minimum guarantee fixed. If the receipts from still-head duty fall below it in any one year, the Abkāri contractor has to make up the deficiency.

The average annual receipts from the still-head duty during the ten years ending in 1890 were Rs. 93,190 and in the next decade Rs. 93,950. In 1902-03 the receipts were Rs. 76,681.

The number and locality of shops for the retail sale of country liquor are fixed by the Collector, with the sanction of the Commissioner. There are now 145 in the province. The shop-keepers are appointed by the contractor, with the approval of the Collector, and the maximum prices of liquor are fixed by the latter.

The spirit distilled from mahua is by far the most popular; there is little demand for toddy. A preparation of mahua liquor mixed with sugar, aniseed, cardamom and orange, of the strength of 15° and 25° under-proof is sold in sealed bottles under the name of *masāla.*

The 15 *tāzīmi istimrārdārs* in the Ajmer district are allowed by Government to maintain private stills for distillation of liquor from mahua or molasses, but solely for their own consumption. These stills are open to inspection by the superior officers of the Excise Preventive staff, and the liquor distilled is subject to limits fixed by the Collector.

In addition to the receipts from liquor, excise revenue is also derived from the vend of the right to sell by retail the intoxicating drugs—*gānja, charas, bhāng* and *majhūn.* The cultivation of the hemp plant in Ajmer-Merwāra has been prohibited absolutely by rules introduced in 1899. *Majhūn,* however, is manufactured locally. A duty of Rs. 4 per seer on *gānja,* Rs. 6 per seer on *charas,* and Rs. 5 per maund on *bhāng* is levied upon their import into the district. The import must come by rail through the Ajmer Railway Station, must be consigned direct to the Collector of Exise Revenue, and must be removed to a bonded warehouse in Ajmer, where it remains until the duty is paid and it is issued for consumption.

The average receipts from drugs during the ten years ending in 1890 were Rs. 4,904. In the next decade the average rose to Rs. 6,976. In 1903-04 the total receipts from duty and vend fees of drugs amounted to Rs. 11,022. There were 17 retail shops in the districts, and the incidence of hemp drugs revenue per head of the population came to 4½ pies.

A preventive establishment is maintained at a monthly cost of Rs. 910, of which half is paid by Government and half by contributions from the liquor, opium and drugs' contractors. The staff tours in the districts on inspection duty during 3 weeks in every month.

Arrangements have been made with neighbouring Native States by which the latter refrain from placing their liquor shops within three miles from the Ajmer-Merwāra border.

The consumption of liquor has decreased considerably during the last 13 years. The liquor revenue which was Rs. 1,36,997 in 1891-92 had fallen to Rs. 76,681 in 1902-03. For this various causes may be assigned. The depletion of people's resources by famine has made them resort to the cheaper intoxicants, such as drugs, and the surplus available for luxuries has been considerably restricted. Certain classes are debarred from drinking by religious and moral principles, and among others a tendency is said to be growing to confine the consumption of liquor to the occasions of festivals. The excise measures of the Government have the same effect, and the facility and ease with which liquor could formerly be obtained no longer exist.

English education and the general spread of modern ideas is leading, especially in the towns, to an increased demand for imported and European spirits in preference to country liquors, so far as the richer classes are concerned. The duty paid on imported spirits rose from Rs. 2,168 in 1886-87 to Rs. 10,974 in 1896-97, but fell to Rs. 9,426 in 1902-03. In this year 2,355 gallons were imported as against 567 in 1886-87.

Stamps.

The system of stamp revenue is under similar rules to those prevailing in the rest of British India. Licenses are granted to vendors, who are allowed discount upon the sale of stamps, according to a fixed schedule. The Assistant Comissioners of Ajmer and Merwāra are Collectors for the purposes of the rules.

Between 1880 and 1890 the average receipts were Rs. 1,13,543 for non-judicial stamps, and Rs. 86,171 were derived from judicial stamps. In the next decade the average receipts from the latter had risen to Rs. 89,798, while the former had fallen to Rs. 1,10,123. In 1902-03 receipts from judicial and non-judicial stamps were Rs. 86,209 and Rs. 45,129 respectively. The increase and decrease in the revenue from judicial stamps is due to causes affecting the popularity of litigation. In times of famine, civil suits diminish, as little can be recovered from a debtor upon relief works. On the other hand liabilities are contracted which when prosperous seasons return, result in increased litigation. Over an average of ten years, therefore, the figures are not much affected. Among causes affecting revenue from non-judicial stamps may be mentioned the growing popularity of the money order system and the use of currency notes, leading to a decreased demand for foreign bills and hundi stamps, and the growing appreciation of the advantages of legal security for debts resulting in an increased sale of impressed sheets.

Income-tax.

The Assistant Commissioners of Ajmer and Merwāra are the Collectors of Income-tax in their respective charges. An appeal to the Commissioner lies from their decisions.

The net revenue from income-tax from 1886-87 to 1889-90 amounted to Rs. 3,87,686, and in the next decade to Rs. 736,390. In the former period the incidence per head of the population averaged 3 annas $3\frac{1}{2}$ pies per annum, while the number of assessees per thousand averaged 6·5. In the latter period the average annual incidence per head of population came to 2 annas $2\frac{1}{5}$ pies, and the average number of assessees per thousand to 4·2. In 1902-03 the income-tax yielded Rs. 63,245, showing an incidence of 2 annas 1 pie per head of population. The number of assessees amounted to four per thousand.

CHAPTER XVI.

LOCAL AND MUNICIPAL.

District Board.

There is one District Board for both Ajmer and Merwāra, which came into existence on the 1st December 1888. The District Magistrate of Ajmer is chairman, and there are 40 members. Of these 9 are nominated by the Local Government, 6 are elected from Ajmer and 10 from Merwāra. The remaining 15 are composed of the *tāzīmi istimrārdārs* of Ajmer, who are "ex-officio" members. The electorate body is restricted by various qualifications of property and position.

The principal functions of the Board are the upkeep of Local Fund roads, roadside trees and dāk bungalows, and the general management of fairs and tolls throughout the district. It also assists to maintain out of its funds the district dispensaries and the village schools, and decides questions connected with them. In times of scarcity it has frequently started road works in order to relieve local distress. In 1895-96 the Sendra, Kotra, Bhīm-Tītrī, and Beāwar-Nayānagar roads were undertaken chiefly with this object, and in 1896-97 the Chachiāwās-Ararka road was improved for the same reason. But in times of real famine, these obligations are more restricted; regular relief works are started by Government, and it frequently happens that even Local Fund roads are repaired by famine labour paid from Imperial Funds. The Board holds a position of responsibility with reference to the well-being of the district, and upon occasion it has made free distributions of quinine throughout the villages during the prevalence of fevers.

During the ten years ending 1900 the average receipts amounted to Rs. 35,121 and the average expenditure to Rs. 36,541. The largest source of receipts was Provincial rates, which averaged Rs. 20,081. In the expenditure the heaviest items were education (Rs. 8,284), medical (Rs. 6,277), and public works (Rs. 13,667). This last item was exceptionally heavy owing to the number of works undertaken to relieve local scarcity. In 1902-03 the receipts rose to Rs. 76,622 and the expenditure to Rs. 41,188. Only Rs. 4,014 were spent on public works in 1900-01, as Government had undertaken relief operations on a large scale, and, as explained above, the usual repairs to many District Fund roads were carried out from Imperial Funds by famine labourers. Medical expenses were, however, heavy, amounting to Rs. 8,814 and were necessitated by the epidemic of fever which swept the country during the cold weather. In 1902-03 the charges under public works and medical were Rs. 16,543 and Rs. 7,038 respectively.

There are three municipalities in the district, at Ajmer, Beāwar and Kekri. Beāwar was first established in 1867, Ajmer followed in 1869 and Kekri in 1879. Until 1889 they were under the provisions of the North-West Provinces and Oudh Municipalities Act, but in that year it was repealed and replaced by Regulation V of 1886, which continues in force at present. Local rules applying to each municipality have been framed under the various sections of the Regulation. **Municipalities.**

Until 1884 the Ajmer municipal committee, consisting both of Europeans and natives, was entirely nominated by the district authorities. Its chairman was the District Magistrate. After 1884 the elective system was introduced, and in the year 1888 the municipality came under the provisions of Regulation V of 1886. Under the rules the Committee consists of 18 elected members, including a chairman and a number of members nominated by the Local Government who cannot exceed one-fourth of the total number of the Committee. They usually amount to five. For elective and executive purposes the municipality is divided into four wards, *viz.*, the City, Kaisarganj, Suburban and Railway wards. These wards are entitled to return nine, two, three and three members respectively. The electorate body is restricted by residence, educational and property qualifications. There are no ex-officio members among them. As a rule the committee contains some 6 or 7 Europeans, including the nominated members. **Ajmer.**

The chief source of the municipal revenues is the octroi, the incidence of which, per head of the population of 73,839 persons, amounts to Rs. 1-12 per annum nearly. Its average for the ten years ending 1900 was Rs. 1,16,617. The average total income for the same period was Rs. 1,94,286. The year 1902-03 showed a decrease from this average, only Rs. 1,83,551 being received. The expenditure during the decade averaged Rs. 1,84,286, out of which conservancy claimed Rs. 32,203, and administration and collection of taxes Rs. 38,752. The expenditure on public works averaged Rs. 11,621. In 1902-03 municipal expenditure amounted to Rs. 1,56,913.

The efficiency of the working of the municipality is shown by the various improvements that have taken place since 1885. In 1886 a conservancy tramway was constructed at a cost of about Rs. 1,00,000, by which the sweepings and nightsoil are taken 3 miles away from the city to the trenches. An Assistant Health Officer has been appointed, the conservancy staff has been strengthened, and the number of public sanitary conveniences increased. The health of the town has further been ensured by the completion upon sanitary lines of the suburb of Kaisarganj, which has relieved the congestion in the city. The Rājputāna-Mālwā Railway has built good houses for its employees near the workshops and in the suburb known as Jones Ganj. New roads have been constructed giving easy access to the Railway Station from all parts of the city. In 1900 the Trevor Town Hall was built, and provides a large hall for public purposes as well as a municipal office. The municipal committee subscribed Rs. 19,000 towards the cost of its construction.

The water supply of the town has received attention. The Foy Sāgar scheme was completed in 1892. In 1886 the dhōbis' *ghāts*, bathing *ghāts*, and a cattle trough in the Bīsla tank were constructed at a cost of Rs. 40,000, and ensure a supply of clean water for washing clothes, bathing and watering cattle. The drinking supply has been further extended by sinking a large well in the Daulat Bāgh. The Ana Sāgar catchment area was increased in 1885-86 by the making of the east feeder.

Other departments have also improved. Vaccination has been made compulsory, and a special staff is employed for the registration of vital statistics. A bonded warehouse has been constructed for storing dutiable articles which are intended re-export. Five new police outposts have been established and the force has been strengthened. Cattle pound and slaughter-house arrangements have been improved. Trees have been planted along the roads and in the public gardens. Owing to municipal supervision the class of hackney carriages available has risen considerably. Larger grants are now made for educational purposes. The municipal accounts are audited by the Examiner, Public Works Accounts, Rājputāna and Central India.

Beāwar. The population within Beāwar municipal limits in 1901 was 21,928 persons. The town was first given a system of municipal government in 1867. Before 1881 the municipal committee consisted of 15 members, of whom 12 were elected and 3 were ex-officio members. After 1888 the committee was increased to 20 members, at which strength it now stands. Out of these 4 are "ex-officio" members, one is nominated by Government and the rest are elected. The Assistant Commissioner, Merwāra, is the chairman. Of the elected members there must be 9 Hindus, 4 Muhammadans and 2 Christians. Including the chairman there are generally two or three European members. The electorate is restricted by a tenancy or property qualification. Prior to 1888 elections were held triennially; thereafter till 1897 a third of the elected members went out of office annually; since 1897 elections are held triennially, when all elected and nominated members go out of office.

During the ten years ending in 1900 the total annual income averaged Rs. 49,525, of which octroi accounted for Rs. 39,184. The annual expenditure averaged Rs. 49,712, of which the largest item was Rs. 18,603 for charges on account of administration and the collection of taxes. In 1902-03 the receipts and expenditure were Rs. 57,016 and Rs. 60,196 respectively. Of the latter figures the chief items, besides administration and collection charges (Rs. 29,263), were public safety (Rs. 6,072), education (Rs. 5,387,) and conservancy (Rs. 7,360). In this year the incidence of octroi taxation per head of the population was Rs. 2-7.

Since the changes of 1884-85 came into operation, considerable improvements have been effected in the working of the municipal system in Beāwar. They are to be found in all the departments. Vaccination has recently been made compulsory instead of optional, and the contributions paid to the medical institutions have increased steadily. The police force has risen from a strength of 36 to one of 48. Improved rules for the registration of vital statistics were introduced in 1894. Taxes are still collected by direct agency, but changes in detail have taken place leading to increased powers of check and efficiency, specially in the octroi department. The limit of refunds of octroi was raised from 4 annas in 1891 to Rupee 1 in 1896, and recently has been further raised to Rs. 2. Conservancy arrangements have been improved, iron carts have been substituted for those of wood, and the nightsoil sweepings are sold as manure. Wells have been deepened to secure a more permanent water supply, and the town has recently come through a period of prolonged drought without serious inconvenience or any epidemic arising. In 1900 it was decided to entertain the services of a paid European secretary, with qualifications as engineer and overseer, in order to secure efficient control over the various departments.

Tho population of Kekri municipality according to the 1901 census was 7,053. The only municipal taxation is the octroi. The average income from the tax during the ten years ending in 1900 has been Rs. 9,182, which gives an incidence of Rs. 1-4-8 per annum per head of the inhabitants. The average income from all sources during the ten years has been Rs. 11,112, and the average expenditure Rs. 10,690. Of the latter amount administration expenses and refunds account for Rs. 4,069, while expenditure on public works averaged Rs. 1,578. In 1902-03 the total income was Rs. 14,874 and expenditure Rs. 13,982. The incidence of octroi taxation per head of population was Rs. 1-13-5. **Kekri.**

The Extra Assistant Commissioner in charge of Kekri is the chairman of the municipal committee, which consists of 8 members besides himself. The members are not elected, but are nominated by the Chief Commissioner on the recommendation of the chairman, through the Assistant Commissioner, Ajmer. They retire by rotation every three years, but the outgoing members are eligible for re-appointment. The sanitary condition of the town and the water supply are fair, and no epidemic disease has so far occurred within its limits. The town owes its importance and the establishment of a municipality to the fact that at one time it bade fair to become a chief entrepôt for the cotton trade of Mewār. In this respect it is now eclipsed by Beāwar.

CHAPTER XVII.

PUBLIC WORKS.

Public Works Department.

Ajmer-Merwāra is, for purposes of Public Works, a Provincial division under an Executive Engineer, assisted by three sub-divisional officers. The sub-divisions are Ajmer, Nasīrābād and Merwāra. The two first are in charge of two upper subordinates, and the last is under the charge of a lower subordinate, who has his head-quarters at Beāwar. Five sub-overseers are attached to the division to assist the three sub-divisional officers. The Public Works Department looks after all the civil Government buildings, the roads and irrigation tanks in the Division and military buildings, except at Nasīrābād. District Fund and municipal suburban roads are also in its charge, the Executive Engineer being the professional adviser of the president of the District Board, and of the chairmen of the Ajmer, Beāwar and Kekri municipalities respectively.

Road and tank construction.

Between the date of the British occupation of the district and 1869 the attention of the Public Works was mainly confined to the roads. During these years the Nasīrābād-Deoli road, the Grand Trunk road from the Jaipur border to Mārwār, the Ajmer-Nasīrābād and the Ajmer-Pushkar road were constructed. Before 1869 all the tanks built in Ajmer and Merwāra were constructed by the Civil Department, and chiefly through the energy of Colonel Dixon. In this year an Irrigation division was added to the Public Works Department, and all tank works since constructed have been carried out by it. Among the more notable may be mentioned the Nadi Nala tank in 1872, Balād in 1873, Jāliā in 1875, Bīr in 1876, Dānta in 1877, Makrera in 1879, Lādpura in 1881, and Kāir tank in 1892-93. During the famine years 1898-00 the department carried out the doubling of the railway embankment line between Tilaurniā and Madārpura and between Ajmer and Kharwa. It also constructed the earthworks of the projected lines between Nasīrābād and Kekri, Kekri and Sāwar and part of the embankment for the Bārān-Mārwār line.

The department is also responsible for the construction of the fine public buildings erected in Ajmer during recent years. The Ajmer Government College was built in 1869-70, and the Ajmer District Courts between 1873 and 1876. The Mayo College was constructed in 1878-1885, the Ajmer Court of Wards Office in 1890-91, the Victoria Jubilee Clock Tower in 1891-92, the Ajmer General Hospital in 1894-95, and Trevor Town Hall in 1899-1900.

Water schemes.

The only large municipal water scheme completed by the department is that which supplies Ajmer with water from the Foy Sāgar reservoir, situated 3 miles to the south-west of the town. The reservoir was constructed from municipal funds in 1892 by throwing a dam across the Bāndi river. The tank when full is 30 feet deep, and has a cubic capacity of 150 million cubic feet, sufficient to supply all the requirements of Ajmer city, civil station and railway for about two years. The water flows by gravitation through a 12-inch iron pipe, and commands the general level of the town. If, however, the depth of the water in the reservoir falls below 6 feet, the height of the outlet bed, it has to be raised into the pipe by pumping operations. It is sufficiently pure for most purposes, and undergoes scarcely any filtration. During the past decade the severe droughts have seriously affected the Foy Sāgar, and it has twice been found necessary to bring water from the Budha Pushkar lake, 5 miles to the north-west of Ajmer. The water there is of a very pure quality, and is never known to fail, but as a high barrier exists between it and Ajmer, it can only be obtained by costly pumping. For this reason the line of iron piping between this lake and the town is only used in case of any temporary failure of the Foy Sāgar supply.

In the case of famine the provision of a programme of works, and supervision of them when started, are duties of the Public Works Department.

CHAPTER XVIII.

ARMY.

Nasīrābād.

There are three military stations in the district—Nasīrābād, Deoli and Ajmer, the two latter being garrisoned by local corps.

The cantonment of Nasīrābād is situated on a bleak, bare plain, which slopes eastward from the farthest range of the Arāvalli Hills in this direction. The drainage is good, but there is a great lack of sweet water. All the wells in the cantonment are brackish and many are quite bitter. Water for the troops is carried a distance of about three miles. There is also a pipe, by which water is brought from the wells at Dānta some four miles away.

The lines of Nasīrābād were laid out in 1818 by Sir David Ochterlony, who early in the year had marched into Rājputāna with a force of eight regiments of infantry, one of cavalry and a proportionate amount of artillery, with a view of effecting the dispossession of Amīr Khān's forces, and confirming the newly-formed and renewed treaties of alliance and protection with the States of Rājputāna. Two accounts are given of the origin of the name. According to one it was after a fakīr, Nasīr Shāh, whom the General found living in the place. According to the other the name is derived from the title of Nasīr-ud-daula, which Shāh Alam conferred on Sir David Ochterlony for his defence of Delhi against Holkar in 1804. The cantonment is laid out in a continuous stretch of over a mile in length, the lines of the troops being to the windward of the officers' bungalows, to the leeward of which is a large irregularly-built open town with about 20,000 inhabitants. The garrison consists of a battery of Royal Field Artillery, 6 companies of British infantry, a regiment of Bombay infantry and a squadron of Bombay cavalry from the regiment at Nīmach. It is directly under a Colonel on the Staff, but forms part of the Mhow division of the Western Army Corps.

As a military station Nasīrābād is important in being most centrally situated for operations in Rājputāna. It is the nearest considerable military station to Jaipur and Jodhpur, and well placed for the rapid despatch of troops in the direction of Udaipur, Bīkāner or Indore.

The cantonment is administered by a cantonment committee, under the Cantonment Code of 1899, and the Cantonment Magistrate exercises civil and criminal jurisdiction within its limits. Nasīrābād possesses a chaplain of the Church of England appointed by the the Bishop of Bombay, and a Roman Catholic chaplain. The former is supposed to minister to the spiritual wants of the European inhabitants of Tāragarh, Beāwar and Deoli also. The Cantonment Magistrate is the Registrar of Births and Deaths under the Commissioner, Ajmer-Merwāra, as Registrar-General. The Administrator-General of Bengal takes charge of the estates of persons dying intestate.

The cantonment of Deoli is about 70 miles from Ajmer, in the midst of native territory, but the cantonment itself is considered part of the Ajmer district. It is garrisoned by a local crops called the 42nd Deoli Regiment, formerly called the Deoli Irregular Force. After the Mutiny a regiment of Bengal cavalry was also stationed at Deoli, but it was removed at the time of the last Afghān war. Deoli.

The 42nd Deoli Regiment consists of a squadron of cavalry and and a battalion of infantry, with a total of 7 British officers and 812 native rank and file. The infantry is recruited from the Mīnās, a predatory tribe who have been enlisted with a view to weaning them from unlawful pursuits; the sawārs are principally Sikhs. The commandant of the force is also Cantonment Magistrate, and disposes of the few magisterial cases which arise from time to time.

The 44th Merwāra Infantry, formerly known as the Merwāra Battalion, whose head-quarters were removed from Beāwar to Ajmer in 1871, deserves a more extended notice, as it was largely instrumental in the pacification and civilization of Merwāra; and the Resolution of the Governor-General in Council, dated 20th June 1822, which directed the formation of a local corps in Merwāra, yields to none in the importance among the measures adopted to reclaim the Mers from their predatory habits. The nucleus of the regiment then raised was composed of drafts from the Rāmpura local battalion, which in its turn had been formed from the remnants of the army of the notorious Amīr Khān. The total strength of the new battalion was fixed at 680 of all ranks, divided into 8 companies. Vacancies for 340 Mers as sepoys were reserved, and a certain proportion of the commissioned and non-commissioned posts were set apart for those Mers who should qualify themselves to hold them. The corps was cantoned near the old town of Beāwar, about 30 miles south-west of Ajmer, then in the midst of a waste and uncultivated tract of country. At first there was considerable difficulty in obtaining recruits, but 100 Mers of ages from 50 to 14 years were induced to enlist by a largess of five rupees and the favorable influence of a general feast. Not only was it difficult to enlist men, but it was still more difficult to retain them after they had enlisted. Many returned to their villages, being unable to brook the restraints of military service. The regiment, however, soon found no difficulty in attracting men to its standard; some of the most smart and deserving recruits were rapidly promoted; the first feeling of mistrust soon gave way to one of attachment to the service, and while the battalion gained in popularity it also gained a creditable standard of efficiency from a military point of view. Ajmer. 44th Merwāra Infantry.

During the early years of the existence of the battalion many Mer sepoys used to take their discharge on the completion of three years service, by which time they had generally managed to save sufficient money to purchase a pair of bullocks. They then returned to their villages and took to agriculture. In this way the number of those who in the new regiment had learned what duty was, and who had acquired habits of discipline, obedience, cleanliness, and good faith, was sufficiently great to influence the inhabitants of Merwāra in the direction of industry and order. In 1835 a system of agricultural advances was established, and from that date discharges, though still numerous, were much less frequent. In 1823 the cantonments were moved 4 miles south, adjacent to what was subsequently the site of the town of Nayānagar. In 1825 the battalion was augmented by the addition of ten men per company, thus raising its strength to 760 of all ranks. The immediate cause of the augmentation was severe detachment duty on the outposts in the Merwāra hills. This did not, however, prevent two companies being detached to Ajmer in 1832—one as the escort of the Agent Governor-General, the other as a city guard. In 1838 this quota was reduced by half on account of the excessive strain on the corps.

It was not till the year 1839 that the battalion saw any active service, but in that year it was found necessary to despatch a force composed of the Merwāra Battalion and the Jodhpur Legion against several outlawed thākurs of Mārwār, who, under the leadership of one Chiman Singh Champāwat, had for several years devoted themselves to pillage and highway robbery, and whom the Mahārāja of Jodhpur was unable to subdue. The outlaws had established their head-quarters in the wild country near the town of Kot in Merwāra, at the entrance of the Dewair pass. The two regiments, under the command of Captain Dixon, moved on the enemy from different directions, and after a sharp struggle succeeded in completely dislodging the outlaws and breaking up the band, many of whom with their leader, Chiman Singh, were killed in the action. The loss of the regiment was only 8 men killed and wounded, and the thanks of the Governor-General were accorded to Captain Dixon, while the conduct of the battalion met with high commendation. In the autumn of the same year the services of the regiment were again put into requisition for the expedition against Jodhpur, but as Mahārāja Mān Singh submitted to all demands, no hostilities occurred, and the force was marched back to its quarters at Beāwar. With this event ends all that need be said of the Merwāra Battalion till the Mutiny of 1857.

The troops at Nasīrābād mutinied on the 28th May 1857. Early notice having been conveyed to Colonel Dixon, commanding the battalion at Beāwar, he at once ordered a company to move on Ajmer. By a forced march of 33 miles during the night, Lieut. W. Carnell, commanding the detachment, was enabled to occupy the magazine at Ajmer before information of the occurrences at Nasīrābād had reached the company of the 15th Native Infantry then garrisoning the magazine. It consequently permitted itself to be relieved and marched to Nasīrābād, and by this prompt measure the safety of Ajmer was assured. The detachment was subsequently strengthened by further re-inforcements from Beāwar. During the course of the mutiny, a detachment of the battalion was employed with the Rājputna field force under Major-General Sir G. St. Patrick Lawrence, and moved against the mutineers of the Jodhpur Legion, who had established themselves in the walled town of Awāh in Mārwār. For its services and for the unshaken fidelity and loyalty displayed by the corps, all men serving with the battalion on 1st July 1857, were rewarded with the grant of the same pay and privileges for pension as soldiers of the line.

In December 1857 the Government of India authorized the formation of a second Mer regiment to be stationed at Ajmer. The Merwāra Battalion was reduced by two companies, which were drafted into the new regiment. The strength of the united corps was 1,500 men, but the new battalion enjoyed only a short existence. In 1861 it was reduced and amalgamated with the old Merwārā Battalion, which was raised to a strength of 1,000 of all ranks, the new battalion being called the Merwāra Police Battalion, and put under the control of the Police Department of the North-West Provinces. By this measure the battalion, with tbe exception of the men on whom special privileges had been conferred as a reward for loyalty during the mutiny, was deprived of the advantages in respect of pay and pension, which were afterwards conferred on the local military corps of Rājputāna. The men were consequently discontented, while the regiment was practically useless for police purposes. These among other cogent reasons induced Lord Mayo in 1870 to re-organize the battalion into a purely military corps. The numbers were reduced to 712 of native ranks divided into 8 companies. The pay of the men was raised from Rs. 5-8 to Rs. 7 a month, and they were granted the same privileges as regard pension and allowances as the other local infantry corps in Rājputāna. At the same time the head-quarters were transferred from Beāwar to Ajmer, where they are at present.

In 1878 the regiment took part in the Afghān campaign, and in 1901 were mobilized for service in Jubaland, but the expedition terminated without the necessity of sending re-inforcements. In 1897 the battalion was placed under the orders of the Commander-in-Chief in India. Its present strength consists of 4 British officers, and 712 native rank and file. The Civil Surgeon, Ajmer, is in medical charge of the regiment. Although during its earlier history many outsiders were found in the ranks, it is now recruited entirely from Mers and Kāthāt Merāts.

The regiment., however, has ceased to be what it was in former days, a school through which the greater part of the youth of the country passed; and more especially since the removal of the head-quarters to Ajmer, its influence on what may be called the home aspects of the corps has been much diminished. While the battalion was at Beāwar, the soldiers, who enlisted for the most part from the villages immediately adjacent, were allowed to go to their homes after parade in the morning, they worked all day in their fields, and were back to cantonments by night. Leave was often applied for by those whose homes were at a greater distance, and freely granted. The men therefore continued practically to form a part of the agricultural population: they met their relations frequently, and their pay went often to the common stock, whereas soldiering has now become a profession. Men who enlist do so for their lifetime, and only take their discharge when invalided or entitled to their full pension. After their term of service is over, they invariably settle down on their ancestral land, and have probably saved enough to dig a well for its improvement. Here they spend the remainder of their days, and have generally considerable influence in the villages, especially those who have attained to the rank of *subahdār* or *jamādār* in the battalion.

Volunteers. Ajmer is also the head-quarters of the 2nd Battalion, Bombay, Baroda and Central India Railway Volunteer Rifles. The corps originally formed part of the Agra Volunteer Rifle Corps, with the title of Rājputāna-Mālwa Volunteer Rifle Corps. In 1887 its title was changed to the present designation. It consists of 11 companies, including a cadet company at Mount Abu. Its strength in June 1903 stood at 344. The grand total of troops of all arms within the province on 1st June 1903 was 2,515, of which 789 were British and 1,726 Native.

CHAPTER XIX.

POLICE AND JAILS.

Before 1861 Ajmer-Merwāra had no regular police. The general peace of the district was maintained by the local military force, known as the Merwāra Battalion, whose head-quarters were at Beāwar: the village watchmen and the pecuniary responsibility of *istimrārdārs*, *bhumiās*, and *jāgīrdārs* assisted to prevent crime in local areas. About Rs. 35,000 were spent annually upon the upkeep of the *chaukidārs* in the villages and towns. **Early Police.**

Owing to the loyal spirit shown by the Merwāra Battalion in the mutiny, a second Mer regiment was raised in 1857, with head-quarters at Ajmer. Financial reasons, however, led to its reduction in 1861, or rather to its amalgamation with the old Merwāra Battalion, the strength of which was raised to 1,000 of all ranks, the designation of the latter being changed to Merwāra Police Battalion, the corps being removed from the military establishment and placed under the orders of the Inspector-General of Police, North-West Provinces. Out of the savings resulting from the abolition of the Mer regiment, an organized constabulary consisting of 548 men, under a District Superintendent of Police, was established from the 1st January 1862. From the same date the provisions of the Police Act (V of 1861) were extended to the districts.

The arrangement by which the Merwāra Battalion was classed as police was soon found to be unsatisfactory. It was extremely unpopular with the men, while for regular police purposes the regiment was practically useless. So in 1870 it was restored to its purely military character.

In 1871 when Ajmer-Merwāra was taken under the direct management of the Government of India, the local police force was transferred from the control of the Inspector-General of Police, North-West Provinces, to that of the Commissioner, Ajmer-Merwāra. Since then the District Superintendent of Police has acted under his orders. Between 1862 and 1882 successive schemes of reorganization caused fluctuations in the numbers of the police force, but since the latter date there has been little change. In 1902 the strength was 704 of all grades, which gives a policeman to every 3·8 square miles, and to every 677·4 of the population of the district. The supervising staff consists of a District Superintendent and 3 Inspectors. There are 13 sub-inspectors, 93 head constables, 37 mounted constables and 556 foot constables. The force is distributed among 18 police stations and 38 outposts throughout the districts. Ajmer has 7 first class and 6 second class stations. In Merwāra there are 3 first class and 2 of the **Organization and strength.**

second class. The cost of maintenance has risen from Rs. 86,423 in 1881 to Rs. 1,14,689 in 1902. Of the latter amount Rs. 27,128 is paid from sources other than Imperial.

The recruiting for the force is done locally, but men come in for service from the Panjāb, the United Provinces of Agra and Oudh, and the surrounding Native States. As a rule there is no difficulty in obtaining recruits. The men are trained at the Ajmer head-quarters before being drafted to other stations and outposts. The general attitude of educated natives towards the police is satisfactory, and men of good family and educational attainments are willing to take service in the force.

Rural Police. As a connecting link between the villagers and the regular police, both for the detection of crime and supervision of bad characters, a good *chaukidāri* or village police is most valuable. This has always been recognized in Ajmer-Merwāra, and in 1871 the numbers of the rural police stood at 398. About that time the minimum pay was raised from Rs. 3 to Rs. 4 per month. In 1902 the rural police force in *khālsa* and *jāgīr* villages numbered 205 and in the *istimrāri* areas 191. The cost of the former was Rs. 11,044 and of the latter Rs. 9,564. Besides the *chaukidārs* there are in many villages menial classes, who for a small annual contribution of corn from the villagers perform in a perfunctory way some of a watchman's duties.

The railway police on the Rājputāna-Malwā Railway belong to the Bombay establishment, and are under the orders of the Inspector-General of Police of that province.

Cognizable Cases. During the average of five years ending in 1901 the number of cognizable cases reported was 4,699. Of these 3,445 were decided in the criminal courts, 237 cases ending in acquittal and 3,208 in convictions. The period includes the famine of 1898-1900, when the crime incidence was above the normal. The averages show one crime per ·57 square miles of area and 101 of population. Detection is fairly successful, in spite of the facilities for criminals of escaping and hiding in the surrounding Native States. Finger impressions have proved useful in tracing previously-convicted offenders.

Jails. There is only one jail in the districts—the Ajmer central jail. The average number of prisoners daily was 540 in 1902, as compared with 407 in 1891 and 429 in 1881. The famine of 1898-1900 and the conditions in Merwāra in 1901 resulted in a criminality which raised the jail population to the highest point yet reached.

Although the jail is built on one of the most healthy sites in Ajmer, it did not escape the epidemics of fever and pneumonia that swept the country in 1891 and 1902. In these years the death-rate was 27 per mille and 29·6 per mille respectively. In 1881 under normal conditions it was only 4·66 per mille. Carpets and rugs of excellent quality and good cotton *durrīs* are made to order in the jail. A coarse cotton cloth is also manufactured and dyed, which finds a good market locally for the clothing of the poorer classes. The profits in these manufactures have risen steadily from Rs. 2,883 in 1881 to Rs. 3,472 in 1891 and to Rs. 3,881 in 1902.

The expenditure on jail maintenance was Rs. 18,769 in 1881, Rs. 26,686 in 1891 and Rs. 25,385 in 1902. The cost per prisoner in each of these years works out at Rs. 43-15-9, Rs. 65-8 and Rs. 46-15-4 respectively.

In addition to the central jail there are three lock-ups at Ajmer, Nasīrābād and Beāwar for prisoners under trial in the courts at these places. One at Kekri is also under contemplation for the same purpose. In the event of courts being held in other places the prisoners are kept in the ordinary lock-ups attached to police stations.

CHAPTER XX.

EDUCATION.

Education in former times.

In the early days of the British occupation of Ajmer, with the exception of a monthly subsidy of Rs. 300 to an English missionary who had established a school in the city, little attempt was made by Government to provide for the education of the people.

Instruction was confined to the indigenous schools, which in the year 1845-46 numbered 56, of which 42 with a roll of 807 pupils were Hindi and Sanskrit schools, and 14 with 266 pupils Persian and Arabic schools. The cities of Ajmer and Shāhpura, capital of the present Shāhpura chiefship, had 13 Persian and 20 Hindi schools, and the rest were situated in the villages. It was noted as significant of the aversion of Rājputs to intellectual improvement, that very few of that caste were to be found in the Hindi schools and not one in the Persian schools. In the year 1836 a Government school was established in Ajmer, with a European head-master and two native teachers for Hindi and one for Urdu. At the end of 1837 the number of pupils stood at 219, and for some years the school was fairly prosperous. But afterwards it declined both in numbers and efficiency, and was finally abolished in 1843. The next decade showed a desire for improvment on the part of the people, and Colonel Dixon points out that not only had the vernacular schools increased in Ajmer but one for teaching English had been started by private effort. The time appeared favourable, and Government decided to open a school in 1851, with an idea that it might ultimately become a college, if funds permitted. A Superintendent was appointed, with one English and nine Native assistants, and in the year 1853 there were 230 students, of which 44 were Muhammadans and 186 Hindus. In 1861 the school was affiliated to the Calcutta University, and in 1868 was raised to the position of a college, but with a staff of teachers limited to the requirements of the First Arts examination of the Calcutta University.

Ajmer Government College.

The College at Ajmer is a commodious building, situated about a mile from the city. It teaches up to the B. A. standard, and in the same building the higher classes of a High School. The staff consists of a European Principal, a Vice-Principal, three professors and thirteen assistant professors and teachers. Attached to the College is a lower school, the staff of which consists of 9 English and 14 vernacular teachers. Also in connection with the College there is a boarding house for the accommodation of boys from the village schools who have obtained scholarships, and 54 boys resided here on the 31st March 1903. Provision is being made for the accommodation of 20 more.

The number of students in 1891 was 411, and 266 in 1903. The efficiency has steadily increased: the University results in 1881 were 4 Matriculation and 2 Intermediate passes; in 1891 there were 15 Matriculation passes and 1 Intermediate. In 1903, 23 students passed the Matriculation examination and 10 the Intermediate, and 8 obtained the B.A. degree.

The cost of the College in 1902-03 was Rs. 32,119, of which Provincial revenues paid Rs. 23,539, District and municipal funds Rs. 2,580, while the balance come from fees and other sources.

Secondary Schools.

Connected with the Government College at Ajmer through a system of inspection, are the secondary schools, aided and unaided, and the primary schools of Ajmer-Merwāra. The inspection of those schools has long been a duty attached to the office of the Principal of the College, who is assisted in it by two Deputy Inspectors. The public secondary institutions in Ajmer-Merwāra numbered 14 in 1903, with a total of 2,465 pupils. Of these 5 are high schools with 1,567 pupils, and 9 are middle schools. There were also 19 advanced private schools with 450 pupils. The public institution figures showed a satisfactory advance upon those of 1891, which were 11 schools (3 high schools and 8 middle schools) with 1,837 pupils, but the famines had reduced the number of higher private schools, which in 1891 stood at 33 with 1,168 pupils.

Primary Schools.

Primary education before 1850 was left entirely in the hands of the indigenous schools supported by the people, and without interference from Government. But shortly after Colonel Dixon's assessment in that year, 75 schools were established in Ajmer-Merwāra, and the people were induced to defray a large portion of their cost by means of a cess. The number was subsequently reduced to 57, and the contributions were continued as long as Colonel Dixon lived. An inspector for village schools was appointed for the Ajmer district in 1851, and one for Merwāra in 1852. After Colonel Dixon's death, however, the clamours of the people against the cess became so violent, that Government authorized the cessation of the contribution, and all schools except those supported by Government were closed. The intensity of the unpopularity may be gathered from the fact that, when the sister-in-law of the Bhinai Rājā performed *sati* in 1857, the last request of Brāhmans who surrounded the pyre was that she would use her influence for the abolition of the cess for village schools. The teachers in the indigenous schools were as a class badly paid and incompetent, and the Government inspector writing in 1858 gave it as his opinion that, as long as they continued to be so, "popular education through the indigenous schools existing in this province is a hopeless sham and a delusion." An earlier report had noted the small amount of knowledge acquired in spite of the great length of time during which the boys prosecuted their studies—"when they leave school after having spent some 10 or 12 years in the Persian, 12 or 13 years in the Arabic schools, they possess little beyond a mechanical knowledge of the Korān and an equally mechanical knowledge of office style."

In 1871 upon the transfer of the province to the direct control of the Government of India, the educational department was also severed from that of the North-West Provinces and was placed under the Commissioner, Ajmer-Merwāra, as Director of Public Instruction. In 1891 there were 47 upper primary schools, with a total attendance of 3,082 pupils. Besides these public institutions 2,777 children were being educated in 83 elementary private schools. The famines of the next decade caused a distinct retrogression in primary education. But it was made up in 1903, when, though the number of private elementary schools had fallen to 71, the number of pupils had increased by 848. The public primary schools had risen to 50, but the number of pupils did not keep pace and had sunk to 2,843. Both years, however, show an improvement compared with 1881, in which year there were 67 public and 60 private primary schools, with a total attendance between them of 4,785 pupils. The proportion of boys under education to those of a school-going age was 12·8 per cent. in 1881, 13·5 per cent. in 1891, and 12·5 per cent. in 1903. The public primary schools are managed by the educational department, under the Commissioner as Director of Public Instruction. The department receives and disburses not only Government funds in the case of schools that are maintained entirely by Government, but also District Funds and municipal contributions towards the expenses of these schools. The department also receives the school fees and spends them. The pay of the teachers varies from Rs. 100 per month paid to the head-master of the Government Branch School at Ajmer to Rs. 6, the salary of the lowest grade masters in the department. Out of the 50 primary public schools, 7 are girls' schools and 42 are village schools (*halkābandi*). In 1903 the total cost of the primary public schools was Rs. 17,722, of which Imperial revenues paid Rs. 6,105, cesses and municipal funds Rs. 7,351; Rs. 3,232 were derived from fees and Rs. 1,034 from other sources.

Normal and Industrial Schools.

A training school for male teachers in the primary and secondary schools in the province was started in Ajmer in 1864. In 1867 a similar institution was begun for the training of female teachers. In 1890-91 there were 20 males and 4 females under instruction. The female normal school was found not to work well and was abolished in 1893. There were 9 pupils at the male normal school in 1902-03.

The United Free Church of Scotland mission at Beāwar maintains a normal school for training the teachers for its village schools. The same mission supports the only industrial school in the districts at its Ashāpura orphanage. Eight workshops are now established there, and the boys are taught carpentry, smiths' work, pottery, tailoring, masonry, shoemaking, weaving and gardening. In 1901 there was an average daily attendance of 481.

Female education.

As was to be expected among the conservative and backward population of Ajmer-Merwāra, female education has progressed but slowly. Even now it is confined to the public primary, and elementary private schools. Of the former there are, as already mentioned, 7 schools for girls only. In the ordinary village schools girls, when they attend, are educated along with the boys and in the same subjects. In the special girls' schools, besides reading, writing and arithmetic, they are taught knitting and sewing.

Taking private and public institutions together, we find that in 1890-91 there were 567 girls being educated in 19 schools. Their percentage to the female population of a school-going age was 1·5. Similarly in 1903 the total number of female schools and scholars was 30 and 1,840 respectively, giving a percentage to the female population of a school-going age of 5·4. This progress shown in a decade of famine is satisfactory, and indicates that prejudices against female education are gradually disappearing. The tendency is most marked among the Brāhman and Mahājan communities. The Muhammadans with their traditional *pardāh* system, and the Rājputs with their invincible conservatism lag far behind.

Schools for European children. In the year 1881 there was only one school in the province for European children—the Railway school at Ajmer. In that year the number of pupils was 29, and in 1891 it had risen to 94. In 1896-97, however, a school for European boys and girls was started by the Roman Catholic Convent at Ajmer. This at once attracted all the children of Roman Catholic parentage, and the numbers at the Railway school decreased accordingly. In 1903 they stood at 57, as against 88 pupils attending the Convent school. Both are classed as secondary schools and receive grants, the former of Rs. 75 and the latter of Rs. 100 per month from Government.

Hindu and Muhammadan education. As the Hindu population is considerably in excess of the Muhammadan, it is only to be expected that their numbers in the various schools should also be greater. If, however, percentages of the school-going population of either class be taken, the Muhammadans have, if anything, the advantage so far as male education is concerned. In 1891 there were 1,757 male and 2 female Muhammadans under instruction, as against 6,331 male and 415 female Hindus, but the percentages of Muhammadan males and females to their populations of a school-going age respectively were 28·4 and ·04, against 18·4 and 1·3 of the Hindus. Of Muhammadans attending the College the percentage was less satisfactory, being ·7 as against 1·3 for the Hindus. In 1903 both in the College and in the schools, percentages of Muhammadan and Hindu males under instruction to their populations of school-going age amounted to 17·8 and 19·0 in both cases respectively. The number of Muhammadans in the College was 31, and in other public and private schools 1,015. Hindus, however, had the advantage in female education with 802 girls, representing 2·9 per cent, while the Muhammadans had only 67 or 1·3 per cent. The general conclusion from these figures appears to be that so far as the boys are concerned the common reproach of backward education among Muhammadans cannot fairly be applied to those of Ajmer-Merwāra. Many of them are in the police, army or other branches of the public service, where the benefits of educating their children are brought prominently before them.

Finances. The direct cost of the Educational Department in the province in

1903 amounted to Rs. 78,218. Of this Rs. 37,060 were paid from Imperial revenues, Rs. 18,155 were contributed from District and municipal funds, Rs. 12,961 were derived from fees, and Rs. 10,042 from other miscellaneous sources, including endowments and subscriptions. In the same year the average cost per pupil in the College came to Rs. 133-1-3, in training and special schools to Rs. 118-9-9, in secondary schools to Rs. 12-13-2 and in primary schools to Rs. 6-8-3. The census returns of 1901 showed that out of the total male population only 12 per cent. and of the total female population only ·8 per cent. were educated.

Mayo College.

Quite apart from the general education of the province there is the Mayo College at Ajmer. In the latter part of the year 1870 the late Earl of Mayo held a Darbār at Ajmer, and proposed to the assembled chiefs of Rājasthān that a College should be established at Ajmer, where their sons and nobles might receive such an education as would fit them for their high position and important duties. He invited subscriptions from the chiefs, promising on behalf of the Government of India a sum equal to the aggregate amount collected. Fifteen of the eighteen principalities in Rājputāna responded by promising subscriptions amounting to over 6 lakhs, which was later increased to nearly 7 lakhs, the interest on which sum added to a subsidy from the Government of India forms the income of the College. Of the three States Dholpur, Jaisalmer, and Dungarpur, which did not subscribe originally, the two last have since contributed to the endowment. The States of Jaipur, Udaipur, Jōdhpur, Kōtāh, Bharatpur, Bikāner, Jhālāwār, Alwar and Tonk have also built boarding houses in the College park at a cost of Rs. 4,28,000, and maintain them at an annual cost of approximately Rs. 18,600, including the salaries of house *motamids* and servants. The most liberal donor was Jaipur, whose total contributions exceed 2 lakhs, while those of Jōdhpur, Udaipur, Kōtāh and Jhālāwār exceed one lakh each. The British Government on its part presented the College park, comprising 167 acres, formerly the site of the old Residency, built the main building, the residences of the Principal and Vice-Principal, and the Ajmer boarding house, which is occupied by boys from the Ajmer district and also by boys from elsewhere who have not been provided with accommodation by their own States. It also provides for the salaries of the English staff and the upkeep of the main roads and the four Government buildings.

The main building, which costs approximately Rs. 4,01,400, is built of white marble in the Indo-Saracenic style, after designs prepared by Major Mant, R.E. The foundation-stone was laid on the 5th January 1878 by Mr. (now Sir) Alfred Lyall, then Agent to the Governor-General for Rājputāna, and the building was opened by H. E. the Earl of Dufferin on the 7th November 1885. In front stands a statue of the founder, Lord Mayo, the work of Mr. Noble, and erected from funds subscribed by British and Native residents of Rājputāna. The ten boarding houses, of which 9 are Hindu and one Muhammadan, are arranged in the form of a horse shoe, with the

College in the centre of the base. The Jaipur house alone stands at some distance apart to the south of the main building.

The first Principal to be appointed was the late Colonel Sir Oliver St. John, at the close of 1874. Major (now Colonel) Powlett, officiated as Principal for two months in the autumn of 1878, after which he was relieved by Colonel W. Loch, A.D.C., who held the post for over 24 years, retiring on 1st January 1903. Mr. H. Sherring, the Head master, officiated as Principal from that date to 3rd March 1903, when Mr. C. W. Waddington, late Principal of the Rājkumār College, Rājkot, was appointed Principal.

The College was opened for the reception of boys in October 1875. The first boy to join was the late Mahārāja Mangal Singh of Alwar. and the number of admissions up to August 1903, was 322, of whom 56 are now on the College rolls. The total includes the ruling chiefs of Alwar, Bikāner, Dholpur, Dungarpur, Jhālāwar, Jaisalmer, Karauli, Kōtāh, Manipur, Tehri, Farīd-kōt, and Panna, and the heirs-apparent of Bharatpur, Partābgarh, Shāhpura, Tonk, Kuch Bīhār, and Lunawāra. The greater number come from Rājputāna, but some 20 have been sent from other provinces.

The different boarding houses are supervised by the English staff, and in addition there is a native resident guardian in each house. There is accommodation in all for about 100 boys, with stabling for about 150 horses. Riding is not compulsory, but the majority of boys keep one or two horses.

The College curriculum is not fettered by having to conform to any prescribed code, but if desired, students are prepared for the Entrance examination of the Allāhābād University. The teaching of Sanskrit and Persian is provided for, when a satisfactory test in the vernacular has been passed. With a view to making the course of studies as useful and practical as possible, instruction is also given in law, political economy, agriculture, veterinary science, physics and chemistry.

To the south of the Jaipur house is the College temple, built from subscriptions of Rs. 4,000 raised from among the boys, and a donation of Rs. 5,000, given by Mahant Dewa Dās of the Kāyasthās of Ajmer. All Hindu boys attend service at the Temple on Sundays, and sermons and general instructions are also given there by a Shāstri. The religious training of the Muhammadan boys is attended to by a Hāfiz attached to the Tonk boarding house.

The boys undergo a thorough course of physical training in riding, gymnastics, dumb-bells, Indian clubs, drill, target practice and athletic sports, to one or other of which an hour is devoted every morning. Cricket, foot-ball, hockey, lawn-tennis and racquets are played in the afternoons and evenings.

In February 1902, a conference was held at Calcutta under the presidency of H. E. Lord Curzon, to discuss the question of increasing the efficiency of the Chiefs' Colleges in India. As a result of this the number of the English staff has been raised from 2 to 4, *viz.*, 1 Principal, 1 Vice-Principal, and 2 Assistants. The Native staff has also been strengthened and improved and other reforms initiated.

In continuation of the same movement a conference of Chiefs was held at Ajmer in March 1904, under the Agent to the Governor-General in Rājputāna, and agreeing with its resolutions the Government of India have since reconstituted the Council of the Mayo College as follows:—There is a General Council, of which His Excellency the Viceroy is President and the Agent to the Governor-General in Rājputāna is Vice-President, composed of (1) all Chiefs who are now members, (2) such Chiefs from places other than the Bombay Presidency, the Punjab and the North-West Frontier Province as may be nominated by the Viceroy, after qualifying for membership by contributing Rs. 10,000 or more to the Mayo or Daly College, and by sending a son or ward to the former, (3) the Agent to the Governor-General in Central India, (4) the Principal of the Mayo College, (5) the Commissioner of Ajmer, (6) three Political Officers each from Rājputāna and Central India, nominated by their respective Agents to the Governor-General, and (7) such other members as the Viceroy may see fit to nominate.

There is also a Working Committee consisting of (1) not more than ten Ruling Chiefs elected by ballot from members of the General Council, (2) the Commissioner of Ajmer, and (3) one Political Officer from Central India. The members serve for two years and are eligible for re-election. Subject to the general control of the Vice-President and of the Committee, the ordinary business of the College is conducted by the Principal.

Press and Newspapers.

There is no indigenous literary class, nor was there any printing press in Ajmer till 1871, when a native gentleman from the Panjāb established one. From this press the Rājputāna Official Gazette issued in triglot form—English, Hindi, and Urdu, and the publisher was allowed to publish a supplement, which was an ordinary newspaper. The Rājputāna Official Gazette ceased to exist in 1880.

In 1891 the number of printing presses from which periodicals issued rose to thirteen. Two of these, the "Rājputāna Gazette" and the "Rājasthān Samāchār" were ordinary newspapers, one, the "Veda Bhashya," was a Vedic commentary in the form of a monthly magazine, while the others were periodicals relating to either social or religious reform.

In 1902 there were 12 printing presses in Ajmer and one in Beāwar. The number of periodicals fell to eight, of which five relate to social and religious reform.

The two newspapers above mentioned still continue, and one, the "Muin-ul-Hind," has been added. All these papers are in the vernacular of the district, one religious periodical only, the "Arya," having an English duplicate. Their circulation is purely local and very limited, and their influence corresponds with these conditions.

The registered publications in the province are for the most part merely pamphlets, frequently on religious subjects, and do not deserve detailed discussion. Eleven such pamphlets, amounting to 14,800 copies were registered in 1901, but seven of them were merely new editions of previous works.

CHAPTER XXI.

MEDICAL.

Since 1881 there has been no increase in the number of civil hospitals and dispensaries in Ajmer-Merwāra. There are seven situated at Ajmer, Kekri, Pisāngan, Deolia, Rāmsar, Beāwar and Todgarh. The first charitable public dispensary in the districts was, by the initiation of Colonel Dixon, opened in Ajmer on the 15th January 1851. It was constructed within the city, near the Agra gate, at a cost of Rs. 6,000, subscribed by the inhabitants. It had accommodation for 25 beds, 21 for males and 4 for females. For many years this dispensary did admirable service in giving medical and surgical aid to the inhabitants not only of Ajmer but of other parts of Rājputāna. But after a time it became unable to meet the demands for increased in-door accommodation, for operations and for general hospital work, and in 1895 a larger "General Hospital" was built outside the city walls at a cost of Rs. 43,250. The sum was raised partly by subscriptions from wealthy citizens and from the municipality, and partly by sale of the old dispensary. The new hospital is a handsome building containing several large wards. It has accommodation for 55 in-door patients, 33 males and 10 females, and 12 beds were till recently allotted for men of the Ajmer police. They are now to be accommodated in a ward separate from the hospital. When the new hospital was opened, the old police hospital in the magazine was done away with, in consideration of which Government contributed towards the cost of the buildings. The dispensaries at Kekri, Pisāngan, Rāmsar and Beāwar were all opened in 1869, the one at Todgarh in 1880, and the Deolia dispensary in 1890. There was a dispensary at Masūda between the years 1869 and 1890, but it was closed shortly after the Deolia one was opened. Hospitals and dispensaries.

In 1881 the average daily attendance of in-door and out-door patients was in round numbers 28 and 231 respectively. In 1891 there was a slight rise in the average of out-door patients, the figures being 27 and 281. In 1902 the daily average of both classes of patients had increased largely, that of the in-door patients being 49 and of the out-door 414. The figures show that medical work is steadily extending. Medical statistics.

The civil hospital and the dispensaries are maintained by contributions from Government, from municipal and local funds, and from private subscriptions. Both income and expenditure have risen of late years. On the side of income, that from Government payments has increased from Rs. 3,869 in 1881 to Rs. 4,990 in 1891, and to Rs. 6,353 in 1902; that from municipal and local funds has Finances.

risen from Rs. 900 in 1881 to Rs. 1,435 in 1891, and to Rs. 2,475 in 1902; from other sources the income in 1902 was Rs. 5,803, as against Rs. 2,796 in 1891 and Rs. 2,616 in 1881. Expenditure on establishments has risen from Rs. 4,197 in 1881 to Rs. 6,426 in 1902, and that upon medicines, diet, etc., from Rs. 3,549 to Rs. 6,320 within the same period.

The excellent medical work done by the United Free Church of Scotland Mission at its Ajmer and Nasīrābād dispensaries has already been noticed.

Diseases.

Although, with the exception of the miasmatic fevers after the rains, there are no diseases which can be called endemic, there is always a wide field for medical assistance. Diseases of the skin of every variety are common among the poorer classes, favus being a parasitic skin disease often met with, while ophthalmia and allied eye diseases are common. Many children are carried off every year by measles, owing to the general ignorance as to suitable treatment.

The hospital and dispensaries are generally popular with the common people, but the well-to-do banias in towns still show some reluctance in availing themselves of the Western methods of treatment, and the number of *baids* and *hakīms* as well as of quacks of every description is not inconsiderable. Shops are common in Ajmer, where country drugs in crude or prepared forms are obtainable. In diseases requiring surgical interference, however, the dispensaries are more frequently resorted to, though *jarrāhs* (native barber surgeons) and *sattias* (a class of quack surgeons who undertake the cure of eye diseases) are not rare.

In surgical practice, operations for cataract and for the removal of stone from the bladder, a not infrequent complaint among children, are common.

The villagers have great faith in the efficacy of quinine for driving away fevers, and frequently resort to the dispensaries for the yellow chinchona febrifuge, or the Government pink pills. The pice packet system has not been a success, owing probably to the fact that they are sold at Post Offices. In 1894 only two packets were sold and in 1901 only six. The people prefer to go to the dispensaries. The men of the 44th Merwāra Infantry, when they return to their homes, help to enlighten the rural population as to the efficacy of dispensary treatment.

Lunatic asylum.

There is no separate lunatic asylum for the province. Such lunatics as appear to require restraint are received temporarily in the Ajmer jail, and cases requiring prolonged treatment are sent to the lunatic asylum at Lahore. Their average daily attendance number is insignificant, being ·50 in 1881 and 1·01 in 1902.

Vaccination.

Vaccination was started in Ajmer-Merwāra by Dr. Lord, the Civil Surgeon, in 1853. At first only two vaccinators were employed, and the operations were performed at the dispensary. In 1866 house-to-house vaccination was started, and in 1867 a native Superintendent was appointed, with four vaccinators paid by Government and two paid by the municipalities of Ajmer and Beāwar.

Vaccination increased steadily, and in 1886-87 the number of vaccinators was raised from six to eleven; it now stands at fourteen. The Vaccination Act was introduced within the limits of the Ajmer, Kekri and Beáwar municipalities from the 1st October 1895, 1st October 1901, and 1st January 1902 respectively, and vaccination is now compulsory in these places.

It is carried out among all classes of the people in the districts, and vaccinators of good castes are employed. The total number of persons successfully vaccinated was 4,433 in 1881, 12,226 in 1891 and 12,179 in 1902, or per 1,000 of population 9·62, 22·54, and 25·54 respectively. The total cost of the department was Rs. 839 in 1881, Rs. 1,549 in 1891, and Rs. 2,267 in 1902. The cost of each successful case in these years came to 3 annas, 1 anna 11 pies, and 3 annas respectively.

The good results of vaccination are seen in a steady decrease of the blind in the last 20 years.

The general sanitation in the towns will compare not unfavourably with that of towns in other provinces. In certain villages simple rules have been brought into force and have worked smoothly. Sanitation.

CHAPTER XXII.

SURVEYS.

Trigonometrical Survey of 1847-48.

A trigonometrical survey of Ajmer-Merwāra was made in 1847-48, the area of the two districts being given as 2,059 and 602·5 square miles respectively. They were divided into 19 *parganās* and 591 villages. An index map was prepared on the scale of 4 miles to an inch; the *pargana* map scale was 1 mile to an inch; that of the village maps varied from 20 to 80 chains to an inch. Subsequent to the completion of these survey operations, Colonel Dixon carried out the first regular settlement of the two districts. Under it two separate standards of measurement were used in Ajmer and Merwāra, the *bigha* in the former measuring 1,936 square yards, and in the latter 1,764 square yards.

Topographical Survey of 1868-1875.

When the term of Colonel Dixon's settlement was approaching completion, a topographical survey of the district was commenced in 1868. It was finished in 1875, and showed the areas of Ajmer and Merwāra as 2069·816 square miles and 640·864 square miles respectively. It was followed by the settlement of the districts by Mr. LaTouche in 1875. During the survey there was the first attempt to initiate the *patwārīs* into survey work. Two special *patwāri* instructors were appointed and were fairly successful. Out of a total of 792,413 acres surveyed, the *patwārīs* measured 400,506 acres, or rather more than one-half. The survey was carried out by means of the plane table, and to each 4 or 5 measuring parties a *munsarim* was appointed to test the measurements and entries. These were again noted by superior officers. The outside boundary of the village was in all cases laid down and thoroughly tested by diagonal lines before the field survey was commenced. In the preparation of village maps a scale of 20 inches to the mile was adopted. The whole district, including Merwāra, was on this occasion measured by the standard of the Ajmer *bigha* of 1,936 square yards.

Survey of 1884-85.

As the expiry of this decennial settlement was approaching, Mr. Whiteway was in January 1883 deputed for its revision. Instruction in survey work was given to the *patwārīs*, and a select few were sent to Rurki for special training to act as instructors to the rest after their return. The work of bringing the old maps up to date was then begun, but was soon found to be impracticable. The boundaries were often incorrect, and no attempt had been made by the *patwāris* to keep the maps up to date. A boundary and traverse survey was therefore determined on, and was carried out by the professional agency of the Survey Department. The same causes which had so soon rendered obsolete the maps of former measurements, prevented the introduction of a professional cadastral survey. The problem was to get the skeleton of the village drawn by trained surveyors in such a way that the flesh and bones of the field survey could be added by the *patwāri* staff. To carry out this, the Survey Department mapped the boundaries of each village, and laid down a number of points so fixed by marks in the ground that the *patwārīs* could always utilize them in measuring cultivation. One such map of each village was prepared, on a scale of 16 inches to the mile. The Survey Department worked with the theodolite only, and not with the plane table and chain. This method, though well suited to taking up fixed points, can only with great difficulty be applied to taking up a boundary. As a result, when the map was received by the settlement officials the boundaries of almost every village were found to be incorrect and had to be gone over again. When finally corrected, the work of filling in the fields in the maps was undertaken by the *patwārīs*, each of whom was supplied with a plane table, chain, compasses, a scale and a cross staff. This work was subjected to continual and rigorous tests, and nothing but pencil entries were allowed until the final check had taken place. No survey of unculturable ground and topographical features, beyond roads, railways and streams, was attempted. Unlike previous surveys, which had been confined to *khālsa* and *jāgīr* areas, this one was extended to six minor *istimrāri* villages as well. The total area surveyed was 734,578 acres. It was completed in 1886. The *patwāri* staff, which had been described as quite ignorant by Mr. Risdale in 1868, was warmly praised by the last settlement officer as an exceptionally able class of men showing a great aptitude for their work.

It is well if this continues to be so, for the maintenance of the results of the survey lies in their hands. Under section 106 of the Ajmer Land Revenue Regulation II of 1877, rules have been framed by which *patwārīs* are bound to inspect all traverse survey and boundary marks within the limits of the village and report as to their condition. At the time of each *girdāwari*, the *patwāri* prepares slips of changes that have taken place during the preceding six months and the village maps are amended accordingly. They also maintain registers relating to the record of rights in prescribed forms, and must keep them up to date by periodical entries.

Survey training of Patwārīs.

Out of 193 *patwārīs* and *naib patwārīs* in Ajmer-Merwāra, 150 have either passed the local *patwārīs'* examination held twice a year, or have been exempted. The examination requires an elementary knowledge of survey work. There is a *patwāri* class in Ajmer for the instruction of such as have not yet passed the test, and such *patwārīs* as can be spared from each *tahsīl* are sent to attend it.

Forest Survey.

A set of forest maps was prepared in 1884-85 by the Revenue Survey Department on a scale of 4 inches to a mile, but as they were merely skeletons, showing only the boundaries of the forests and of the village lands included in them, a fresh survey of the tracts, showing the topographical details was commenced in 1898, under a surveyor of the Forest Survey Department. The scale of the maps is the same as before. The work is not yet completed.

BIBLIOGRAPHY

Rājputāna Gazetteer, 1879, Volume II.

District Gazetteer of Ajmer-Merwāra, 1875.

Mr. (now Sir James) LaTouche's Settlement Report, 1875.

Tod's "Rājasthān," 1829 (frequently re-published).

Dixon's "Sketch of Merwāra," 1848.

King G. "Flora of Rājputāna."

Article on the Arts and Manufactures of Ajmer by Colonel Hendley, I.M.S., in Volume III of the Journal of Indian Art.

Census Reports of Ajmer-Merwāra for 1881, 1891 and 1901.

Talboys Wheeler's History of India gives a good account of the Mughal court at Ajmer at the time of Sir Thomas Roe's visit, and the *Ain-i-Akbarī* describes Akbar's pilgrimages there.

INDEX.

T.

U.

V.

W.

Y.

Z.

RAJPUTANA DISTRICT GAZETTEERS.

VOLUME I.—B.

AJMER-MERWARA.

STATISTICAL TABLES

COMPILED BY C. C. WATSON, I.C.S.

AJMER:
SCOTTISH MISSION INDUSTRIES CO., LTD.

1904

CONTENTS.

I.—DESCRIPTIVE.

II.—ECONOMIC.

STATISTICAL TABLES.

Statement No. 1.

Temperature—Ajmer-Merwāra

Station.	Height of Observatory above Sea-level.	AVERAGE TEMPERATURE FOR 25 YEARS ENDING WITH 1901 IN—							
		January.		May.		July.		November.	
		Mean.	Divisional range.*	Mean.	Divisional range.*	Mean.	Divisional range.*	Mean.	Divisional range.*
1	2	3	4	5	6	7	8	9	10
	Ft.								
Ajmer	1,611	59·4	28·5	91·5	24·5	84·9	14·5	67·9	32·8

* Average difference between maximum and minimum temperatures of each day.

Statement No. 2.

Rainfall—Ajmer-Merwāra.

Station.	AVERAGE RAINFALL (IN INCHES) FOR THE 25 YEARS ENDING WITH 1901 IN—												Total of year.
	January.	February.	March.	April.	May.	June.	July.	August.	September.	October.	November.	December.	
1	2	3	4	5	6	7	8	9	10	11	12	13	14
Ajmer	0·44	0·20	0·16	0·13	0·59	2·26	7·11	7·04	2·36	0·34	0·23	0·32	21·18

Statement No. 3.

Temperature of Ajmer-Merwāra.

Years.	May.			July.			December.			Remarks.
	Maximum.	Minimum.	Mean.	Maximum.	Minimum.	Mean.	Maximum.	Minimum.	Mean.	
1	2	3	4	5	6	7	8	9	10	11
1881 ..	100·0	86·0	93·0	97·0	78·0	87·5	75·0	63·0	69·0	
1882 ..	105·0	82·2	93·6	94·0	75·5	84·7	85·5	65·0	75·2	
1883 ...	109·0	81·0	95·0	93·0	75·0	84·0	82·0	60·0	71·0	
1884 ...	107·0	87·0	97·0	99·0	79·0	89·0	78·0	57·0	67·5	
1885 ...	102·0	79·0	90·5	97·0	76·0	86·5	81·0	58·0	69·5	
1886 ...	113·0	90·0	101·5	98·5	76·5	87·5	81·5	59·0	70·4	
1887 ...	111·5	88·5	100·0	98·0	75·0	86·5	84·0	61·5	72·5	
1888 ...	110·5	84·0	97·2	102·5	78·5	90·5	79·0	61·0	70·0	
1889 ..	111·5	75·5	93·5	99·5	78·5	89·0	84·0	61·0	72·5	
1890 ...	109·0	66·6	87·8	95·4	72·1	83·7	84·5	39·0	62·2	
Total ...	**1078·5**	**819·8**	**949·1**	**973·9**	**764·1**	**869·0**	**814·5**	**585·4**	**699·8**	
Average	**107·8**	**82·0**	**94·9**	**97·4**	**76·4**	**86·9**	**81·5**	**58·5**	**70·0**	
1891 ...	108·5	68·1	88·3	107·5	72·6	90·0	85·0	41·4	63·2	
1892 ...	107·5	62·2	84·4	106·9	74·1	90·5	74·9	35·0	54·9	
1893 ...	107·4	72·6	90·0	89·4	74·1	81·7	79·9	41·4	60·6	
1894 ...	107·9	73·6	90·7	92·4	72·1	82·2	84·4	39·4	61·9	
1895 ...	111·0	83·5	97·5	101·0	78·0	89·5	80·0	44·0	62·0	
1896 ...	110·8	77·2	94·0	98·2	74·3	86·2	81·0	37·0	59·0	
1897 ...	110·0	84·5	97·2	104·0	77·0	90·5	81·6	42·0	61·8	
1898 ...	109·0	72·0	90·7	101·0	74·0	87·7	81·8	43·5	62·6	
1899 ...	96·0	82·0	89·0	85·0	77·0	81·0	59·5	50·0	54·7	
1900 ...	93·0	79·0	86·0	91·0	79·5	85·4	67·5	45·5	56·5	
Total ...	**1,061·1**	**754·7**	**907·8**	**976·4**	**752·7**	**864·7**	**775·6**	**419·2**	**597·2**	
Average	**106·1**	**75·5**	**90·8**	**97·7**	**75·3**	**86·5**	**77·6**	**42·0**	**59·8**	
1901 ...	95·5	78·0	86·7	95·0	78·5	86·7	62·5	51·0	56·7	
1902 ...	93·0	76·0	84·5	90·0	77·50	83·70	63·0	39·0	51·0	

These months are taken as fairly representing the hot weather, the rains and the cold seasons respectively.

Statement No. 4.

Rainfall of Ajmer-Merwāra.

Years.	Average of the Ajmer district.	Average of the Merwara district.	Ajmer Observatory.	Remarks.
1	2	3	4	5
1880-81	15·1	19·2	19·2	
1881-82	17·9	20·3	22·1	
1882-83	24·3	24·0	26·5	
1883-84	14·3	20·1	17·3	
1884-85	23·9	28·5	26·9	
1885-86	19·3	19·3	24·6	
1886-87	18·2	17·3	15·2	
1887-88	22·0	20·3	23·7	
1888-89	18·7	20·9	22·3	
1889-90	21·4	16·8	23·0	
Total ...	195·1	206·7	220·8	
Average ...	19·6	20·7	22·1	
1890-91	12·05	13·56	16·34	
1891-92	8·50	10·24	8·18	
1892-93	37·28	37·33	22·18	
1893-94	25·20	30·26	31·22	
1894-95	25·33	28·51	26·61	
1895-96	17·05	15·00	23·53	
1896-97	23·02	21·41	26·64	
1897-98	20·93	24·30	23·26	
1898-99	14·05	10·66	12·69	
1899-00	8·36	4·92	10·00	
Total ...	191·77	196·19	200·65	
Average ...	19·2	19·6	20·1	
1900-01	28·18	29·84	26·94	
1901-02	12·91	10·81	11·90	
1902-03	15·57	18·69	17·38	

1890-91, 1895-96 and 1898-99 were years of severe scarcity. 1891-92, 1899-1900 and 1901-02 were famine years throughout the districts, and 1902-03 a year of scarcity in Merwāra.

Statement No. 5.

Distribution of population of Ajmer-Merwāra.

Administrative Divisions.	Area in square miles.	Number of Towns.	Number of Villages.	Total Population.			Urban Population.			Persons per square mile in rural areas.
				Persons.	Males.	Females.	Persons.	Males.	Females.	
1	2	3	4	5	6	7	8	9	10	11
Ajmer	2,069·816	3	425	3,67,453	1,93,384	1,74,069	1,03,386	55,000	48,386	130·0
Merwara ...	640·864	1	315	1,09,459	57,642	51,817	21,928	11,146	10,782	136·9
Total ...	2,710·680	4	740	4,76,912	2,51,026	2,25,886	1,25,314	66,146	59,168	131·8

Statement No. 6.

General Statistics of population of Ajmer district.

Particulars.	1901.			1891.		
	Persons.	Males.	Females.	Persons.	Males.	Females.
1	2	3	4	5	6	7
Religion.						
Hindu	2,92,713	1,53,464	1,39,249	3,41,543	1,79,701	1,61,842
Jains	14,409	7,723	6,686	19,687	10,502	9,185
Musalmāns	56,378	29,892	26,486	57,223	31,029	26,194
Christians { Native Christians	1,899	985	914	885	481	404
Christians { Others	1,330	839	491	1,438	887	551
Others	724	481	243	1,583	947	636
Civil condition.						
Unmarried	1,31,666	84,747	46,919	1,67,297	1,04,076	63,221
Married	1,83,529	92,251	91,278	2,10,760	1,07,448	1,03,312
Widowed	52,258	16,386	35,872	44,302	12,023	32,279
Education.						
Literate ... { Total literate ...	26,887	25,219	1,668	27,909	26,522	1,387
Literate ... { In English ...	4,577	3,959	618	*	*	*
Illiterate...	3,40,566	1,68,165	1,72,401	3,94,450	1,97,025	1,97,425
Languages Spoken.						
Ajmeri	1,48,431	78,115	70,316	1,11,534	59,539	51,995
Dhundhāri	3,771	1,537	2,234	23,636	10,577	13,059
Hāraoti	1	...	1	945	452	493
Hindi	87,400	46,596	40,804	2,077	1,190	887
Mārwāri	76,699	39,701	36,998	2,08,667	1,10,049	98,618
Merwāri	1,435	964	471	2,123	1,096	1,027
Mewāri	4,347	2,092	2,255	24,137	12,394	11,743
Mewāti	131	92	39	1,474	848	626
Rājasthāni	105	58	47	..	...	...
Total Vernaculars of the Province ...	3,22,320	1,69,155	1,53,165	3,74,593	1,96,145	1,78,448
Other languages	45,133	24,229	20,904	47,766	27,402	20,364

* Details not forthcoming by districts. In all Ajmer-Merwāra they are as follows:—

Persons	2,842
Males	2,521
Females	321

The general decrease in population is due to the famines of the decade, and the malarial fevers, following the famines. The losses were almost entirely among the rural population. Total literates in 1891 exclude "persons under instruction" in this as well as in next table. The fluctuations in the language figures are due to different methods of enumeration. Dialects returned as Mārwāri, Mewāri and Dhundhāri have evidently been largely included in Hindi at the last census. The increase of persons returned as speaking Ajmeri is probably due to more accurate enumeration.

Statement No. 7.

General statistics of population of Merwāra district.

Particulars.	1901.			1891.		
	Persons.	Males.	Females.	Persons.	Males.	Females.
1	2	3	4	5	6	7
Religion.						
Hindus	87,740	45,202	42,538	95,288	50,514	44,774
Jains	5,513	2,921	2,592	7,252	3,924	3,328
Musalmāns	15,653	9,188	6,465	17,042	10,101	6,941
Christians { Native Christians	463	281	182	324	181	143
Christians { Others	20	10	10	36	18	18
Others	70	40	30	57	40	17
Civil condition.						
Unmarried	44,672	29,196	15,476	57,460	35,442	22,018
Married	49,391	24,218	25,173	52,783	26,698	26,085
Widowed	15,396	4,228	11,168	9,756	2,638	7,118
Education.						
Literate { Total Literate ...	5,201	4,947	254	5,745	5,592	153
Literate { In English ...	221	193	28	*	*	*
Illiterate	1,04,258	52,695	51,563	1,14,254	59,186	55,068
Languages spoken :—						
Ajmeri	213	125	88	1,634	687	947
Dhundhāri	2,166	1,156	1,010	3,673	1,993	1,680
Hāraoti	...	...	...	14	12	2
Hindi	2,551	1,251	1,300	557	291	266
Mārwāri	17,479	8,593	8,886	20,200	10,541	9,659
Merwāri	81,045	43,328	37,717	85,175	46,422	38,753
Mewāri	3,752	1,883	1,869	5,292	2,718	2,574
Mewāti	2	...	2	157	67	90
Rājasthāni	173	104	69	...	...	...
Total Vernaculars of the province	1,07,381	56,440	50,941	1,16,702	62,731	53,971
Other languages	2,078	1,202	876	3,297	2,047	1,250

* Details not forthcoming by districts.

Statement No. 8.

Vital statistics—Births of Ajmer-Merwāra.

Years and districts.		Population under registration.	Total number of births registered.	Ratio of births per 1,000.	Highest district rate.	Lowest district rate.	Mean birth-rate of previous 5 years.
1		2	3	4	5	6	7
1881 ...	Ajmer ..	3,59,288	10,493	29·20	50·14	3·26	25·73
	Merwāra ..	1,01,434	2,298	22·65	25·91	18·51	23·60
1891 ...	Ajmer ...	4,22,359	9,676	22·90	76·85	11·50	21·88
	Merwāra ...	1,19,999	1,890	15·75	20·11	10·75	18·03
1901 ...	Ajmer ...	3,67,453	5,769	15·70	29·41	5·67	30·02
	Merwāra ..	1,09,459	1,910	17·45	30·33	12·59	40·23
1902 ...	Ajmer ..	3,67,453	12,945	35·23	49·37	23·11	26·29
	Merwāra ...	1,09,459	4,262	38·94	44·92	33·64	34·31

The decrease in the 1891 and 1901 figures is due to famine. The high figures of 1902 point to a reaction, consequent upon returning prosperity and probably also to improved registration.

Statement No. 9.

Vital statistics—Deaths of Ajmer-Merwāra.

Years and districts.		Population under registration.	Total number of deaths registered.	Ratio of deaths per 1,000.	Highest district rate.	Lowest district rate.	Mean death-rate of previous 5 years.
1		2	3	4	5	6	7
1881 ...	Ajmer ...	3,59,288	8,856	24·65	39·83	5·47	26·13
	Merwāra ...	1,01,434	1,893	18·66	27·71	15·10	22·05
1891 ...	Ajmer ...	4,22,359	9,315	22·05	77·51	11·46	18·51
	Merwāra ...	1,19,999	1,657	13·81	22·16	8·92	16·65
1901 ...	Ajmer ...	3,67,453	12,619	34·34	62·30	13·85	49·91
	Merwāra ..	1,09,459	3,179	29·04	36·47	22·71	58·65
1902 ...	Ajmer ...	3,67,453	12,220	33·26	62·44	17·28	50·22
	Merwāra ...	1,09,459	3,452	31·54	36·78	26·25	58·48

The largely increased death-rate in 1901 and 1902 was due to the severe fever epidemics which followed the great famine.

Statement No. 10

Vital statistics.—Deaths according to causes in Ajmer-Merwāra.

Years and districts.		Deaths per 1,000 from—						
		Plague.	Cholera.	Small-pox	Fever.	Bowel complaints.	Injuries.	All other causes.
1		2	3	4	5	6	7	8
1881	Ajmer	...	·05	3·79	15·45	2·03	·37	2·96
	Merwāra ...	...	...	2·39	9·44	2·78	·48	3·57
1891	Ajmer	...	1·26	1·28	13·76	2·71	·73	2·31
	Merwāra ...	...	...	·18	10·53	1·53	·39	1·18
1901	Ajmer	..	·13	·01	27·42	1·67	·49	4·62
	Merwāra ..	...	...	·02	27·54	·47	·42	·59
1902	Ajmer	...	·05	·01	25·91	1·19	·41	5·69
	Merwāra ...	...	·11	·02	29·86	·35	·61	·59

Statement No. 11.

Statistics (in acres) of agriculture and irrigation of the khālsa area of Ajmer-Merwāra.

Particulars.	Average of (1881-1890).		Average of (1891-1900).		1902-03.		Names of principal crops raised by means of irrigation.
	Ajmer.	Merwāra.	Ajmer.	Merwāra.	Ajmer.	Merwāra.	
1	2	3	4	5	6	7	8
Total area ...	3,50,858	4,05,392	3,33,304	3,74,909	3,33,394	3,74,965	Maize, Cotton, Chillies, Wheat, Opium, Barley, and Tobacco.
Total uncultivated area.	2,38,150	3,34,873	2,25,953	3,05,318	2,29,080	3,08,547	
Culturable but not cultivated	1,09,347	22,040	1,19,329	23,267	1,21,270	29,473	
Unculturable	1,28,803	3,12,833	1,06,624	2,82,051	1,07,810	2,79,074	
Total cultivated area ...	1,12,708	70,519	1,07,351	69,591	1,04,314	66,418	
Irrigated by wells and tanks	28,816	23,319	26,127	24,602	20,622	16,349	
Irrigated by other sources	162	12	26	438	10	65	
Total irrigated area ...	28,978	23,331	26,153	25,040	20,632	16,414	
Unirrigated area ...	83,730	47,188	81,198	44,551	83,682	50,004	
Total crop acreage:—							
Wheat	8,607·4	5,151·2	3,665·4	3,660·0	2,153	2,710	
Barley	24,214·5	20,475·3	15,697·0	17,667·1	12,699	12,046	
Maize	12,412·2	26,005·3	12,882·6	28,291·2	15,857	26,612	
Bājra	10,850·6	2,170·3	11,804·4	1,762·6	21,546	6,627	
Joār	24,827·0	5,975·9	29,544·3	8,467·0	30,346	14,530	
Other food grains and pulses	24,958·9	17,307·2	19,264·9	12,428·8	13,262	5,001	
Oilseeds	8,396·0	3,893·5	9,375·8	5,287·3	6,467	4,194	
Sugarcane	1,130·9	148·5	162·3	172·6	139	3	
Cotton	8,019·1	4,407·1	13,608·9	7,401·4	8,351	4,405	
Tobacco	42·1	25·0	5·1	12·9	...	12	
Opium	44·5	2,638·5	2·0	1,349·5	...	852	
Miscellaneous	3,292·3	2,490·0	2,146·4	1,721·2	1,464	1,758	
Total ...	1,26,795·5	90,687·8	1,18,159·1	88,221·6	1,12,284	78,750	
Area cropped more than once	14,087·4	20,168·8	10,808·4	18,630·1	7,970	12,332	
Net area cropped during the year ...	1,12,708·1	70,519·0	1,07,350·7	69,591·5	1,04,314	66,418	

Under "culturable but not cultivated" are included the figures for current fallows.

The decrease in the total area shown in 1891-1900 is due to the new survey of the districts in 1882-84, by which the errors of the previous survey were corrected. Fluctuations are in general due to good or bad seasons.

Statement No. 12.

Live-stock, ploughs and carts in the khālsa area of Ajmer-Merwāra.

Particulars.	1880-81.		1890-91		1900-01.		1902-03.	
	Ajmer.	Merwāra.	Ajmer.	Merwāra.	Ajmer.	Mewāra.	Ajmer.	Merwāra.
1	2	3	4	5	6	7	8	9
Bulls and bullocks	72,148	72,983	21,356	25,253	23,026	6,888	21,082	17,401
Cows			26,898	42,849	26,935	3,273	10,896	9,888
Male buffaloes	...	...	900	2,114	1,519	69	813	268
Cow buffaloes	...	...	7,242	7,966	8,961	1,952	5,293	3,921
Young stock (calves & buffaloe calves)	..	...	23,034	6,167	6,863	3,039	11,772	7,618
Sheep	92,750	1,02,507	44,703	55,198	55,564	20,021	43,403	30,751
Goats			30,074	46,236	33,688	39,342	39,629	87,413
Horses and ponies	930	1,161	742	1,022	703	155	526	244
Mules and donkeys	3,100	2,005	1,634	1,640	2,025	633	1,289	1,030
Camels	145	156	200	82	184	239	297	212
Total live-stock ...	**1,69,073**	**1,78,812**	**1,56,783**	**1,88,527**	**1,59,468**	**75,611**	**1,45,030**	**1,58,749**
Ploughs	9,880	11,628	10,672	12,444	9,483	7,737	8,508	9,877
Carts	2,450	1,103	4,769	1,433	3,307	1,179	3,301	1,894

In 1880-81 the figures entered against bulls and bullocks and cows also include male and female buffaloes and young stock.

During the famine of 1898-00 Merwāra lost 1,55,697 cattle and Ajmer 2,05,457.

Statement No. 13.

Part A.—The prices of certain food grains for the three tahsils of Ajmer, Beawār and Todgarh.

Particulars.	Average for 1873-80.								Average for 1881-1890.								Average for 1891-1900.								1902-03.							
	Tahsils.						Average of the three Tahsils.		Tahsils.						Average of the three Tahsils.		Tahsils.						Average of the three Tahsils.		Tahsils.						Average of the three Tahsils.	
	Ajmer.		Beāwar.		Todgarh.				Ajmer.		Beāwar.		Todgarh.				Ajmer.		Beāwar.		Todgarh.				Ajmer.		Beāwar.		Todgarh.			
	Srs.	Chs.	Srs.	Chs.	Srs.	Chs.	Srs.	Chs.	Srs.	Chs.	Srs.	Chs.	Srs.	Chs.	Srs.	Chs.	Srs.	Chs.	Srs.	Chs.	Srs.	Chs.	Srs.	Chs.	Srs.	Chs.	Srs.	Chs.	Srs.	Chs.	Srs.	Chs.
1	2	3	4	5	6	7	8	9	10	11	12	13	14	15	16	17	18	19	20	21	22	23	24	25	26	27	28	29	30	31	32	33
Wheat	14	13	15	13	16	4	15	10	15	..	16	3	18	5	16	8	11	13	13	1	14	1	13	.	12	11	13	3	12	½	12	10
Barley	22	4	23	12	24	..	23	5	23	½	24	7	23	8	25	4	18	5	20	5	22	8	20	7	16	11½	17	8½	16	2½	16	13
Jowār	20	10	20	4	22	5	21	1	22	7	22	15	19	7	21	10	18	5	18	15	22	..	19	12	17	13	18	..	19	7	18	7
Bājra	19	..	18	12	17	10	18	7	17	10	20	½	17	12	18	8	14	14	15	13	16	2	15	10	16	6	15	8½	16	3½	16	1
Maize	21	12	23	1	24	15	23	4	23	3	25	9	28	12	25	13	18	12	20	11	22	10	20	11	18	7½	18	12	18	11	18	10
Salt	25	5	22	13	18	8	22	3	12	11	13	5	11	7	12	8	11	15	12	15	11	9	12	2	12	10	13	½	11	7½	12	6

In 1873-1880 the average for salt has been worked out on 3 years, and in 1881-1890 on 6 years, as the figures for the other years are not forthcoming.

Since the introduction of the railway the prices in the province depend more upon the harvests in the Panjāb and the United Provinces of Agra and Oudh than upon local conditions. The prices during the acute famines have therefore not been omitted in striking the averages for this Statement. The effects of the general famines throughout India may be seen in the prices for 1890-1900 and in 1902-03.

The grain prices in Merwāra are generally lower than those in Ajmer.

Statement No. 13.

Part B.—The prices of certain food grains according to the 20th Issue of the Prices and Wages Volume from the Government of India for Ajmer from 1873-1900 and for 1902.

PARTICULARS.	AVERAGE FOR 1873-1880.		AVERAGE FOR 1881-1890.		AVERAGE FOR 1891-1900.		1902.	
	Seers.	Chittāks	Seers.	Chittāks	Seers.	Chittāks	Seers.	Chittāks
1	2	3	4	5	6	7	8	9
Wheat	14	12	15	$4\frac{7}{16}$	12	$12\frac{1}{2}$	12	$12\frac{1}{2}$
Barley	22	$\frac{1}{2}$	22	$14\frac{9}{16}$	19	$12\frac{5}{8}$	16	$6\frac{3}{4}$
Joār	19	$14\frac{5}{8}$	22	$3\frac{1}{2}$	19	$11\frac{1}{2}$	16	$15\frac{1}{2}$
Bajra	17	$14\frac{3}{4}$	18	1	16	11	15	$13\frac{3}{4}$
Maize	21	$1\frac{1}{2}$	22	$13\frac{1}{2}$	20	$1\frac{1}{4}$	17	$3\frac{3}{4}$
Salt	29	$13\frac{3}{8}$	13	$7\frac{5}{16}$	12	$6\frac{5}{8}$	12	8

In this statement the period of acute famine (1899-1900) is omitted in obtaining the average for the decade 1891-1900. The height of the prices notwithstanding shows the succession of poor and indifferent seasons since 1891.

Statement No. 14.

The average monthly wages (in rupees) of skilled and unskilled labour in the Ajmer district.

YEARS.	Able-bodied agricultural labourer.	Syce or horse keeper.	Common mason, carpenter and blacksmith.
1	2	3	4
1873	7	6·5	7·5 to 13·5
1881	3 to 4	5 to 8	10 to 20
1891	3 to 4	5 to 8	10 to 15
1902	4·69 to 7·5	5 to 8	7·5 to 15

Wages have shown little tendency to rise along with the increase in prices. Those for unskilled labour have been dominated by the ruling wages upon relief works, which is scientifically calculated from a basis representing the subsistence minimum of the workers.

Statement No. 15.

Factories of Ajmer-Merwāra.

Particulars.		1897.	1902.
1		2	3
Number of mills ...		1	1
Number of looms ...		250	252
Number of spindles ...		12,312	12,312
Hands employed ...		542	606
Out-turn in lbs.	Yarn ...	13,81,080	13,91,290
	Cloth ...	5,18,252	7,78,292
Valuation in Rs.	Yarn ...	4,31,588	3,91,300
	Cloth ...	2,26,735	3,40,503

Statement No. 16.

The principal commodities imported and exported from Ajmer and Beāwar stations.

Names of Principal Commodities.	Ajmer.			Beāwar.		
	1881.	1891.	1902.	1881.	1891.	1902.
1	2	3	4	5	6	7
Imported.						
Grain and pulses ...	1,971	18,355	18,022	3,134	20,075	18,093
Oil-seeds	57	351	329	142	1,774	838
Sugar and jagri ...	2,931	2,248	2,181	10,819	5,797	3,511
Salt	911	581	533	806	1,265	1,318
Cotton (raw)	3	......	19	51	1,075	528
Piece goods	706	666	599	657	350	257
Metals and manufactures of metals ...	559	744	510	406	675	457
Total ...	**7,138**	**22,945**	**22,196**	**16,015**	**31,011**	**25,032**
Remittances received from other treasuries in Rs.	*	... ...	5,75,000	...	...	...
Exported.						
Grain and pulses ...	190	817	571	5,495	4,532	2,123
Oil-seeds...	3	28	40	79	496	356
Sugar and jagri ...	112	82	75	2,599	1,573	962
Salt	160	......	20	14	16	38
Cotton (raw)	2	3	3	3,561	8,471	4,683
Piece goods	63	120	149	115	170	450
Metals and manufactures of metals ...	71	687	482	67	92	99
Total ...	**601**	**1,737**	**1,340**	**11,930**	**15,350**	**8,711**
Remittances sent to other treasuries in Rs.	*	1,09,18,450	1,66,37,091	...	...	...

The figures for Ajmer and Beāwar Railway stations alone are given as they are the chief places of export and import. As statistics of road-borne trade are not available, no complete statement of exports and imports is possible for the districts.

The figures for 1881 and 1891 have been taken from the Administration Reports. Those for 1902 have been supplied by the Chief Auditor and Accountant, Rājputāna-Mālwā Railway.

Decrease in exports of cotton in 1902 is due to restrictions placed on export from Mewār to Merwāra which, although removed in 1900, have since affected trade.

* Figures not forthcoming.

Statement No. 17.

Mileage and cost of the metalled and unmetalled roads in Ajmer-Merwāra.

Years.	Mileage of metalled and unmetalled roads.			Cost of maintenance of metalled and unmetalled roads in Rupees.			Remarks.
	Imperial	Local Fund.	Munici-pal.	Imperial	Local Fund.	Munici-pal.	
1	2	3	4	5	6	7	8
1891	187	304½	26⅜	27,495	9,495	[illegible],035	
1901	187	308¾	29⅛	47,914	3,264	5,025	
1902	187	308¾	29⅛	18,112	13,191	2,712	

The small expenditure on Local Fund roads during 1901 is due to the fact that many of the roads were repaired by famine labour charged to Imperial Funds. In 1902, a year of local scarcity, the Local Funds undertook extensive repairs with a view to relieving distress by employment of labour.

Statement No. 18.

Expenditure incurred during the famines of 1891-92 and 1898-00, in Ajmer-Merwāra.

Heads of Expenditure.	1891-92.	1898-00.
1	2	3
Relief works (including establishments, dependants, kitchens and hospitals.)	12,37,890	31,87,000
Civil kitchens	...	2,00,000
Village relief (gratuitous and home labour)	1,02,739	1,28,000
Poor houses	...	75,000
Civil establishments, contingencies, etc., ...	25,757	71,000
Remission of Land Revenue	46,685	390
Suspension of Land Revenue	1,03,714	4,81,423
Advances under the Land Improvement Loans' Act, XIX of 1883	3,39,775	1,91,842
Advances under the Agriculturist's Loans' Act, XII of 1884	2,69,079	2,58,050
Miscellaneous	...	8,000
Amount given from the Indian Famine Charitable Relief Fund under object IV	...	1,64,161
Total ...	21,25,639	47,64,866

In 1891-92 the cost of village kitchens and poor-houses is included in the figures for "Gratuitous relief." They were used to a very limited extent, and cost only Rs. 434 and Rs. 3,394 respectively.

Of the Land Revenue suspended during the 1898-00 and the 1900-01 famines, Rs. 2,55,000 were remitted later.

Legislation and Justice.

Statement No. 19.

Criminal Justice—Work done by Courts in Ajmer-Merwāra.

Particulars.	Average for ten years ending 1890.	Average for ten years ending 1900.	Year. 1902.
1	2	3	4
Magistrates' Courts.			
Persons tried	8,941·9	8,224·2	7,293
Persons acquitted or discharged	5,148·3	2,871·2	2,321
Persons convicted	3,793·6	5,353·0	4,972
Cases disposed of	4,558·4	5,409·2	4,932
Courts of Sessions.			
Persons tried	30·1	64·2	40
Persons acquitted or discharged	6·4	22·1	26
Persons convicted	23·7	42·1	14
Cases disposed of	19·8*	17·6	20

* Average for 7 years only.

Statement No. 20.

Criminal Justice of Ajmer-Merwāra by offences.

Particulars.	Average for ten years ending 1890.		Average for ten years ending 1900.		Year 1902.	
	Number of persons tried.	Percentage of convictions.	Number of persons tried.	Percentage of convictions.	Number of persons tried.	Percentage of convictions.
1	2	3	4	5	6	7
For offences against persons and property ...	5,519·7	21·1	3,866·7	38·8	3,086	46·1
For other offences against the Indian Penal Code	699·0	36·7	360·4	48·5	270	35·9
For offences against Special and Local Laws	2,782·8	86·7	4,074·9	91·2	3,997	87·1
Total ...	**9,001·5**	**42·6**	**8,302·0**	**65·0**	**7,353**	**68·1**

The **slight** discrepancies in figures between this and the last statement are due to the inclusion in it of a number of persons tried in miscellaneous proceedings under the Criminal Procedure Code. It is according to the Annual Judicial Statements Nos. 2 and 3, while Statement No. 19 is according to Annual Statement No. 4.

Statement No. 21.

Civil Justice—Courts and suits instituted in Ajmer-Merwāra.

Particulars.	Average for ten years ending 1890.	Average for ten years ending 1900.	Year 1902.
1	2	3	4
Subordinate Courts, Civil and Revenue.			
Suits for money or moveable property ...	2,675·2	2,936·2	3,190
Title and other suits	376·4	264·4	317
Rent suits	557·9	461·7	451
Small Cause Courts.			
Suits for money or moveable property ...	5,672·6	4,888·0	4,790·0
Title and other suits	...	...	...
District Courts.			
Suits for money or moveable property ...	·1	·3	1
Title and other suits	·1	...	1
Rent suits	...	...	...

Suits for money or moveable property tend to rise owing to general indebtedness increasing during the famine. Civil litigation in general is reverting to its pre-famine figures.

Statement No. 22.

Civil Justice of Ajmer-Merwāra.

Particulars.	Average for ten years ending 1890.	Average for ten years ending 1900.	Year 1902.
1	2	3	4
Suits for money or moveable property ...	8,347·9	7,824·5	7,981
Title and other suits	376·5	264·4	318
Rent suits	557·9	461·7	451
Total ...	**9,282·3**	**8,550·6**	**8,750**

Statement No. 23.

Revenue and expenditure (in thousands) from 1880-81 *to* 1899-00, *and for* 1902-03 *(in rupees) in Ajmer-Merwāra.*

Heads of Revenue.	Average of ten years ending 1890.	Average of ten years ending 1900.	1902-03.	Heads of Expenditure.	Average of ten years ending 1890.	Average of ten years ending 1900.	1902-03.
1	2	3	4	5	6	7	8
Imperial.				**Imperial.**			
Land Revenue	404·5	385·7	263·9	Land Revenue	101 3	97·4	92·0
Opium	115·5	103·6	130·6	Forest... ..	15·2	16·1	15·5
Salt	150 0	150·0	150·0	Interest ...	4·4	130·5	117·4
Stamps ...	215·2	221·5	147·6	Law and Justice (Courts)	72·1	93·0	95·5
Excise	106·2	114·2	121·6	Jails	26·7	22·2	32·9
Assessed taxes	38·4	76·9	57·2	Police	85·6	89·4	90·4
Forest	9·1	14·7	11·0	Education ..	43·4	46·2	58·2
Interest ...	19·0	29·1	230·7	Medical ...	15·1	19·9	18·6
Law and justice	32·1	21·2	22·6	Superannuation and Pension, etc., General	..	52·6	95·7
Education ...	1·8	6·4	11·8	Ecclesiastical .	10·7	11·4	12·5
Public works ...	12·4	18·5	16·2	Famine Relief	...	38·2	...
Miscellaneous...	6·2	14·5	23·0	Public Works	84·5	313 0	247·7
	...	...	...	Refunds and drawbacks.	5·2	12·8	2·0
	...	...	...	Miscellaneous.	36·0	49·2	71·5
Total Imperial Revenue	**1,110·4**	**1,156·3**	**1,186·2**	Total Imperial Expenditure	**500·2**	**991·9**	**949·9**
Local.				**Local.**			
Incorporated Local Funds	73·7	73·4	112·0	Incorporated Local Funds	69·4	75·3	80·9
Excluded Local Funds	58·6	71·6	60·0	Excluded Local Funds	59·6	71·2	65·9
Municipal Funds	155·4	208·5	241·0	Municipal Funds	154·3	209·1	217·2
Total Local Receipts	**287·7**	**353·5**	**413·0**	Total Expenditure	**283·3**	**355·6**	**364·0**
Grand Total Receipts	**1,398·1**	**1,509·8**	**1,599·2**	Grand Total Expenditure	**783·5**	**1,347·5**	**1,313·9**

Decrease under most heads of income in columns 3 and 4 is due to the famines of the period 1891-1902. Opium receipt consists of duty on **Receipts.**

chests exported principally to the Punjāb. From 1880-81 to 1903 only estimated figures of value of salt consumed (Rs. 1,50,000) have been entered. The excise figures for 1902-03 shown here do not tally with those in Statement No. 29. In this total—which is according to Financial Statement No. 42—certain balances from the preceding years have been included.

Assessed taxes.—In 1880-1890 the average was worked out on 10 years, but Income Tax only commenced in 1886-87. Increase in income from "Interest" in 1902-03 is on account of interest from takāvi advances made during the famine.

"Miscellaneous" include Customs, Registration, Police, Medical, Pensions, Stationery and Printing, Post Office, etc. In 1902-03 the receipts from Customs were Rs. 13,035, but as in the preceding two decades they averaged below Rs. 10,000 they have been included under "Miscellaneous."

Incorporated Local Funds include the District Fund, Dispensary Fund, Pound Fund and *Patwār* Fund. The increase in 1902-03 is due to the inclusion of the recently sanctioned Government grant of Rs. 23,000 towards the *Patwār* and District Funds, and to the recovery of cesses suspended during famine. Excluded Local Funds include the Nasīrābād Cantonment Fund, Police Clothing Fund, Police *Chanda* Fund, *Chaukidāri* Fund, Rājputāna Veterinary School Fund, Rājputāna Native Hospital Assistants' Reserve Fund, and the Mayo College Fund. Increase in Municipal Funds is due, among other causes, to an increasing population and the raising of limit of octroi refunds.

Expenditure.

For several years in the decade 1880-90 "Law and Justice" figures were included in "Land Revenue." Hence partly increase in the former and decrease in the latter in the succeeding decade. "Interest" is on account of promissory notes. The item commenced from 1889-90, so there was only one year on which to calculate the 10 years' average.

"Superannuation Pensions, etc."—The amount is shown under this head since 1892-93 only.

"Public Works."—These figures are shown separately only since 1883-84. Recent increase is due to famine works.

"Miscellaneous" includes Meteorology, Stamps, Excise, Assessed taxes, Registration, Post Office, Opium assignment, Minor departments, Stationery and Printing, Customs Administration, Civil Works and Settlement charges. Settlement charges, amounting to Rs. 25,000, were only incurred between 1882 and 1884.

Statement No. 24.

Land Revenue (in rupees) in khālsa villages of Ajmer-Merwāra.

Year.	Ajmer.				Merwāra.			
	Demand including balance of previous year.	Collection.	Remission.	Out-standing balance of the end of the year.	Demand including balance of previous year.	Collection.	Remission.	Out-standing balance at the end of the year.
1	2	3	4	5	6	7	8	9
1880—81	1,10,848	1,10,559	188	101	33,334	33,302	32	...
1881—82	1,10,801	1,10,586	186	29	80,658	80,654	4	...
1882—83	1,10,590	1,10,460	29	101	80,728	80,488	...	240
1883—84	1,10,662	1,10,340	195	127	80,832	80,104	...	728
1884—85	1,15,031	1,14,853	163	15	83,210	82,052	...	1,158
1885—86	1,29,888	1,29,873	15	...	90,013	89,142	431	440
1886—87	1,22,320	1,22,313	7	...	90,031	89,539	444	48
1887—88	1,20,664	1,20,649	15	...	90,703	90,677	...	26
1888—89	1,31,995	1,31,380	585	30	94,014	93,982	32	...
1889—90	1,28,454	1,28,360	...	94	1,01,808	1,01,803	5	...
Total ...	11,91,253	11,89,373	1,383	497	8,25,331	8,21,743	948	2,640
Average	1,91,125·3	1,18,937·3	138·3	49·7	82,533·1	82,174·3	94·8	264·0
1890—91	1,34,610	1,33,381	62	1,167	1,01,808	96,323	...	5,485
1891—92	1,00,204	58,110	...	42,094	1,07,297	59,409	2	47,886
1892—93	1,53,811	86,271	3,975	63,565	1,49,697	70,201	...	79,496
1893—94	1,95,772	1,58,570	33,105	4,097	1,81,307	1,25,451	...	55,856
1894—95	1,31,878	1,30,790	...	1,088	1,57,401	1,23,662	266	33,473
1895—96	1,27,150	1,26,965	...	185	1,35,018	1,30,413	287	4,318
1896—97	1,27,931	1,27,752	...	179	1,05,864	1,02,172	3,592	100
1897—98	1,25,069	1,24,939	...	130	1,01,646	1,01,505	...	141
1898—99	1,24,943	1,16,802	...	8,141	1,01,687	73,137	...	28,550
1899-1900	1,17,323	57,968	69	59,286	1,30,096	16,073	...	1,14,023
Total ...	13,38,691	11,21,548	37,211	1,79,932	12,71,821	8,98,346	4,147	3,69,328
Average	1,33,869·1	1,12,154·8	3,721·1	17,993·2	1,27,182·1	89,834·6	414·7	36,932·8
1900—01	1,73,538	76,095	...	97,443	2,15,569	49,682	...	1,65,887
1901—02	2,13,912	1,17,396	..	96,516	2,67,433	77,264	...	1,90,169
1902—03	2,13,763	77,187	59,846	76,730	2,91,715	39,035	1,44,702	1,07,978

The large arrears for 1891-92 and 1892-93 in Ajmer, and in 1891-92, 1892-93, 1893-94 and 1894-95 in Merwāra were due to the famine of 1891-92. The great famine of 1898-1900, and the famine year of 1901-1902 in Merwāra are responsible for the out-standing balances of recent years. The remissions of 1902-03 may be noticed.

Statement No. 25.

The water revenue (in rupees) in khālsa villages of Ajmer-Merwāra.

Years.	Ajmer.				Merwāra.				Remarks.
	Demand including balance of previous year.	Collection.	Remission.	Outstanding balance at the end of the year.	Demand including balance of previous year.	Collection.	Remission.	Outstanding balance at the end of the year.	
1	2	3	4	5	6	7	8	9	10
1880-81	31,426	31,426	...	...	25,527	25,105	352	70	
1881-82	22,628	22,628	...	...	25,221	25,150	9	62	
1882-83	24,674	24,674	...	...	29,751	28,418	194	1,139	
1883-84	31,902	31,845	57	...	33,490	31,327	...	2,163	
1884-85	22,011	21,924	...	87	29,263	26,825	1,621	817	
1885-86	33,334	33,334	...	...	34,889	34,138	457	294	
1886-87	30,246	30,246	...	...	30,914	30,216	698	...	
1887-88	26,690	26,510	...	180	28,397	28,367	30	...	
1888-89	34,139	34,139	...	...	30,673	30,673	...	...	
1889-90	29,487	29,487	...	...	35,273	35,273	...	...	
Total ...	**2,86,537**	**2,86,213**	**57**	**267**	**3,03,398**	**2,95,492**	**3,361**	**4,545**	
Average	**28,653·7**	**28,621·3**	**5·7**	**26·7**	**30,339·8**	**29,549·2**	**336·1**	**454·5**	
1890-91	38,198	37,682	...	516	34,001	30,193	...	3,808	
1891-92	13,281	9,330	...	3,951	28,335	22,695	...	5,640	
1892-93	23,640	18,978	849	3,813	31,657	21,879	782	8,996	
1893-94	42,479	38,926	1,981	1,572	49,745	42,257	1,463	6,025	
1894-95	35,655	35,150	...	505	42,060	38,540	...	3,520	
1895-96	30,068	30,049	...	19	39,887	39,690	..	197	
1896-97	34,938	34,762	...	176	32,617	32,420	197	...	
1897-98	28,560	28,560	...	...	33,856	33,804	...	52	
1898-99	37,312	34,654	...	2,658	31,843	23,004	...	8,839	
1899-00	25,878	9,326	...	16,552	30,276	6,800	180	23,296	
Total ...	**3,10,009**	**2,77,417**	**2,830**	**29,762**	**3,54,277**	**2,91,282**	**2,622**	**60,373**	
Average	**31,000·9**	**27,741·7**	**283·0**	**2,976·2**	**35,427·7**	**29,128·2**	**262·2**	**6,037·3**	
1900-01	39,382	22,800	...	16,582	48,626	15,697	...	32,929	
1901-02	53,733	39,349	...	14,384	72,735	31,989	...	40,746	
1902-03	42,377	21,214	8,674	12,489	68,011	14,412	27,188	26,411	

Vide notes on Statement No. 24.

Statement No. 26.

Land Revenue (in rupees) from the istimrārdārs of Ajmer district.

Years.	Demand including balance of last year.	Collection.	Remission.	Outstanding balance at end of the year.
1	2	3	4	5
	Rs.	Rs.	Rs.	Rs.
1880-81...	1,25,004	1,25,004	...	...
1881-82...	1,24,734	1,24,734	...	...
1882-83	1,24,734	1,24,734	...	...
1883-84...	1,24,734	1,24,734	...	...
1884-85...	1,24,734	1,24,359	...	375
1885-86...	1,25,109	1,24,653	...	456
1886-87...	1,25,190	1,25,150	...	40
1887-88...	1,24,774	1,24,774	...	...
1888-89...	1,24,734	1,24,734	...	...
1889-90...	1,24,734	1,24,734	...	...
Total	**12,48,481**	**12,47,610**	...	**871**
Average	**1,24,848·1**	**1,24,761·0**	...	**87·1**
1890-91...	1,24,734	1,24,697	...	37
1891-92...	1,24,771	1,18,053	...	6,718
1892-93...	1,31,452	1,18,402	552	12,498
1893-94	1,37,232	1,33,361	...	3,871
1894-95...	1,18,606	1,17,979	...	627
1895-96...	1,15,362	1,15,193	...	169
1896-97...	1,14,904	1,14,704	100	100
1897-98...	1,14,835	1,14,685	150	...
1898-99...	1,14,735	1,14,131	...	604
1899-1900	1,15,339	82,050	...	33,289
Total	**12,11,970**	**11,53,255**	**802**	**57,913**
Average	**1,21,197·0**	**1,15,325·5**	**80·2**	**5,791·3**
1900-01...	1,48,024	95,623	...	52,401
1901-02...	1,67,136	1,17,618	...	49,518
1902-03...	1,64,253	1,04,154	...	60,099

Before 1894-95 the annual fixed revenue from *istimrārdārs* was Rs. 1,24,734-9-11. In that year Rs. 10,000, paid annually by Shāhpura Durbār, were, under the sanction of the Government of India, transferred to the head "Tribute," as paid by other Native States in Rājputāna. The annual fixed demand is now Rs. 1,14,734-9-11.

Statement No. 27.

The assessment of the khālsa variable villages (in rupees) according to Mr. Whiteway's Settlement Report, by circles and tahsīls, for Ajmer-Merwāra.

Name of Circle.		Number of Villages.	Assessment.				Remarks.
			Revenue.	Details of included water Revenue.			
				Variable.	Fixed.		
1		2	3	4	5		6
			Rs.	Rs.	Rs.	A.	
Ajmer	Variable ...	3	3,780	...	126	0	
	Fixed ..	13	29,792	413	712	1	
Gangwāna	Variable ...	26	23,038	1,602	1,377	6	
	Fixed ..	8	5,316	...	58	2	
Rājgarh	Variable ...	9	10,422	1,976	608	4	
	Fixed ...	17	23,770	3,332	1,029	15	
Rāmsar	Variable ...	23	23,907	5,307	1,032	13	
	Fixed ...	34	38,363	12,330	1,685	5	
Pushkar	Variable ...	...	...	..	...		
	Fixed ..	9	7,237	...	...		
Total Ajmer Tahsīl.	Fixed ...	**81**	**1,04,478**	**16,075**	**3,485**	**7**	
	Variable ...	**61**	**61,147**	**8,885**	**3,144**	**7**	
	Total ...	**142**	**1,65,625**	**24,960**	**6,629**	**14**	
Beāwar ...	...	134	41,917	9,151	6,708	9	
Chāng ...	...	46	8,605	1,161	1,135	9	
Shāmgarh ...	...	61	21,350	1,180	3,410	9	
Total Beāwar Tahsīl	...	**241**	**71,872**	**11,492**	**11,254**	**11**	
Bhailān ..	...	25	11,485	914	3,495	13	
Dewair ...	...	35	22,735	132	825	5	
Todgarh ...	...	27	27,210	1,406	1,888	9	
Total Todgarh Tahsīl	...	**87**	**61,430**	**2,452**	**6,209**	**11**	
Total Ajmer...	...	142	1,65,625	24,960	6,629	14	
Total Beāwar	..	241	71,872	11,492	11,254	11	
Total Todgarh Tahsīl		87	61,430	2,452	6,209	11	
Grand Total ...	...	**470**	**2,98,927**	**38,904**	**24,094**	**4**	

In the Merwāra villages the Land revenue is fixed: they are only variably assessed in respect of the water revenue. The Ajmer villages, shown as variable, have a variable land revenue, which may or may not be combined with a fixed or variable water revenue. Of the 61 variable villages shown in this Statement 24 have since been given a fixed assessment.

Statement No. 28.

The area (in acres) of each circle in each tahsīl according to Mr. Whiteway's settlement in Ajmer-Merwāra.

Tahsīl.	Circles.	Total Area.	Excluded.			Assessable Area.										
						Uncultivated.			Cultivated.							Total Assessable.
									Wet.			Unirrigated.			Total Cultivated.	
			Barren.	Revenue free.	Total.	Culturable.	Fallow.	Total.	Well.	Tank.	Total.	Abi.	Dry.	Total.		
1	2	3	4	5	6	7	8	9	10	11	12	13	14	15	16	17
Ajmer.	Ajmer	58,993	21,518	3,335	24,853	9,073	4,367	13,440	5,959	85	6,044	1,204	13,452	14,656	20,700	34,140
	Gangwāna	75,405	26,345	6,415	32,760	7,787	9,287	17,074	4,028	859	4,887	1,366	19,318	20,684	25,571	42,645
	Pushkar	20,781	6,128	2,154	8,282	6,455	1,305	7,760	820	201	1,021	934	2,784	3,718	4,739	12,499
	Rājgarh	62,656	21,068	2,209	23,277	7,782	5,351	13,133	5,225	1,208	6,433	1,986	17,827	19,813	26,246	39,379
	Rāmsar	1,40,961	35,537	11,409	46,946	38,602	16,229	54,831	5,790	5,975	11,765	1,813	25,606	27,419	39,184	94,015
	Total Ajmer Tahsil ..	3,58,796	1,10,596	25.522	1,36,118	69,699	36,539	1,06,238	21,822	8,328	30,150	7,303	78,987	86.290	1,16,440	2,22,678
	Total Ajmer Tahsil at 1875 settlement ...	3,59,424	1,11,303	31,480	1,42,783	89.703	18,018	1,07,721	18,553	8,365	26,918	7,746	74,256	82,002	1,08,920	2,16,641
Beāwar.	Beāwar	77,197	39,231	303	39,534	4,580	1,715	6,295	4,019	5,525	9,544	4,622	17,202	21,824	31,368	37,663
	Chāng	46,807	38,800	5	38,805	1,172	468	1,640	1,172	618	1,790	1,053	3,519	4,572	6,362	8,002
	Shāmgar	79,014	63,657	95	63,752	2,862	722	3,584	2,800	1,116	3,916	3,084	4,678	7,762	11,678	15,262
	Total Beāwar Tahsil ..	2,03,018	1,41,688	403	1,42,091	8,614	2.905	11,519	7,991	7,259	15.250	8,759	25,399	34,158	49,408	60,927
	Total Beāwar Tahsil at 1875 settlement ...	2,09,692	1,46,234	391	1,46,625	18,016	3,285	21,301	6,466	7,690	14,156	7,770	19,840	27,610	41,766	63,067
Todgarh	Bhailān	45,553	38,337	95	38,432	721	550	1,271	1,599	1,233	2,832	312	2,676	3,018	5,850	7,121
	Dewair	49,169	37,215	250	37,465	2,783	742	3,525	4,091	254	4,345	105	3,729	3,834	8,179	11,701
	Todgarh	78,042	63,530	131	63,661	3,134	803	3,037	4,289	1,213	5,502	434	4,508	4,912	10,444	14,381
	Total Todgarh Tahsil...	1,72,764	1,39,082	476	1,39,558	6.638	2,095	8,733	9,979	2,700	12,679	881	10,913	11,794	24,473	33,206
	Total Todgarh Tahsil at 1875 settlement ...	2,23,297	1,91,212	479	1,91,691	9,152	1,724	10,576	8,469	2,406	10,875	922	8,933	9,855	20,730	31,606
	Total Ajmer-Merwāra (now)	7,34,578	3,91,866	26,401	4,17,767	84,951	41,539	1,26,490	39,792	18,287	58,079	16,943	1,15,299	1,32,242	1,90,321	3,16,811
	Total Ajmer-Merwāra at 1875 settlement...	7,92,413	4,48,749	32,350	4,81,099	1,16,871	23,027	1,39,898	33,488	18,461	51,949	16,438	1,03,029	1,19,467	1,71,416	3,11,314

Statement No. 29.

Revenue under head "Excise" in rupees from 1880-81 *to* 1902-03.

Years.	Liquor.	Opium.	Drugs.	Fines and forfeitures.	Miscellaneous.	Total.	Deduct amount credited to trust accounts.	Revenue as in Finance Statement No. 25.
1	2	3	4	5	6	7	8	9
1880-81 ..	44,044	1,716	3,675	115	...	49,550	2,834	46,716
1881-82 ...	57,941	2,146	3,485	17	...	63,589	232	63,357
1882-83 ...	71,652	2,761	4,816	289	...	79,518	250	79,268
1883-84 ...	77,427	8,084	4,810	26	...	90,347	275	90,072
1884-85 ..	1,05,607	13,635	5,931	256	...	1,25,429	300	1,25,129
1885-86	90,032	9,710	5,431	56	...	1,05,229	...	1,05,229
1886-87 ..	1,10,294	9,206	5,430	27	...	1,24,957	...	1,24,957
1887-88 ...	1,57,099	7,380	5,900	3	389	1,70,771	...	1,70,771
1888-89 ...	61,155	10,430	5,375	197	4,466	81,623	..	81,623
1889-90 ...	1,56,650	7,925	4,185	...	5,744	1,74,504	...	1,74,504
Total ...	**9,31,901**	**72,993**	**49,038**	**986**	**10,599**	**10,65,517**	**3,891**	**10,61,626**
Average ...	**93,190·1**	**7,299·3**	**4,903·8**	**98·6**	**1,059·9**	**1,06,551·7**	**389·1**	**1,06,162·6**
1890-91 ..	87,704	9,270	7,085	19	4,920	1,08,998	...	1,08,998
1891-92 ..	1,36,997	8,433	6,740	...	4,920	1,57,090	...	1,57,090
1892-93 ...	1,10,330	8,842	7,270	9	5,640	1,32,091	..	1,32,091
1893-94 ...	82,226	5,839	6,110	64	5,640	99,879	...	99,879
1894-95 ...	91,035	6,221	5,425	74	5,680	1,08,435	.	1,08,435
1895-96 ..	99,226	6,785	7,603	...	5,880	1,19,494	...	1,19,494
1896-97 ..	91,040	7,785	8,295	...	5,880	1,13,000	...	1,13,000
1897-98 ...	87,239	8,236	8,987	3	5,880	1,10,345	...	1,10,345
1898-99 ...	86,368	6,142	5,176	...	6,475	1,04,161	...	1,04,161
1899-00 ...	67,338	6,762	7,065	...	7,094	88,259	...	88,259
Total ...	**9,39,503**	**74,315**	**69,756**	**169**	**58,009**	**11,41,752**	...	**11,41,752**
Average ...	**93,950·3**	**7,431·5**	**6,975·6**	**16·9**	**58,00·9**	**1,14,175·2**	..	**1,14,175·2**
1900-01 ..	75,464	6,983	8,792	...	7,091	98,330	...	98,330
1901-02 ..	85,453	11,731	10,474	...	7,012	1,14,670	...	1,14,670
1902-03 ..	76,681	21,446	11,104	...	7,091	1,16,322	...	1,16,322

Columns 2, 3, and 4.—Fluctuation due in general to level of prosperity among the people.

The opium farm and vend fees are now for the whole district instead of only for municipal and cantonment areas, as before introduction of the opium rules in 1900.

Column 5.—Now only forfeitures are entered under "Excise" revenue. Fines inflicted by magistrates are credited to "Law and Justice."

Column 6.—Denotes the distillery rent and establishment charges realized from the contractor. The "Sadar" distillery system was introduced in 1887.

Column 8.—Figures shown up to 1885 are on account of sums due to Mārwār-Merwāra and Mewār-Merwāra. The present settlement was made with Mewār in 1881-82 and with Mārwār in 1885.

Statement No. 30.

Income and expenditure of District Board of Ajmer-Merwāra.

Particulars.	Year.	Average for ten years.	Year.
	1889-90.	1891-1900.	1902-03.
1	2	3	4
Income from:—	Rs.	Rs.	Rs.
Land Revenue	...	..	...
Provincial rates	20,849	20,081	27,349
Interest	280	294	297
Education	1,690	1,920	2,597
Medical	3,364	6,162	37,214
Scientific, &c.	986	1,022	1,270
Miscellaneous	2,532	2,227	4,881
Civil Works	527	1,705	1,214
Pounds	350	1,710	1,800
Ferries	...	...	...
Total Income ...	**30,578**	**35,121**	**76,622**
Expenditure on:—			
Refunds	...	...	...
Land Revenue	...	...	...
General Administration	990	1,289	1,305
Education	6,424	8,284	7,445
Medical	4,011	6,277	7,038
Scientific, &c.	341	408	1,702
Public Works	8,540	13,667	16,543
Civil Works	647	2,114	3,700
Miscellaneous	6,657	4,502	3,455
Total Expenditure ...	**27,610**	**36,541**	**41,188**

Income.

Provincial rates.—In 1902-03 include Rs. 8,800 on account of contribution from Government.

Medical.—In 1902-03, increase is due to inclusion of Rs. 26,426 on account of "Victoria Memorial" subscriptions.

Under "Miscellaneous" in 1902-03 are included Rs. 4,515 on account of refund of arrear pension contributions.

Statement No. 31.

Income and expenditure of the Ajmer Municipality.

Particulars.	Year. 1889-90.	Average for ten years. 1891-1900.	Year. 1902-03.
1	2	3	4
	Rs.	Rs.	Rs.
Octroi	1,10,075	1,16,617	1,39,862
Tax on houses and lands	...	...	...
Other taxes	...	..	...
Rents	7,352	4,890	3,845
Loans	...	23,800	...
Other sources	26,304	48,979	39,844
Total Income	1,43,731	1,94,286	1,83,551
Expenditure on administration and collection of taxes	34,559	38,752	41,190
Public safety	16,330	18,962	20,139
Water supply and drainage:—			
(a) Capital	1,228	26,496	25
(b) Maintenance	183	8,645	11,342
Conservancy	24,289	32,203	30,300
Hospitals and Dispensaries	1,141	3,181	3,826
Public Works	9,300	11,621	9,297
,, instruction	3,683	4,409	5,271
Other heads	45,631	40,017	35,523
Total Expenditure ...	1,36,344	1,84,286	1,56,913

Loans include Rs. **2,18,000** borrowed from Government in 1892 for the Foy Sāgar water scheme and Rs. 20,000 borrowed in 1897 towards payment of compensation for land taken up for the same tank.

On the side of income under "other sources" are included conservancy receipts (other than taxes), fees from markets and slaughter-houses, miscellaneous sales and income from garden produce. Under "Expenditure on administration and collection of taxes" the largest item is octroi refunds.

The high average of capital expenditure on water supply and drainage between 1891-1900 was due to the construction of the Foy Sāgar reservoir during the period.

Under "other heads" of expenditure the chief items are interest on loans, repayments of loans and expenditure on public gardens.

Statement No. 32.

Income and expenditure of the Beāwar Municipality.

Particulars.	Year.	Average for ten years.	Year.
	1889-90.	1891-1900.	1902-03.
1	2	3	4
	Rs.	Rs.	Rs.
Octroi	39,698	39,184	53,833
Tax on houses and lands	...	...	...
Other taxes	...	...	...
Rents	519	860	1,246
Loans	...	...	...
Other sources	5,774	9,481	1,937
Total Income ...	**45,991**	**49,525**	**57,016**
Expenditure on administration and collection of taxes	23,972	18,603	29,263
Public safety	5,109	5,793	6,072
Water supply and drainage :—			
(*a*) Capital	...	963	...
(*b*) Maintenance...	124	1,269	1,603
Conservancy	3,683	5,455	7,360
Hospital and Dispensaries	1,400	1,626	3,248
Public Works	2,604	5,120	4,838
Public instruction	3,659	4,286	5,387
Other heads	3,065	6,597	2,425
Total Expenditure ...	**43,616**	**49,712**	**60,196**

The income under "other sources" for 1891-1900 reaches so high an average because it includes sales of Government paper, amounting to Rs. 58,244-12-7 in the 10 years.

Octroi refunds form the largest item in "Expenditure on administration and collection of taxes." The refund limit was raised to Rs. 2 in 1901-02, leading to a considerable increase in the net income from octroi.

"Other heads" includes expenditure on arboriculture and public gardens and on fairs.

Statement No. 33.

Income and expenditure of the Kekri Municipality.

Particulars.	Year.	Average for ten years.	Year.
	1889-90	1891-1900	1902-03
1	2	3	4
	Rs.	Rs.	Rs.
Octroi	6,387	9,182	12,970
Tax on houses and lands	...	...	...
Other taxes	...	...	...
Rents	411	783	1,382
Loans	...	...	...
Other sources	820	1,147	522
Total Income ...	**7,618**	**11,112**	**14,874**
Expenditure on administration and collection of taxes	2,458	4,069	6,146
Public safety	198	492	1,668
Water supply and drainage :—			
(a) Capital	32	32	...
(b) Maintenance	...	95	219
Conservancy	319	504	1,121
Hospitals and Dispensaries	248	412	553
Public works	685	1,578	421
Public instruction	483	844	1,214
Other heads	2,556	2,664	2,640
Total Expenditure ...	**6,979**	**10,690**	**13,982**

The increase in octroi income in 1902-03 is due to the large imports of grains, gur and ghee, and to the local scarcity.

Under "Expenditure on administration and collection of taxes" are included "octroi refunds."

Statement No. 34.

Police of Ajmer-Merwāra.

Particulars.	1881.	1891.	1902.
1	2	3	4
Supervising Staff.			
District Superintendent	1	1	1
Inspectors	3	3	3
Subordinate Staff.			
Sub-Inspectors	11	13	13
Head Constables...	65	*68	*68
Constables	308	356	324
Mounted Constables	40	40	37
Municipal Police and Cantonment Police.			
Head Constables	15	17	25
Constables	138	174	232
European Sergeants	...	1	1
Total Expenditure on above Police in Rs. ...	86,423	1,07,328	1,14,689
Rural Police.			
(a) In Khālsa and Jāgīr villages	†	†	205
(b) In Istimrāri villages			191
Expenditure on Rural Police in Rs. :—			...
(a) In Khālsa and Jāgīr villages	†	†	11,044
(b) In Istimrāri villages			9,564

* Including a Cashier.
† Figures not forthcoming.

Statement No. 35.

Police cognizable crimes of Ajmer-Merwāra.

Particulars.	Average of 5 years ending 1901.	1902.
1	2	3
Number of cases reported	4,699	3,328
,, ,, decided in the Criminal Courts	3,445	2,161
,, ,, ending acquittal or discharge	237	277
,, ,, ending in conviction	3,208	1,884

Average for the five years ending 1901 was high owing to the famine and increase of petty crime.

Statement No. 36.

Jail of Ajmer-Merwāra.

Particulars.	1881.	1891.	1902.
1	2	3	4
Number of Central Jails	1	1	1
Number of District Jails	...	...	...
Number of subsidiary Jails (lock-ups) ...	3	3	3
Average daily Jail Population :—			
(a) Males ... In Central Jails	405·13	391·32	520·48
(a) Males ... In other Jails	...	...	...
(b) Females ... In Central Jails	24·23	16·06	20·08
(b) Females ... In other Jails	...	...	...
Total	**429·36**	**407·38**	**540·56**
Rate of Jail mortality per mille	4·66	27·00	29·60
Expenditure on Jail maintenance in rupees...	18,769	26,686	25,385
Cost per Prisoner in rupees	43-15-9	65-8-0	46-15-4
Profits on Jails' manufactures in rupees ...	2,883	3,472	3,881
Earning per Prisoner in rupees	6-11-5	8-8-4	8-12-7

The increased mortality per mille in 1891 and 1902 was due to the fever epidemics of those years.

Statement No. 37.

College, School and Scholars of Ajmer-Merwāra.

Institutions.	1883-84.			1890-91.			1902-03.		
	Number of Institutions.	Scholars.		Number of Institutions.	Scholars.		Number of Institutions.	Scholars.	
		Males.	Females.		Males.	Females.		Males.	Females.
1	2	3	4	5	6	7	8	9	10
Public.									
Arts Colleges ...	1	225	...	1	411	...	1	266	...
Secondary Schools :—									
Upper Secondary (High)	2	415	...	3	1,049	...	5	1,493	74
Lower Secondary (Middle)... ...	8	678	5	8	788	...	9	898	...
Primary Schools :—									
Upper Primary schools	49	2,834	121	47	2,912	170	50	2,497	346
Lower Primary schools	...	...	...	...	...	...	...	...	...
Training Schools ...	2	17	6	2	20	4	1	9	...
Total of Public Institutions ...	**62**	**4,169**	**132**	**61**	**5,180**	**174**	**66**	**5,163**	**420**
Private.									
Advanced	30	1,094	25	33	1,168	...	19	434	16
Elementary ...	55	1,732	191	83	2,384	393	71	2,221	1,404
Grand Total ...	**147**	**6,995**	**348**	**177**	**8,732**	**567**	**156**	**7,818**	**1,840**

The increase of private institutions and pupils in 1890-91 was due to the correct classification of the Mission schools in Todgarh *tahsīl*, which had previously been included in the list of village schools.

Statement No. 38.

University results of Ajmer-Merwāra.

Passes in—	1880-81.	1890-91.	1902-03.
1	2	3	4
Matriculation	4	15	23
First or Intermediate Examinations in Arts or Science...	2	1	10
Ordinary Bachelors' Degrees	...	...	8
Higher and Special Degrees	...	...	...

The B.A. class at Ajmer College was started in 1896-97.

Statement No. 39.

Cost of Education in Ajmer-Merwāra.

Particulars.	Expenditure on Institutions maintained or aided by Public Funds in 1902-03 from				
	Imperial Revenues.	District and Municipal Funds.	Fees.	Other sources.	Total.
1	2	3	4	5	6
	Rs.	Rs.	Rs.	Rs.	Rs.
Arts and Professional Colleges	23,539	2,580	4,553	1,447	32,119
Training and Special Schools	1,262	...	...	...	1,262
Secondary Boys' Schools ..	4,954	8,224	4,058	6,331	23,567
Primary Boys' Schools ...	4,587	6,751	1,951	84	13,373
Girls' Schools	2,718	600	2,399	2,180	7,897
Total ..	37,060	18,155	12,961	10,042	78,218

Statement No. 40.

Medical—Ajmer-Merwāra.

Particulars.	1881.	1891.	1902.
1	2	3	4
Hospitals, etc.			
Number of Civil Hospitals and Dispensaries	7	7	7
Average daily number of :—			
(a) In-door patients	28·22	27·42	48·71
(b) Out-door patients	231·32	281·52	414·39
Income in rupees from :—			
(a) Government payments	3,869	4,990	6,353
(b) Local and Municipal	900	1,435	2,475
(c) Fees, endowments and other sources	2,616	2,796	5,803
Expenditure in rupees on :—			
(a) Establishment	4,197	5,116	6,426
(b) Medicines, diet, buildings, etc. ...	3,549	4,122	6,320
Lunatic Asylums :—			
Number of Asylums	1	1	1
Average daily number of :—			
(a) Criminal lunatics	...	...	...
(b) Other lunatics	·50	...	1·01
Income in rupees from :—			
Government payments	113	183	203
Expenditure in rupees on :—			
(a) Establishment	84	132	120
(b) District building, etc....	29	51	83
Vaccination :—			
Population among which vaccination was carried on	4,60,722	5,42,358	4,76,912
Number of successful operations	4,433	12,226	12,179
Ratio of persons successfully vaccinated per 1,000 of population	9·62	22·54	25·54
Total expenditure in rupees on vaccination	839	1,549	2,267
Cost per successful case in pies	36	23	36

There is no separate lunatic asylum in Ajmer-Merwāra. Lunatics are kept in the Ajmer Central Jail, from which, if necessary, they are transferred to the Lahore Lunatic Asylum.